IMAGES
of America

MARCUS HOOK

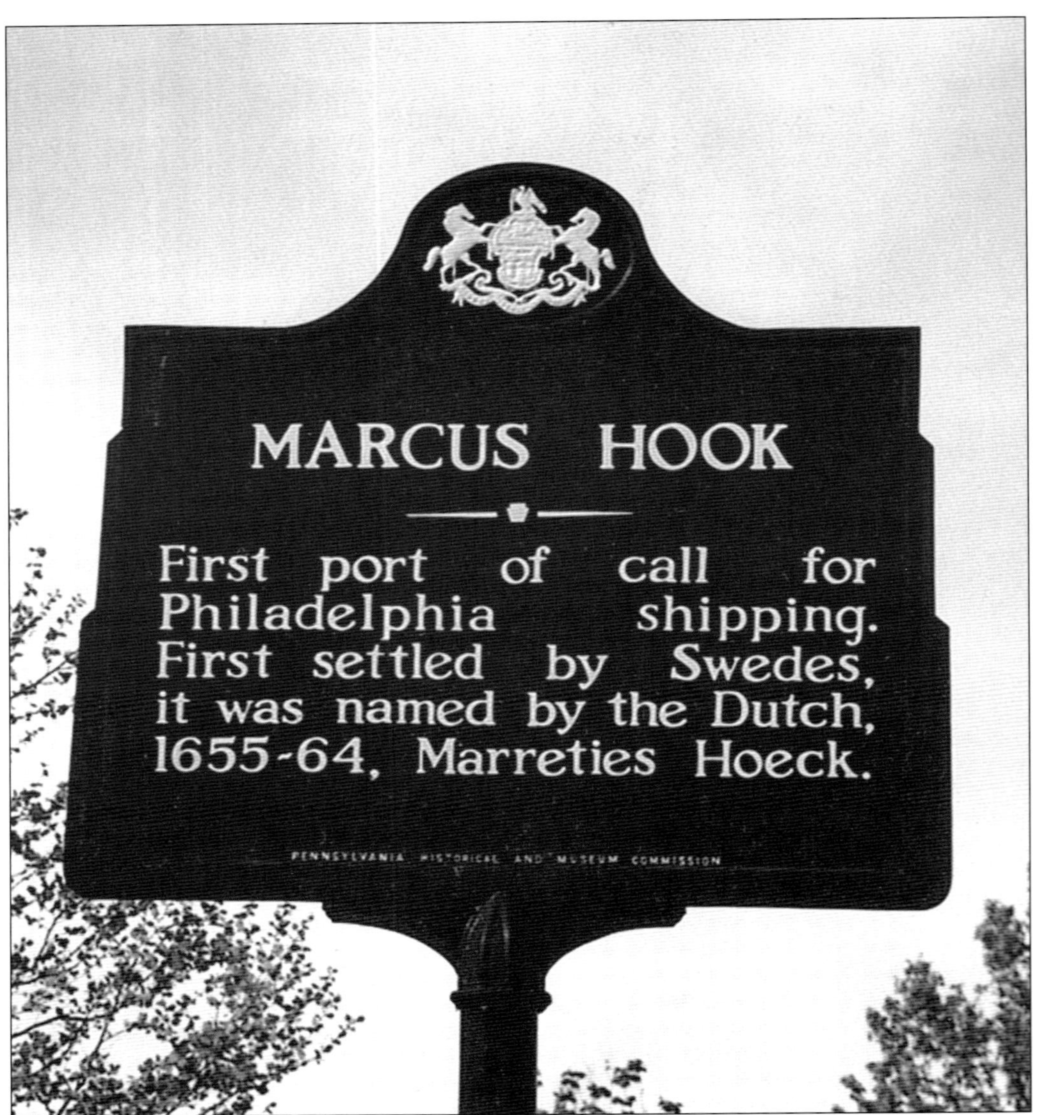

HISTORICAL MARKER. The historical marker coming into town reads, "First port of call for Philadelphia shipping. First settled by Swedes, it was named by the Dutch, 1655–64, Marreties Hoeck." This roadside historical marker is located along Tenth Street (U.S. Route 13) in Centennial Park, across the street from the Marcus Hook Municipal Building.

On the cover: **SUN SEAMAN'S MEMORIAL, 1951.** Embossed in bronze is the Sun Seaman's Memorial. Area residents look up at the memorial, which was dedicated to the 141 men who lost their lives on Sunoco tankers. (Urban Archives of Temple University.)

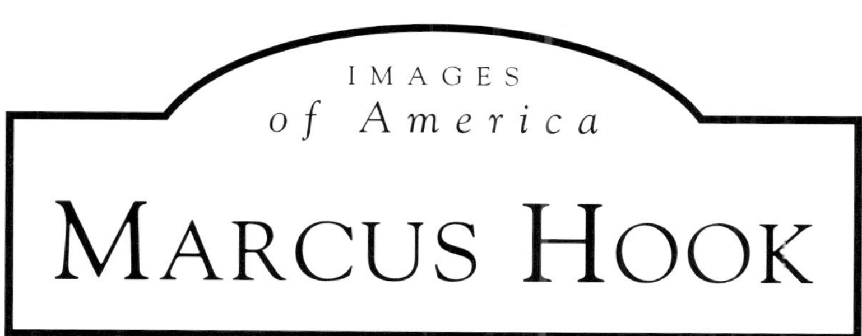

Patricia Ann Miller
for the Borough of Marcus Hook

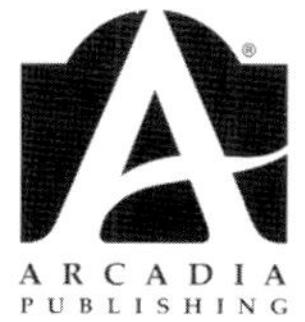

ISBN 978-0-7385-5013-8

Published by Arcadia Publishing
Charleston SC, Chicago IL, Portsmouth NH, San Francisco CA

Printed in the United States of America

Library of Congress Catalog Card Number: 2006940925

For all general information contact Arcadia Publishing at:
Telephone 843-853-2070
Fax 843-853-0044
E-mail sales@arcadiapublishing.com
For customer service and orders:
Toll-Free 1-888-313-2665

Visit us on the Internet at www.arcadiapublishing.com

Dedicated to past and present Marcus Hook residents

Contents

ACKNOWLEDGMENTS

This history of Marcus Hook Borough, Delaware County, is divided into nine chapters. It is a collection of photographs and drawings that date back to the 1600s. I was inspired to keep taking photographs after majoring in journalism at Temple University and taking a photography course. This work was also inspired by the photographer of my wedding, Robert Evans, an excellent photographer who worked for Sun Shipbuilding and Dry Dock Company.

I want to thank Ernie Montella, owner of the Philadelphia Athletics Museum in Hatboro, for continually requesting more copies of my original book and giving me the incentive to redo this history.

I also acknowledge the following individuals: Ralph Montella, a longtime borough resident; Frank Sill of the Chichester Historical Society; Carol Sloan, public affairs coordinator for Sunoco's Marcus Hook refinery; Michael Manerchia of the Marcus Hook Historical Commission and the Marcus Hook Plank Log Cabin Association (MHPLCA); and the borough manager of Marcus Hook, Bruce Dorbian, who helped me collect images and information on the history of the borough and assisted with the editing of this publication.

I collected many images and information courtesy of the following organizations: Delaware County Historical Society, Hagley Museum and Library, Urban Archives of Temple University, and the Houghton Library of Harvard University. During the eight years that I resided in Marcus Hook, I took many photographs and collected images of my observances of the town. I grew to love the close-knit community where everything was within walking distance. Marcus Hook will always bring back memories for me of spending hours in the park on the Delaware River and watching the ships pass by. I also recall the many parades, savoring Clank's upside-down pizza, talking to many longtime residents, and learning all I could about the town's rich history.

INTRODUCTION

The Marcus Hook area of the Delaware River waterfront has attracted settlement since the movement of the Lenni-Lenape into this region. The area from the west bank of Chester Creek to Marcus Hook Creek was originally a part of a large tract granted by Queen Christina of Sweden to Capt. John Ammundsen Besk in 1653; the land west of the latter creek was given to a number of Swedish farmers in 1679. The Dutch called this area Marrieties Hoeck after conquering the Delaware watershed in 1655 to 1664. After the fall of New Amsterdam, these settlements were under the English crown but attracted little interest until Charles II granted William Penn vast acreage for colonization. Some English settlers had migrated to Marcus Hook from Burlington and other West Jersey hamlets, but most arrived in 1682 and 1683. Within six years, the English predominated enough to have the area's name changed to Chichester after the Sussex town from which the most influential citizens had emigrated. In common usage, however, Marcus Hook remained the term for the waterfront settlement, while Chichester became the designation for the hinterland.

During Colonial times, Marcus Hook served as the first port of call for Philadelphia and rivaled Chester in size. It briefly became a notorious haven for pirates in the early 18th century, the most famous cutthroat being Edward Teach, "Blackbeard." The waterfront remained an infamous neighborhood as a result of the many taverns along Discord Lane (present Second Street). The shipbuilding industry was started before 1750 and was well known for coastal traders and herring sloops.

During the American Revolution, a cheval-de-frise was sunk in the channel to prevent the passage of British warships, and the town was bombarded several times. The Continental army camped in the borough in August–September 1777, and there is some evidence that a training camp for the Pennsylvania militia was maintained from 1776 to 1779 on the west bank of Marcus Hook Creek.

During the War of 1812, infantry troops were trained and quartered just north of the crossroads of Market Street and Post Road (U.S. 13). The encampment known as Camp Gaines, and later Fort Snyder, had between 5,000 and 10,000 men stationed there from early September 1814 into early 1815. The troops were mainly Pennsylvania militia with some Delaware units and a sprinkling of U.S. regulars. Following the sack of Washington, D.C., in August 1814, extensive earthworks were hastily constructed along the Marcus Hook waterfront and tidal creeks and cannon were mounted. These entrenchments and the camp were abandoned when winter lessened the likelihood of a British offensive.

The growth of Marcus Hook was gradual and was stimulated by improvement to the local thoroughfares. The construction of the Philadelphia-Wilmington-Baltimore Railroad brought increased commercial and residential development in the later 19th century. Stage inns, waterfront taverns, depots, and similar services augmented income from shipping and fisheries. The shad and herring industries were especially lucrative until the early 20th century.

The first church, St. Martin's Episcopal Church, was established in the 17th century. The Baptist congregation organized in 1789 and have had numerous locations. The Mount Hebron African Methodist Episcopal Church was organized in 1893 and eventually moved to Lower

Chichester. The growth of the river industries in the early 20th century provided employment for a new wave of Catholic immigrants. Immaculate Conception of Lourdes Roman Catholic Church began as a mission church for St. Anthony's parish in Chester. In 1917, the congregation built the present stone church.

The first school in Marcus Hook was organized in 1745 in the old frame church of St. Martin's. It continued there until a brick schoolhouse, which was demolished in 1860, was built. The Marcus Hook Baptist Church was used by the school district from 1854 to 1890 (referred to as the Cedar Grove School). This was followed in 1895 by the Seventh Street Grammar School at Seventh and Green Streets, which consisted of six rooms until World War II. The Central School, which stood at Tenth and Church Streets, was razed in 1921.

Much of the economic development of Marcus Hook has been related to its location on the Delaware River. During the 18th and 19th centuries, it was a center for small ship construction and for the fishing industry. The U.S. quarantine station for the port of Philadelphia was based at Marcus Hook from 1887 to the late 1960s. The growth resulting from these activities warranted the incorporation of Marcus Hook as an independent borough of 1.14 square miles in 1892.

The excellent rail, road, and deepwater ship facilities in Marcus Hook attracted new industries dependent upon water for transport rather than for power. Oil refineries were built on the waterfront, starting with the Bear Creek Refining Company in 1892, giving the borough its primary industry.

A pipeline connected the plant to the oil-producing regions in western Pennsylvania 300 miles away. In October 1901, 82 acres in Marcus Hook were bought by Joseph N. Pew for the Sunoco refinery. The plant was in operation four months later and was immediately prosperous.

The Hardwood Packaging Company was spun off in 1912 to produce wooden barrels for the shipping of oil. The Sunoco Marcus Hook refinery is now connected by pipeline to Sunoco refineries in Philadelphia and New Jersey and, when taken as a group, is the second-largest producer of gasoline in the country.

In 1910, the Union Petroleum Company, quickly to become a wholly owned subsidiary of the Sinclair Refining Company, leased 17 acres in Marcus Hook. It added 242 acres in Trainer in 1921, expanding from a 10,000- to 160,000-barrel-a-day production capacity. The business has had several subsequent owners, the current being ConocoPhillips. Marcus Hook's deepwater harbor allows inexpensive delivery of crude oil from domestic and foreign locations by tanker and efficient export to overseas markets. Pennsylvania Railroad and Reading Railroad lines (now Conrail) provide access to continental markets.

Another significant industry was founded in Marcus Hook when Samuel Agar Salvage first imported British technology to manufacture "artificial silk" in the United States. The American Viscose Company, initially a subsidiary of the English textile firm Samuel Courtauld and Company, built the largest synthetic fiber plant in the world here in 1910. Marcus Hook, therefore, is the American birthplace of rayon, the first mass-produced, man-made fiber in the country. In addition to the industrial complex, American Viscose also constructed an early planned community of employee housing, in the popular English Tudor Revival style, that still goes by the name Viscose Village.

Marcus Hook's population peaked in the 1920s at 5,324, when the first pressures for residential subdivision were generated by burgeoning industries. Subsequent growth of the refineries and related businesses reduced the residential core community to its present-day population of about half that number.

Today the borough of Marcus Hook continues as a family-oriented, pedestrian-friendly community, where the main business district, public parks and buildings, schools, neighborhoods, and riverfront are all within close proximity. The small-town feel and more personalized sense of community prevails in Marcus Hook. Situated in the extreme southeastern corner of the state, Marcus Hook is proudly referred to as "the Cornerstone of Pennsylvania."

One

Marcus Hook's Early History

Located on the northern bank of the Delaware River 17 miles south of Philadelphia is Marcus Hook, one of the first settlements in America and the third-oldest town in Pennsylvania. The Swedes arrived in 1638, and with them came the first Finnish immigrants to the New Sweden colony in North America. The area where Marcus Hook is today was called Finland, or Lapland (which means "region" in Finnish). This is the time period when Marcus Hook appears to have been named. Historians suggest the name is derived from an early settler named "Marcus the Finn" and from the Dutch word *hoeck*, meaning a "corner, point, or spot of land."

The Dutch gained control of New Sweden in 1655. In 1664, England conquered New Netherland, and Pennsylvania became a part of the Duke of York's new territory. In 1673–1674, the Dutch regained control, but soon the colony was back under English rule. William Penn arrived aboard the *Welcome* in 1682. Also in that year, Chester County was created, its name origin from Cheshire, England. Delaware County was created from Chester County in 1789.

In 1701, William Penn granted a local market charter for the long open area of lower Market Street still visible today in Marcus Hook. It was one of three such privileges granted by Penn, the other two located in Chester and Philadelphia.

During the Revolutionary War, French general Marquis de Lafayette was brought to Marcus Hook after being injured in the Battle of Brandywine. George Washington called Marcus Hook an advantageous place for patriots to be located to fire on incoming British ships.

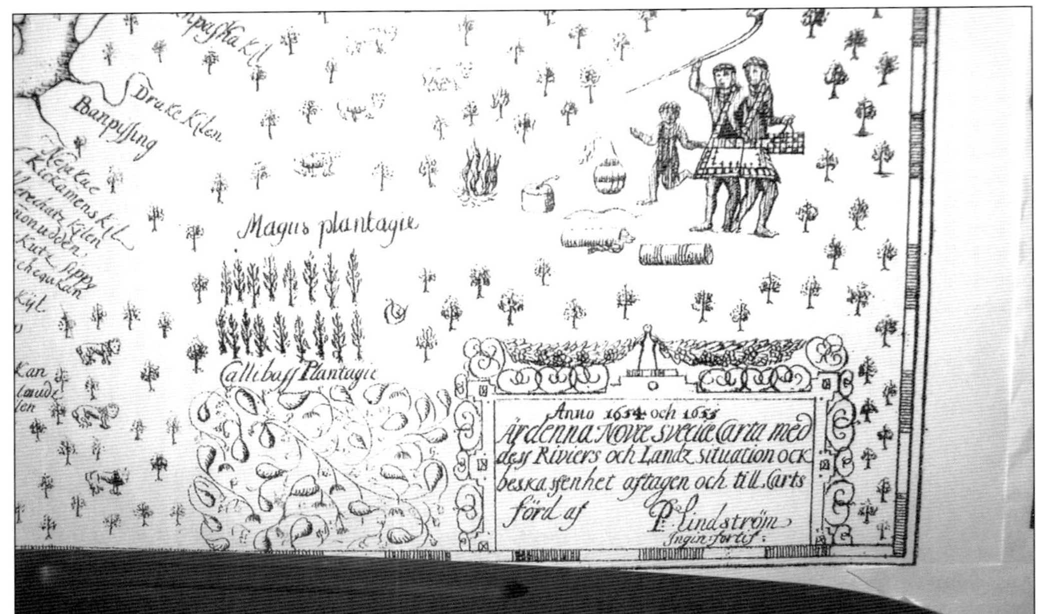

MAP DRAWING OF PETER LINDSTROM. The Marcus Hook area was settled by the Swedes in 1638 when they made a treaty with the Native Americans. This drawing depicts the area possibly from 1654 to 1655. (MHPLCA.)

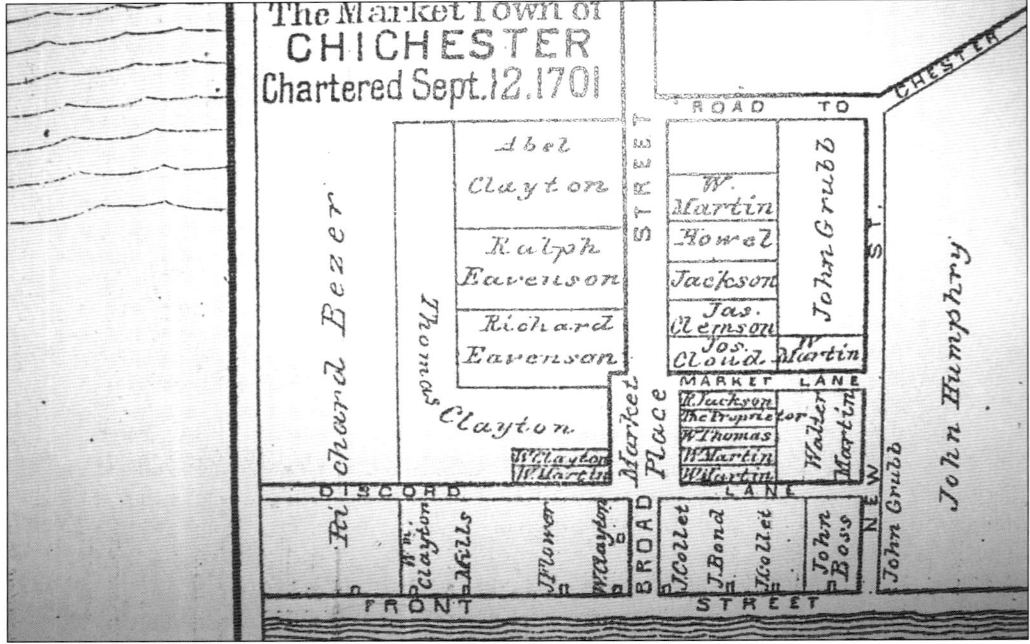

MAP DRAWING OF THE MARKET TOWN OF CHICHESTER. At the court at Upland in 1682 the inhabitants requested the change of the borough's name to Chichester, as this British map labels the charter of William Penn. Marcus Hook grew apace at the time of Penn's charter, which this drawing depicts. At the time of this drawing Chester and Marcus Hook had 100 houses. (MHPLCA.)

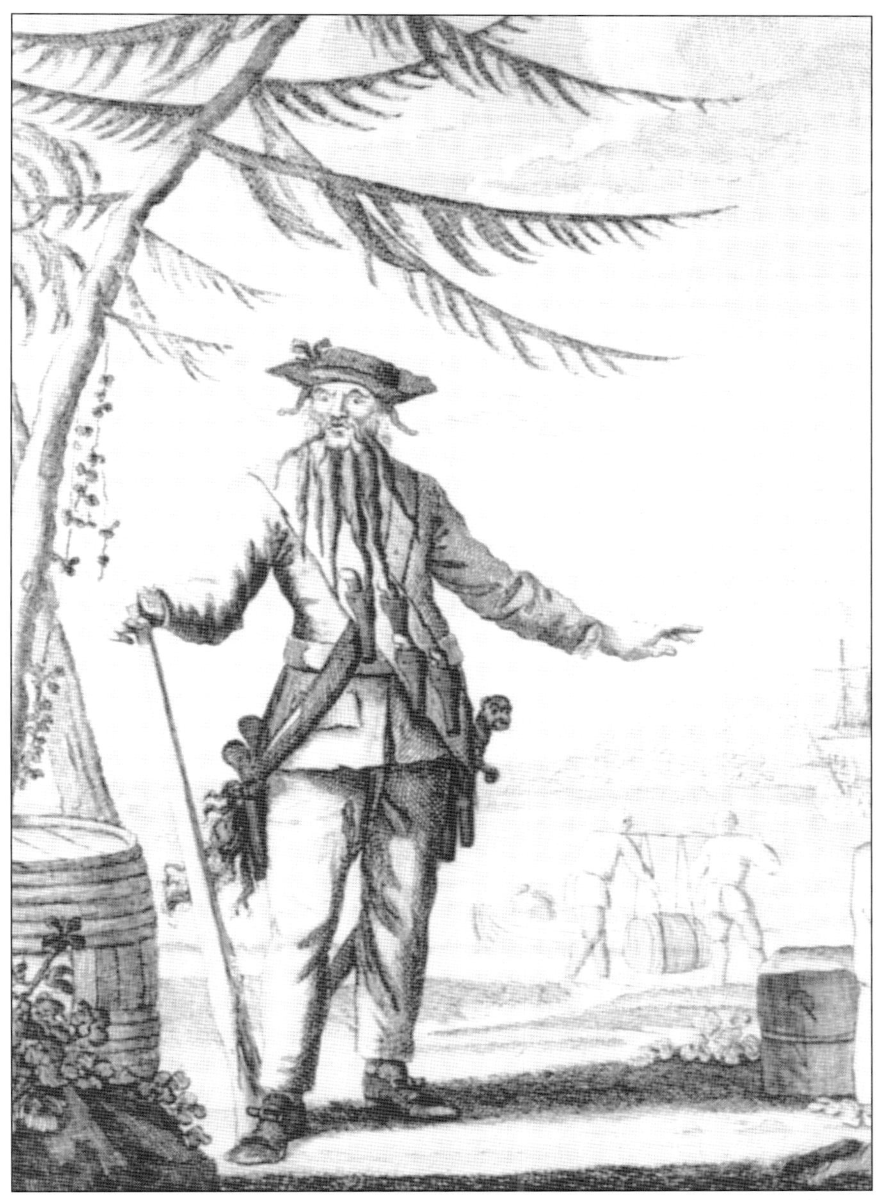

Illustration of Blackbeard, or Edward Teach. Little exists in the way of illustrations of Marcus Hook before 1890, but this illustration is of one of the earlier visitors to the town. During the last years of the 17th century and early part of the 18th century, pirates were a plague in Marcus Hook and other areas on the Delaware River. Governor Keith in 1716 of the provincial council quoted, "The great losses which the colony had already sustained beyond any of its neighbors, by our Trade's being blocked up and infested with pirates at the Capes of this river and bay." They often hid their ships in inlets, safe from the prying eyes of the British navy. Here is a full-length view of one of the most notorious of these pirates, Edward Teach, or "Blackbeard." Some local residents believe Blackbeard built a secret escape tunnel to the Delaware River. Blackbeard was killed in a sea battle in 1718. (Harry Elkins Widener Collection, Houghton Library, Harvard University, HEW 6.8.5.)

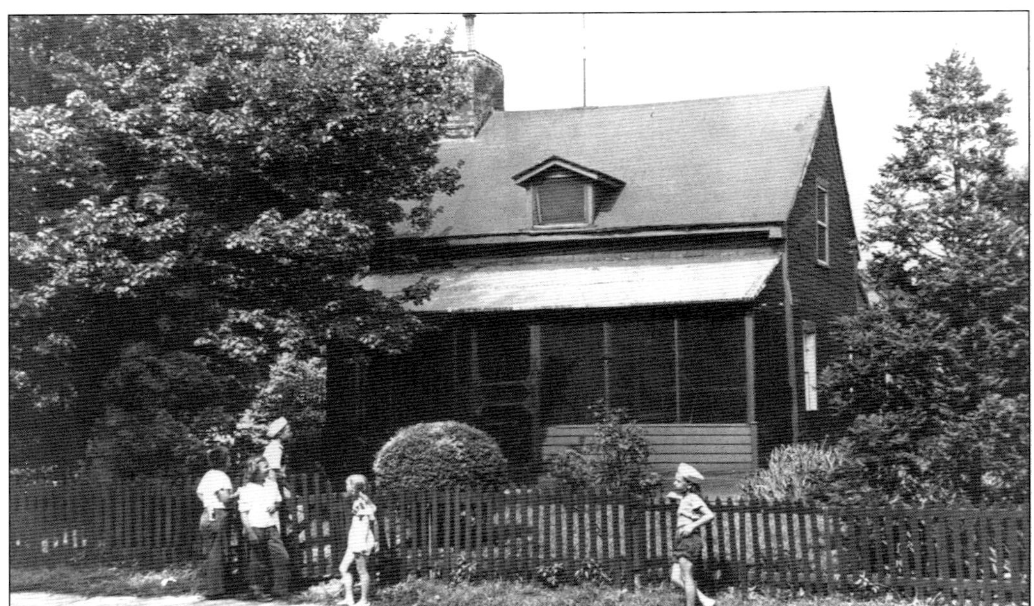

The Oldest House in Marcus Hook. When Blackbeard and other pirates disembarked, they would head for a cabin at 221 Market Street, a few hundred yards from the water's edge. These five children gaze at this historic homestead, which Blackbeard was reputed to visit and was once called the Wanner House, named after a former owner. Nearby Second Street was once called Discord Lane when Blackbeard and his companions created noisy brawls and frequented the taverns that lined the narrow dirt street. The dwelling located at Market Street and Market Lane was owned by patrolman Ernest Fleming and his wife when this photograph was taken on August 13, 1951. In Blackbeard's time this house is reputed to have been inhabited by his mistress Margaret. (Urban Archives of Temple University.)

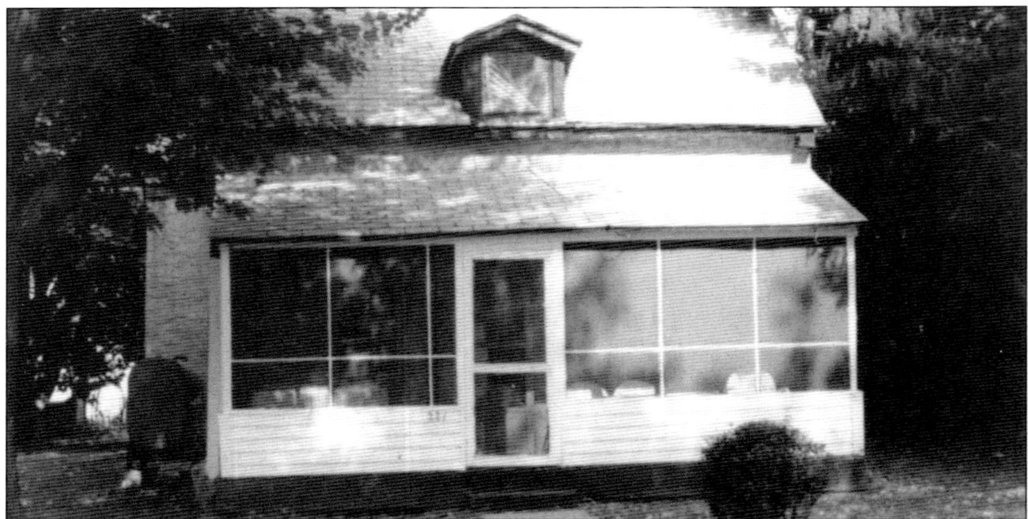

Blackbeard's Mistress's House. Located at 221 Market Street, this is how the house looked in August 1984. The house is now officially called the Marcus Hook Plank Log House. According to the owner of this house, Michael Manerchia, the house dates back to the late 1600s or early 1700s.

Two

THE DELAWARE RIVER WATERFRONT

Marcus Hook exists on the Delaware River, and life on the river has been an ever-changing scene from year to year and decade to decade. Much of the economic development of Marcus Hook has been related to its location on the river. During the 18th and 19th centuries, it was a center for small ship construction and for the fishing industry (particularly noted for shad and herring).

Marcus Hook once had an amusement park called Lindenthorpe Park and a beach before Sunoco bought the park in 1901. A number of inns and elegant houses lined the waterfront, and the area was noted for quail hunting and fishing. The Lindenthorpe Park, with novelty attractions such as county fairs and balloon races, operated in Marcus Hook from 1897 to 1901. The Chester Traction Company operated a trolley to the park on weekends. Marcus Hook was a fishing village at the dawn of the 20th century. At that time the principal industry was boatbuilding.

In the 1980s, the waterfront changed drastically as McClure Park was expanded and became Market Square Memorial Park, with new trees, tall lamps, new park benches, a new fishing dock, and a refined shoreline.

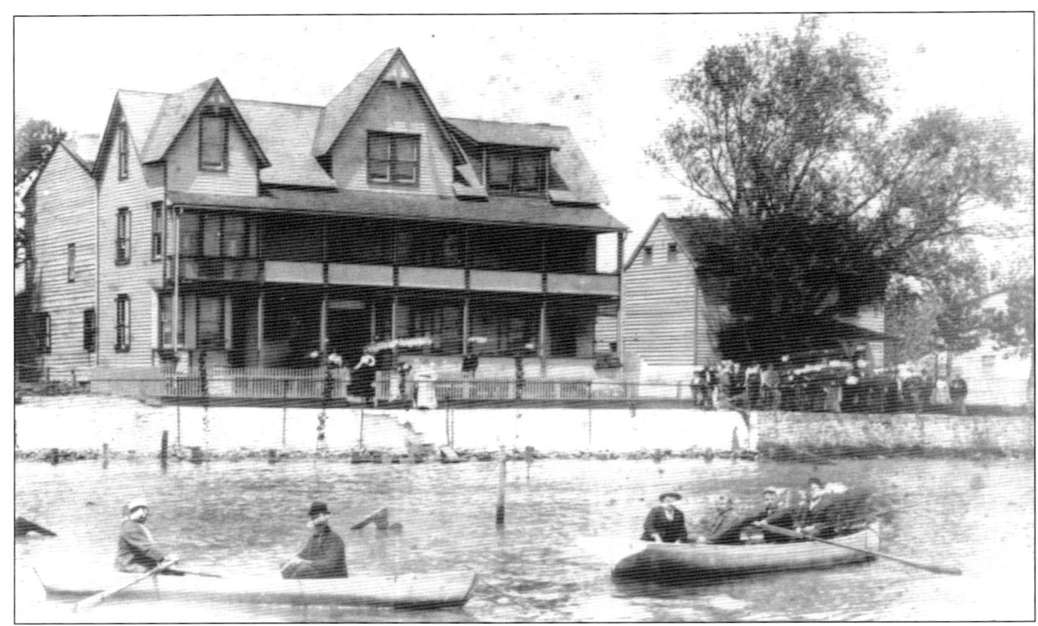

THE DELAWARE RIVER WATERFRONT, 1890S. This is how Marcus Hook's Delaware River waterfront looked in the 1890s, just east of Blueball Avenue. The cradles in the water are part of Samuel J. Burton's shipyard. A gunning bateau is at left, and a fishing skiff is at right. This assemblage is the Heacock family, a longtime prominent family in Marcus Hook. Ed Heacock sits left of the left boat. A member of the Heacock family, Lydia Heacock, was the postmistress in Marcus Hook at the beginning of the 20th century. (Delaware County Historical Society.)

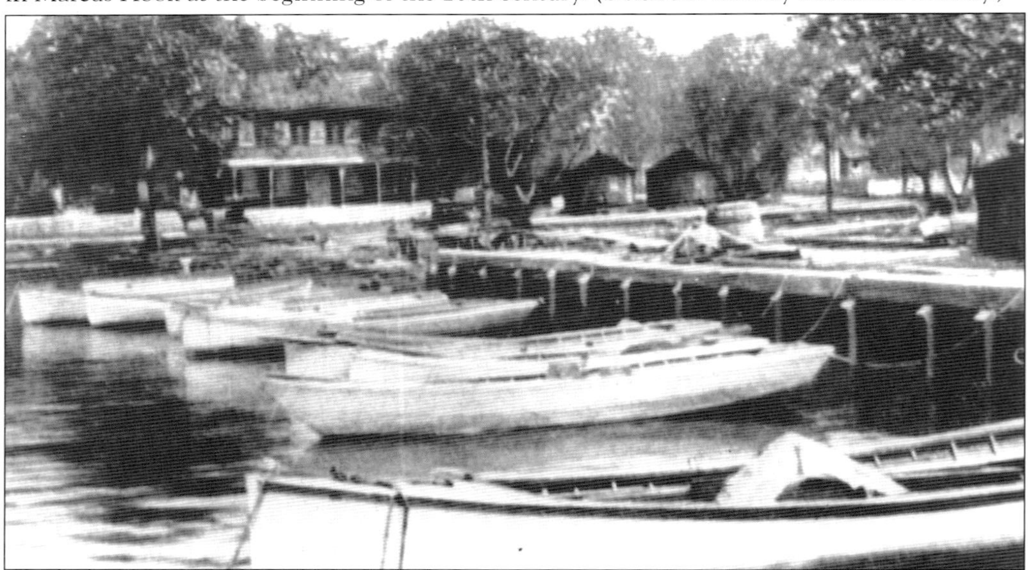

EARLY PHOTOGRAPH OF THE DELAWARE RIVER WATERFRONT. This 1900 photograph shows a horse and buggy in the background. Marcus Hook was a fishing village in the late 1800s and early 1900s. The Middle Wharf can be seen here, where fishing craft and pleasure boat enthusiasts congregated until its removal in 1925. The home of Marcus Hook resident Jasper Phillips is in the background. (Delaware County Historical Society.)

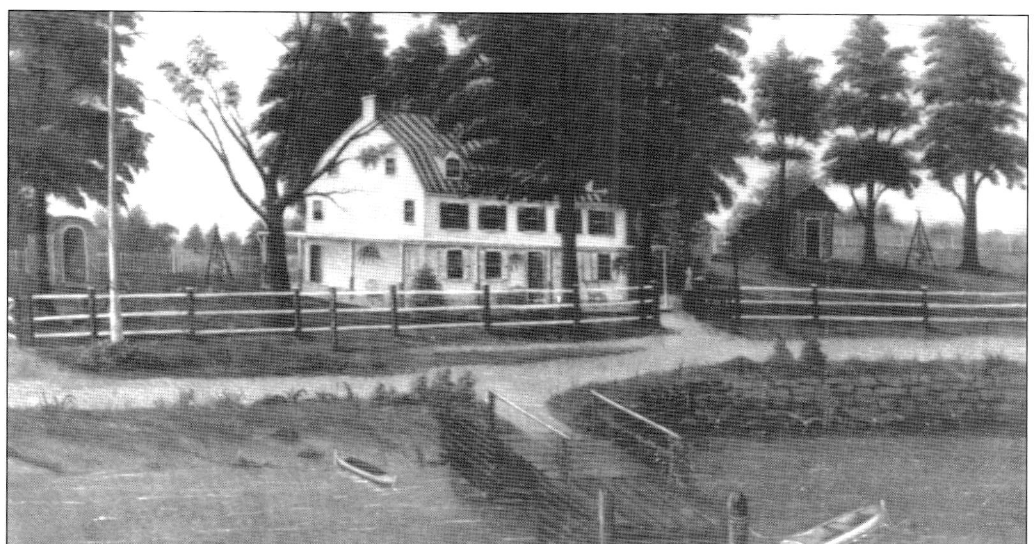

LINDENTHORPE PARK. This is a painting of Lindenthorpe Park, an amusement park that once stood on the Delaware River. This painting was found in a building when Joseph N. Pew purchased the property for the establishment of Sunoco. This painting shows the mansion that was erected in 1723. Lindenthorpe Park, opened in 1896, took its name from the huge linden trees on either side of the front entrance. The drawing is accurate, as a later 1904 photograph of a rock wall exists. (Hagley Museum and Library.)

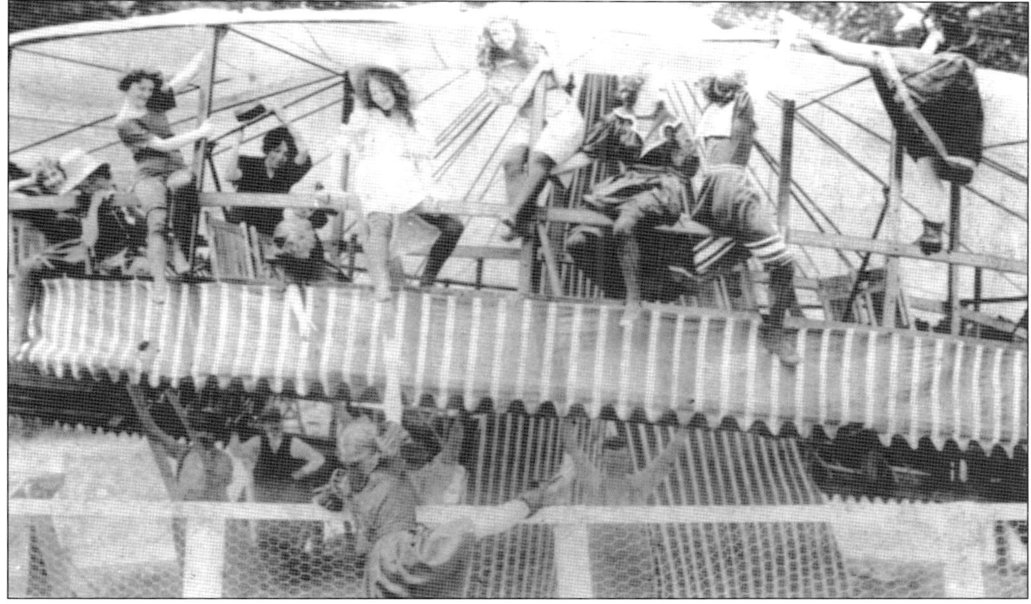

LINDENTHORPE PARK, 1890S. This very early photograph from the 1890s depicts one of the park's amusement rides called the Razzle-dazzle. The ride was 40 feet in diameter with one big seat all around and cost only 5¢. Each year the Pennsylvania State Fair was held at this park. In the park were palmists, lemonade stands, and sideshows. For two years a county fair was held with oddities like four-legged chickens, two-legged goats, and ostriches racing against racehorses. The park was purchased by Sunoco in 1901. (Hagley Museum and Library.)

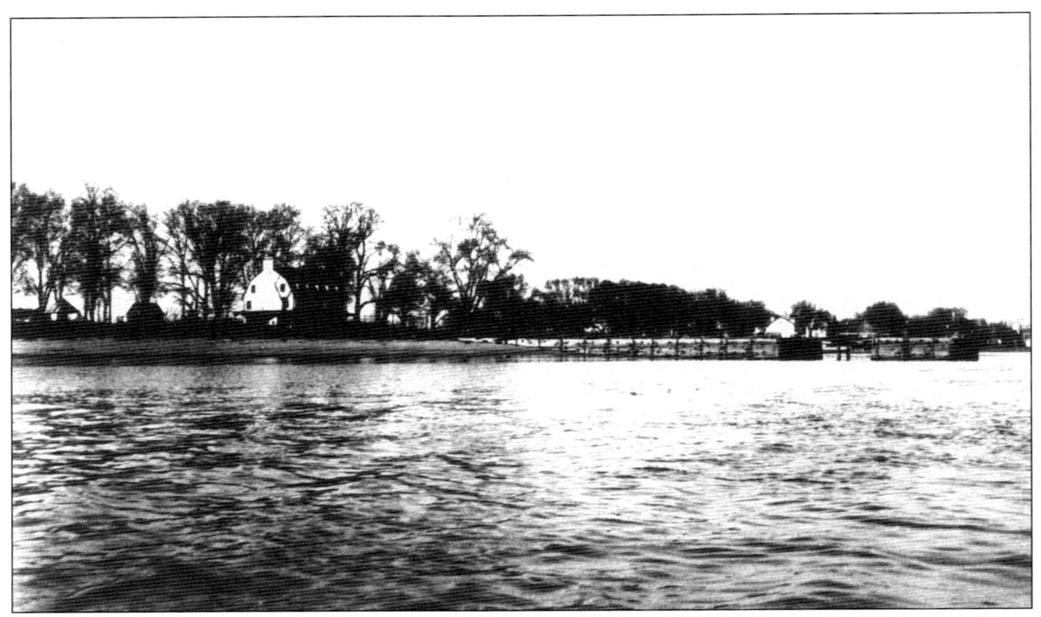

LINDENTHORPE MANSION. This original photograph, dated 1900, shows the Delaware River waterfront and the old Lindenthorpe mansion. The Lindenthorpe mansion was once a plantation on the Delaware River owned by William Hewes, a member of the Chichester assembly. The mansion was included in the land purchased by Joseph N. Pew for the Sunoco refinery in 1901. (Ralph Montella.)

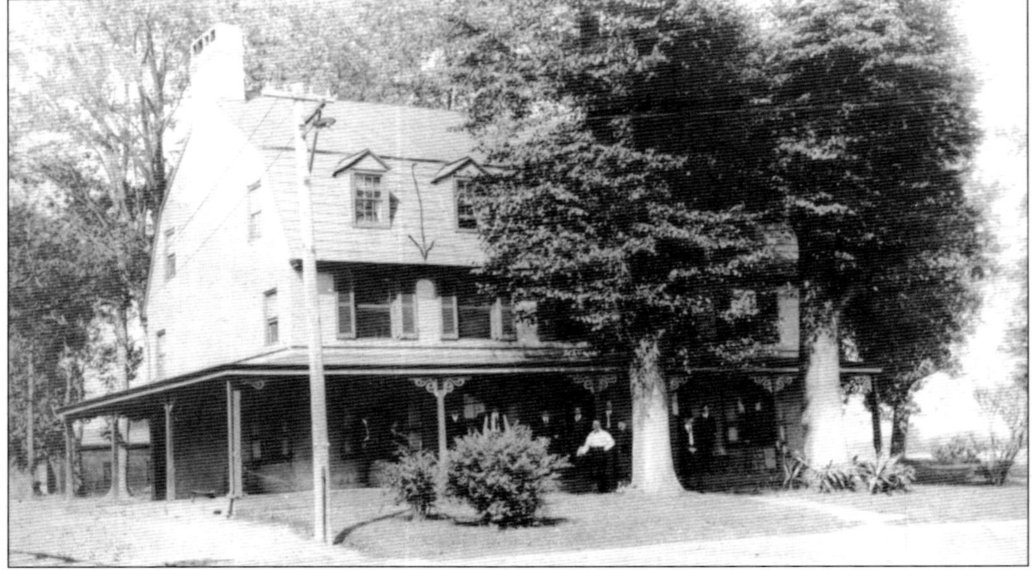

FIRST SUNOCO OFFICE. This close-up front view of the mansion shows the first Sunoco Marcus Hook refinery office in 1903. It housed the plant headquarters. The arrow in the photograph points to the worn date stone located on the outside wall that read "WHM-1723." Thomas Hargreaves, operator of Lindenthorpe Park, once said this stood for William Hewes and his wife, Mary, who lived in the old Hewes mansion at the same site. The mansion was torn down in 1955 to make way for a new extension to the office building at Sunoco.

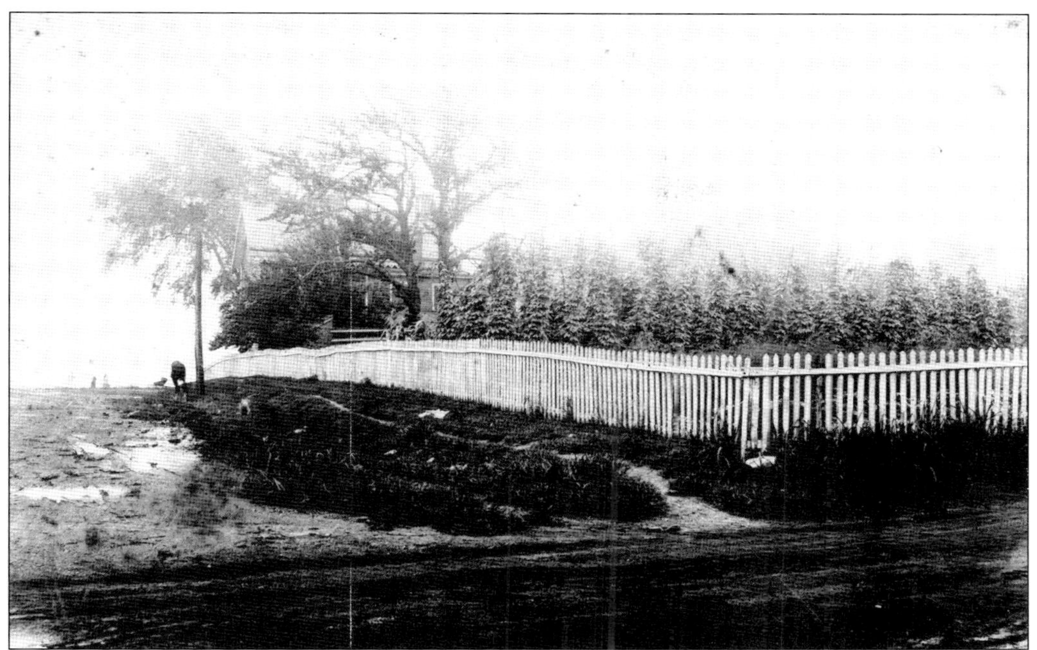

EARLY DELAWARE RIVER PHOTOGRAPH. This photograph was taken of Delaware Avenue from Second Street in 1906. This is the present site of the Sunoco gate on Delaware Avenue. If one looks closely at the photograph, one can see the trolley tracks leading to what was once the Lindenthorpe amusement park. (Ralph Montella.)

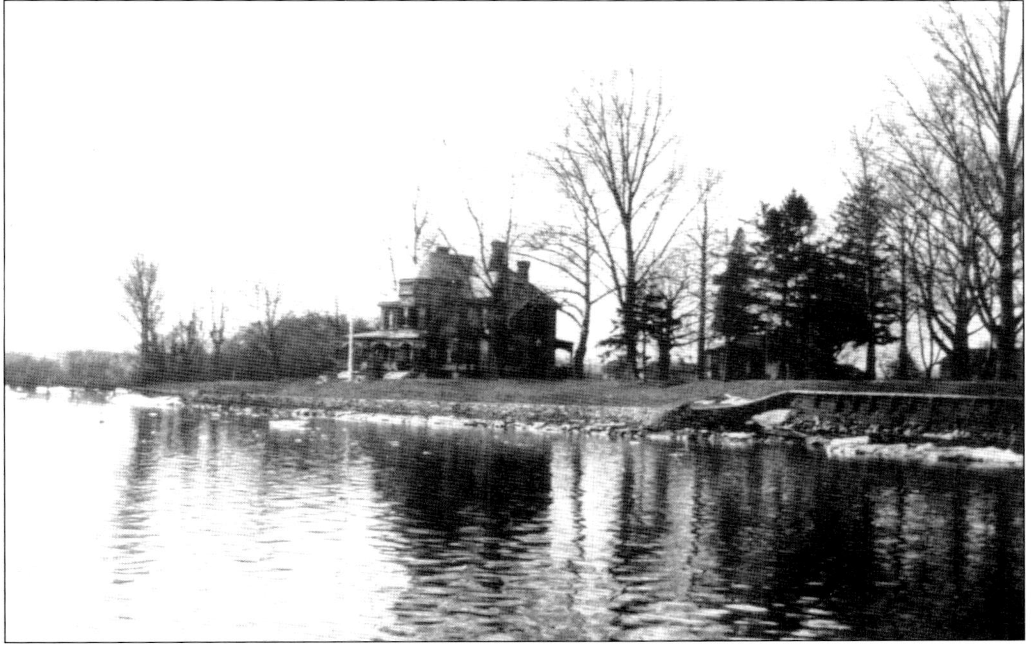

THE DELAWARE RIVER WATERFRONT, 1903. This is a photograph of the Delaware River at a time when fishing was very popular. The camera is focused on the western part of the quarantine station on the H. T. Sloan house. (Delaware County Historical Society.)

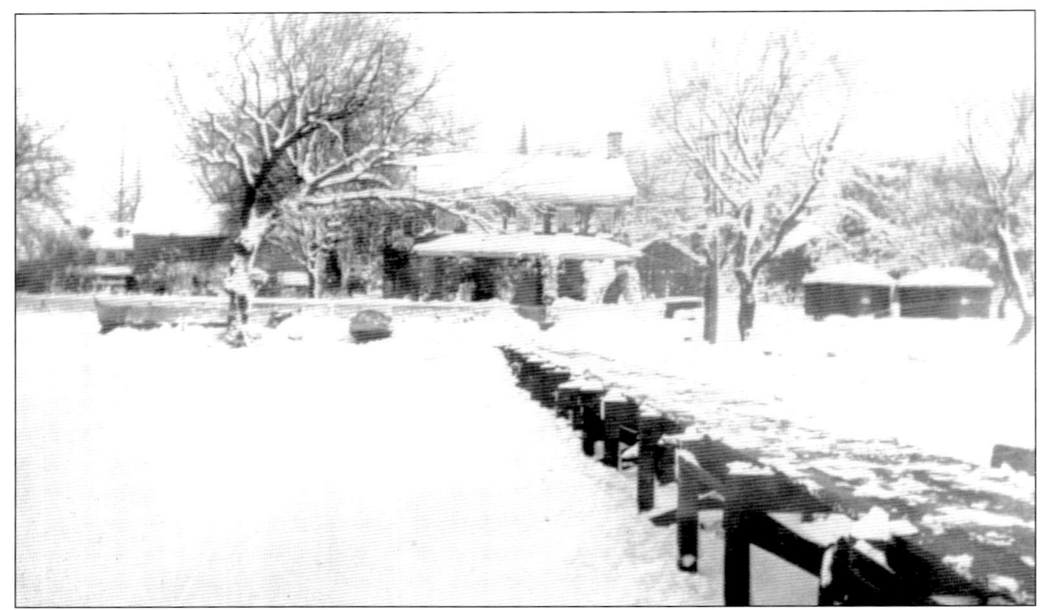

A SNOWY DELAWARE RIVER WATERFRONT. This photograph was taken by Harry Hueber in 1902 from a pier that once stood where Market Square Memorial Park and the Marcus Hook Community Center are now located. The home of Jasper Phillips, which was demolished in the 1950s by Sunoco, can be seen. The steeple of the old Marcus Hook Baptist Church, built in 1854 and razed in 1950, is visible on Market Street between Second and Third Streets. This photograph demonstrates how, according to Petey Pearson, an early Delaware County newspaper reporter, the hulls of ships were cut through by the ice. (Delaware County Historical Society.)

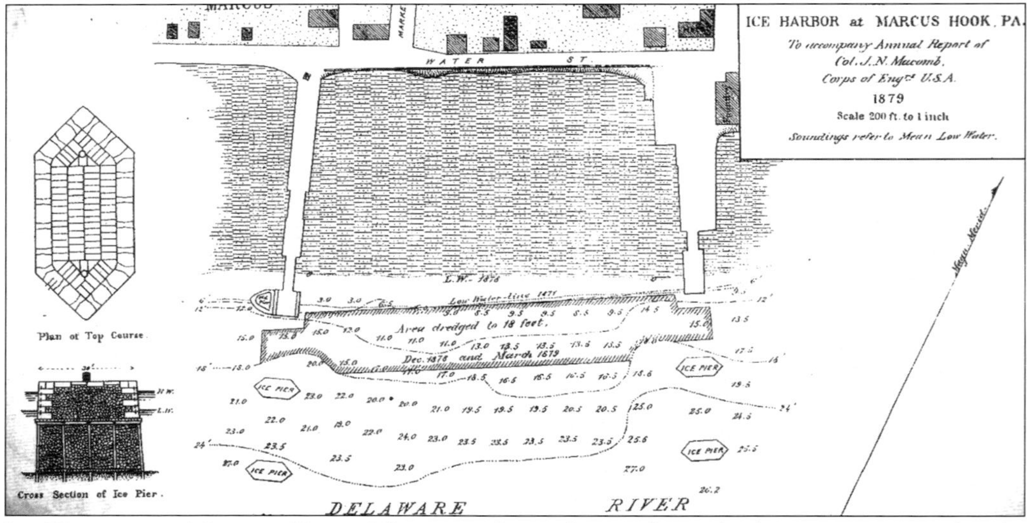

ICE HARBOR AT MARCUS HOOK. This map of 1879 depicts the ice harbor at Marcus Hook. The harbor, with deep water close to the shore, was always a haven for vessels. During winter it was necessary for a government iceboat to constantly sail up and down the channel and keep the ice moving. In 1785, a petition was presented to the state government asking that piers be erected for the protection of ships and for loading and discharging cargoes. The petition was granted, and the two wharves were finished in 1787. (MHPLCA.)

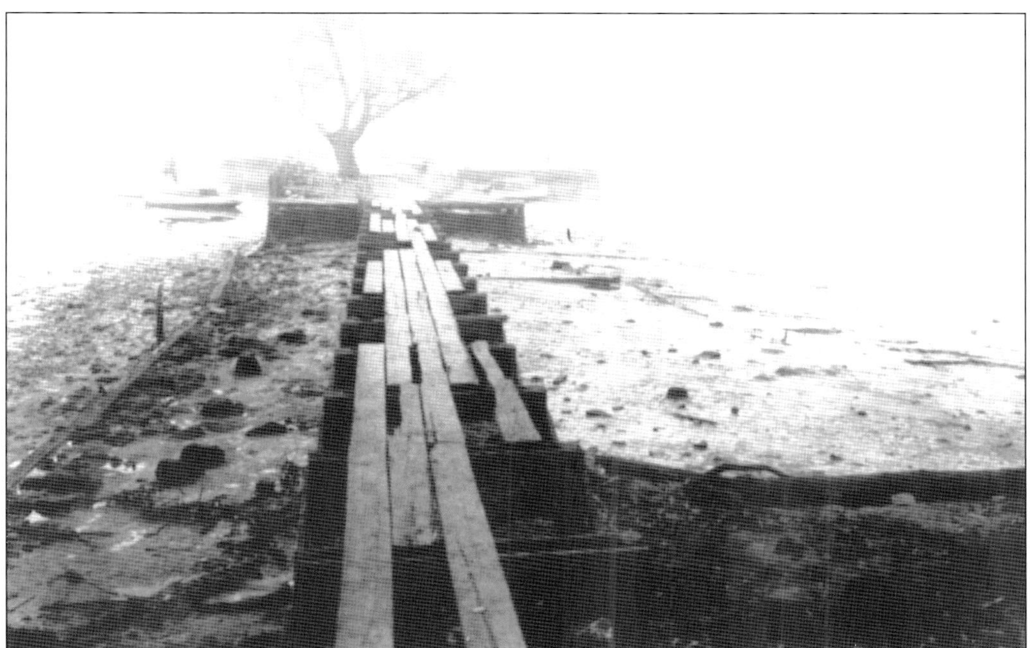

UPPER GOVERNMENT WHARF. This photograph was taken on October 15, 1930. The wharf was part of the indenture of June 2, 1930, under which the piers were leased to the borough of Marcus Hook for a period of five years from July 1, 1930. The wooden piers of Marcus Hook have the distinction of being erected by the State of Pennsylvania prior to the American Revolution. In 1785, Philadelphia merchants petitioned the state government to construct the piers along the Delaware River in the interest of the commercial supremacy of that city. (Delaware County Historical Society.)

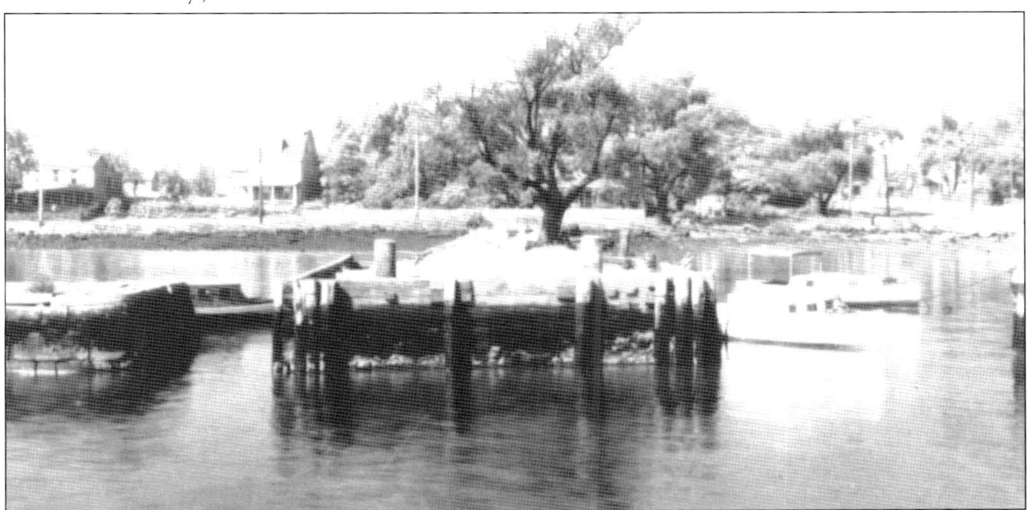

LOWER GOVERNMENT WHARF. There were originally eight piers and two landings in Marcus Hook. This photograph was taken in 1932. In the middle of this photograph under the large tree, people are having a picnic. The photograph is too bright to pick them up. The lower wharf later became the site of the U.S. quarantine station and later the U.S. Army Marine Maintenance Shop and U.S. Army Reserve Center. (Delaware County Historical Society.)

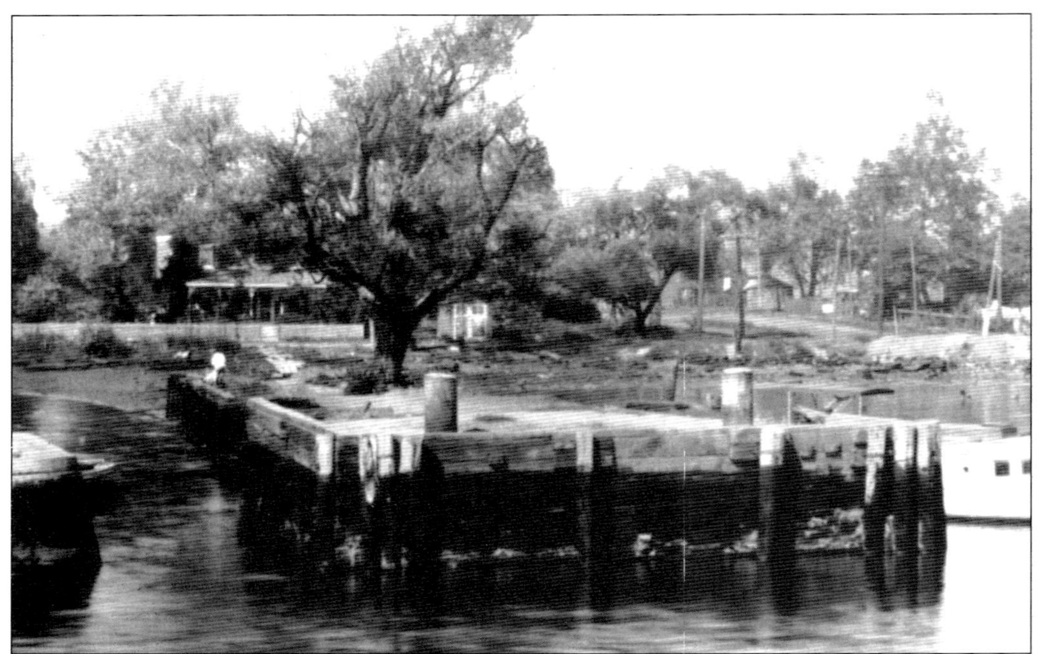

LOWER GOVERNMENT WHARF, 1930S. This is a Lower Government Wharf photograph from the 1930s. Later pictures of this area show great changes to the Delaware River waterfront, but one thing will not change. The boy with his back to the camera is fishing. If one looks closely, there is line going into the water. (Delaware County Historical Society.)

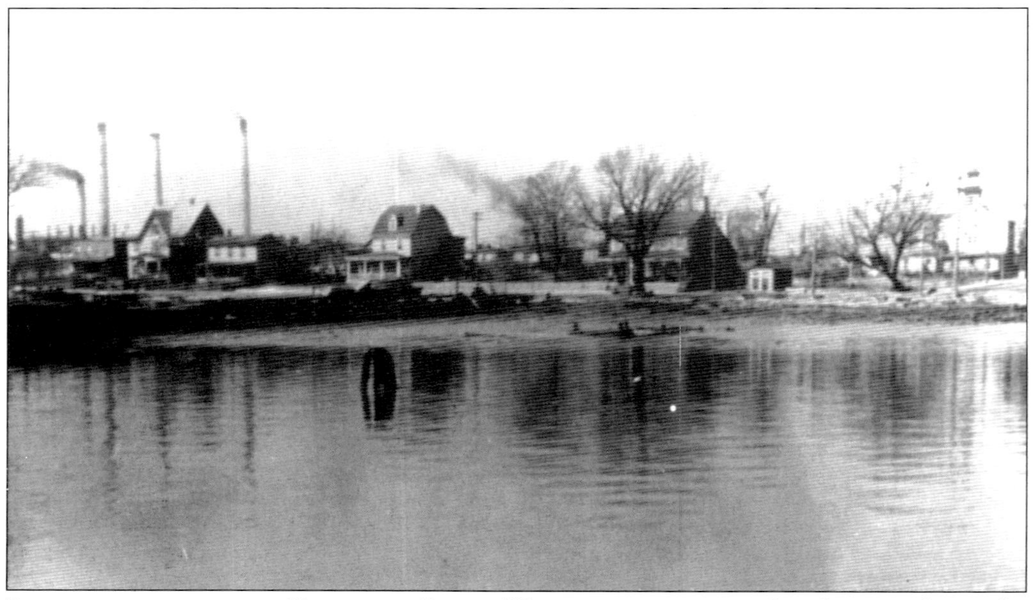

BOATBUILDING ON THE DELAWARE RIVER WATERFRONT, 1940S. On the waterfront, the first principal industry was boatbuilding. Boatbuilding continued to be the chief occupation of the people until the middle of the 19th century, when it was discontinued because of the introduction of ships too large for the resources of the plant at Marcus Hook. (Delaware County Historical Society.)

Three

THE GROWTH OF BUSINESS IN MARCUS HOOK

Marcus Hook has always benefitted from its central location and excellent access and the efficiency of transportation in the area. Geographically one-third of the American population lives within 500 miles of Marcus Hook. Thirty million are within 125 miles. Four interchanges with Interstate 95/Interstate 495 lie just outside the borough. Marcus Hook is served by Southeastern Pennsylvania Transportation Authority (SEPTA) rail and bus and Conrail freight.

Many of the businesses got their start on Market Street and on Post Road (now Tenth Street). A longtime borough resident said that the lights along Market Street resembled gaslights. Marcus Hook was the scene of various small businesses. In the early years, there was Green's corner and his general store, Wood Brothers, and Lipschutz's 44 Cigars. Baker and Baker built a sugar mill on the riverfront at the foot of Church Street. Hyde and Glover operated a machine shop known as the Pioneer Iron Works.

The population of the town tripled from 1,573 to 5,324 between 1910 and 1920 as major businesses like the Sunoco refinery grew and the American Viscose Company got its start. A 1927 property map shows 31 retail businesses fronting on Tenth Street between Viscose Village and Market Street. Among those listed were W. J. Thornton Drug Store, Presto Café, F. Vasil Candy Kitchen, John Bell Tailors, Spielmont Theater, Tabak's Dry Goods Store, Vernon's Electric, Marin's Drug Store, Cambridge Trust Company, Bergman's Cigar Store, H. Sachs Shoe Repair, Dorio's Tailor Shop, Mark's Department Store, C. Blumenkrantz Mens Furnishings, and Wood's News Stand.

By the late 1950s and early 1960s, many of the downtown businesses such as Mark's Department Store, C. L. Morris Furniture Store, the Congress Theater, Richards five-and-dime, and the M&H Restaurant disappeared. The arrival of the shopping malls and a massive downtown fire took their toll upon the small borough. Added to this was the opening of the Interstate 95, a major highway that completely bypassed the business district. Within a 20-year period, 42 of the 76 remaining businesses located in Marcus Hook closed their doors.

Community and economic development revitalization efforts that began in the late 1970s and have continued through to the present day successfully reversed this economic decline and led to the borough's resurgence. Today there are over 100 businesses located in Marcus Hook. The largest employer is the Sunoco Marcus Hook refinery, followed by Epsilon Products Company and Alan McIlvain Company.

Marcus Hook has long been a community supportive of commercial and industrial uses that supply beneficial service and employment to the borough and area residents. Borough officials have long recognized that the borough thrives when its businesses prosper.

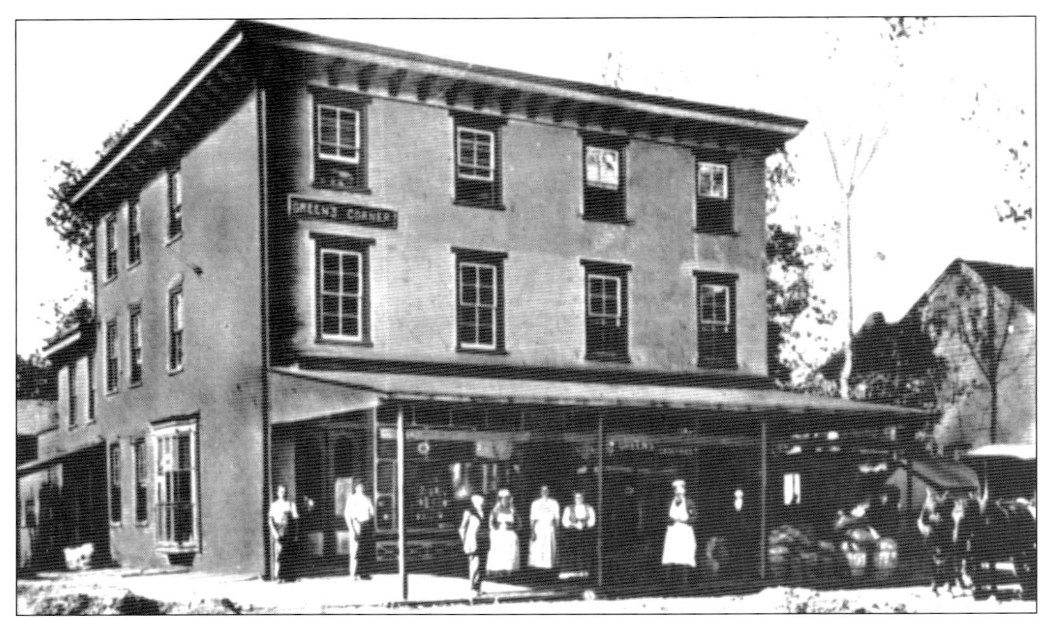

GREEN'S CORNER. Here is a pre-1900 photograph of Green's corner and his general store on the northwest corner of Third and Market Streets. Another name for this business was Joshua E. Green's Ship Chandler Store. For a number of years seafaring men were his customers when their vessels sailed into Marcus Hook. The first post office in Marcus Hook opened here on June 4, 1892. This was the same year that the Borough of Marcus Hook was incorporated (March 7, 1892.) (Delaware County Historical Society.)

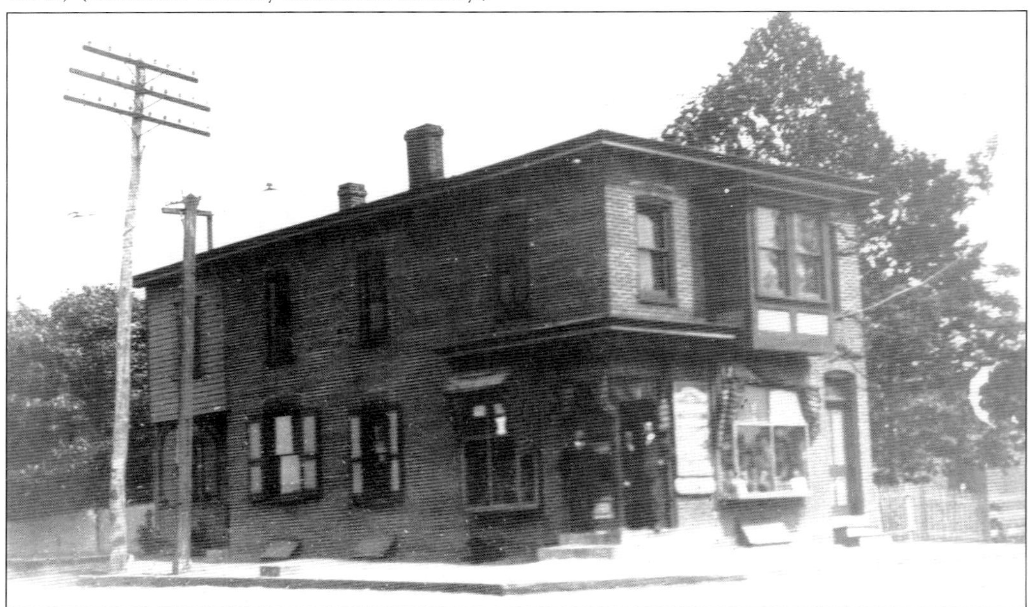

PECHMANN'S DRUG STORE. Here is a photograph of Pechmann's Drug Store located on the southeast corner of Tenth and Market Streets in 1907. Before public ambulances were used in the town, the druggist William Pechmann treated many patients at this drugstore. The drugstore later became Marin's Drug Store.

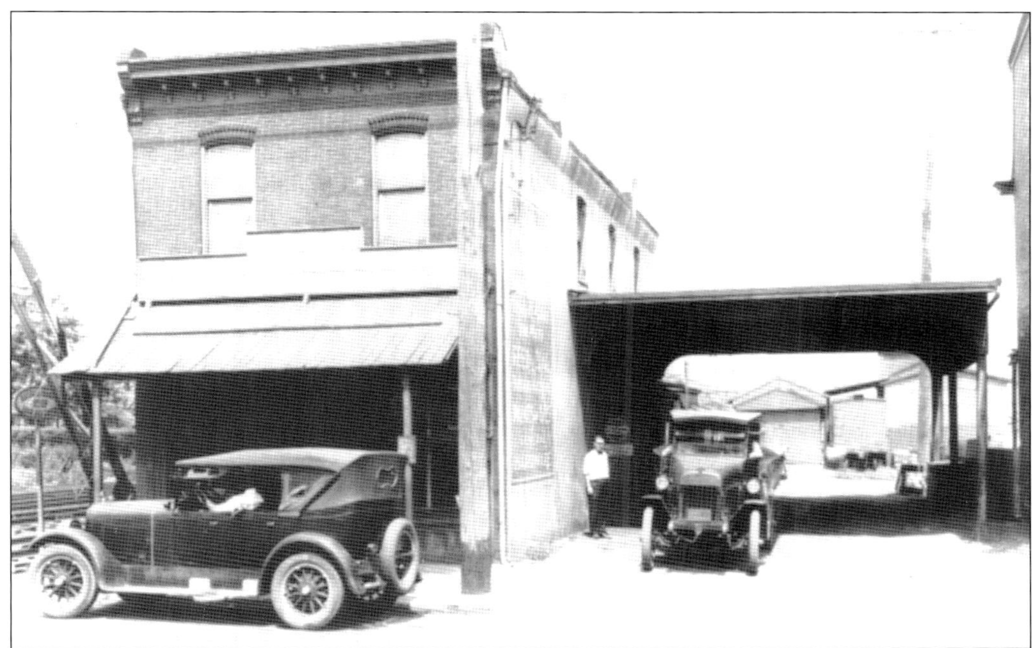

WOOD BROTHERS. Wood Brothers, a wood, lumber, and coal business, stood on Market Street on the Marcus Hook side of the railroad tracks. The proprietor of this business, John Heacock, is facing the camera. The Heacock family was a prominent family in Marcus Hook. They were Quakers and first came from England in 1711 in the sailing vessel called the *Three Sisters*. (Delaware County Historical Society.)

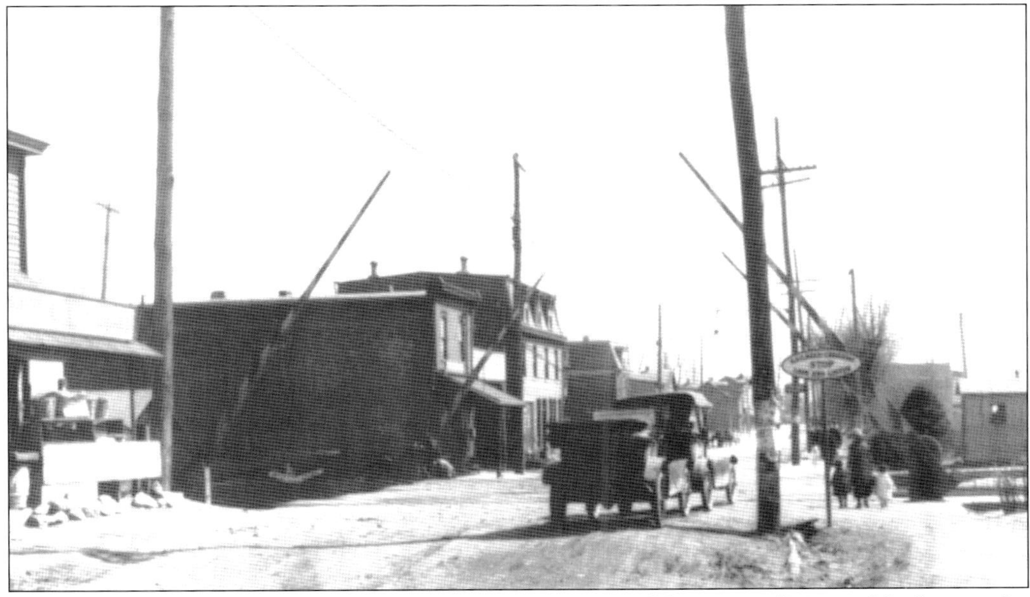

RAIL CROSSING AT MARKET STREET, 1920S. Another small business of Marcus Hook is on the left, Lipschutz's 44 Cigars. The photographer caught this scene just as a train was nearing. It is clear that this is a *c.* 1920 photograph because of the Model Ts in the background. (Delaware County Historical Society.)

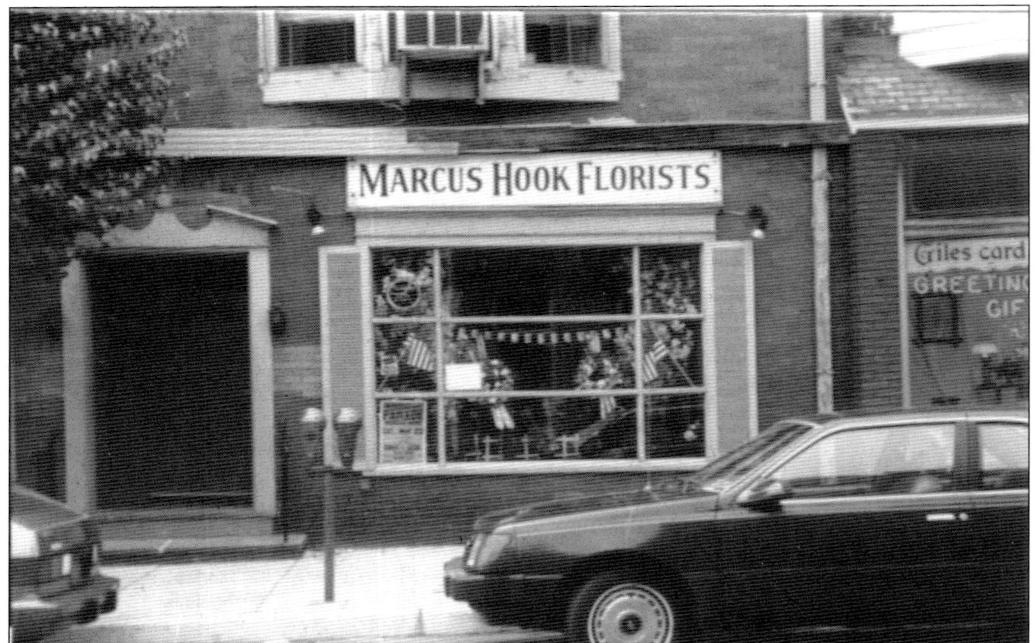

THE MARCUS HOOK FLORISTS AND GILES CARD AND GIFT SHOP. This picture window was an ever-changing scene from season to season and holiday to holiday. Giles Card and Gift Shop was started in 1960 by Covington Giles, who first operated a hardware store in this spot until it became the gift shop in 1932. This photograph was taken in 1984.

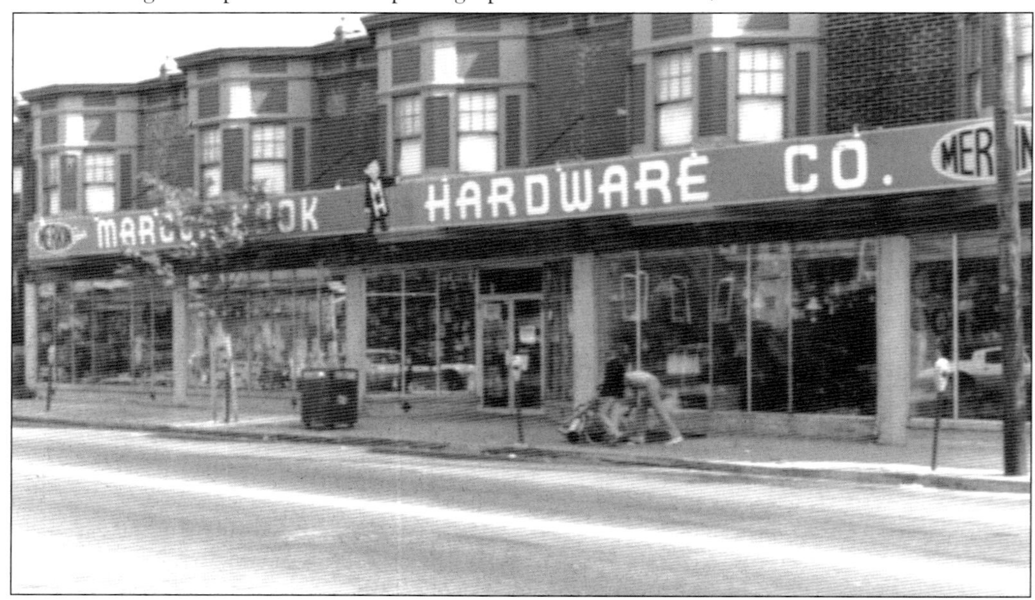

MARCUS HOOK HARDWARE COMPANY. The Marcus Hook Hardware Company has been in operation since 1924. Jules and Helen Tabak, who came from Romania, started this business as a small one-room dry goods and variety store. It is a community tradition for do-it-yourselfers. Prices vary in the store from a 2¢ nut and bolt to a $700 tractor-type lawn mower. This photograph was taken in 1984.

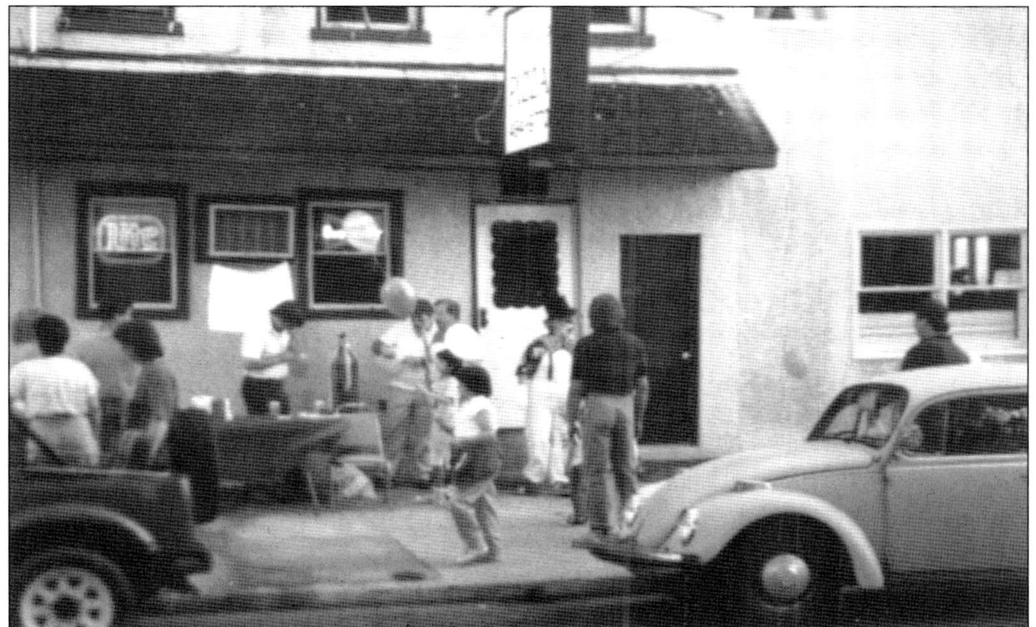

CLANK'S BAR AND PIZZERIA. Located on Market Street near Fourth Street, this bar and pizzeria was started in the early 1900s by Clarence Mingoia and offers different varieties of a Sicilian pie that many travel miles for in the Delaware County and Wilmington area. According to a few longtime residents of the borough, these pies were first cooked outside on an open stove, and they have the distinction of being "upside-down" pies where the cheese is put on the dough before the tomato sauce.

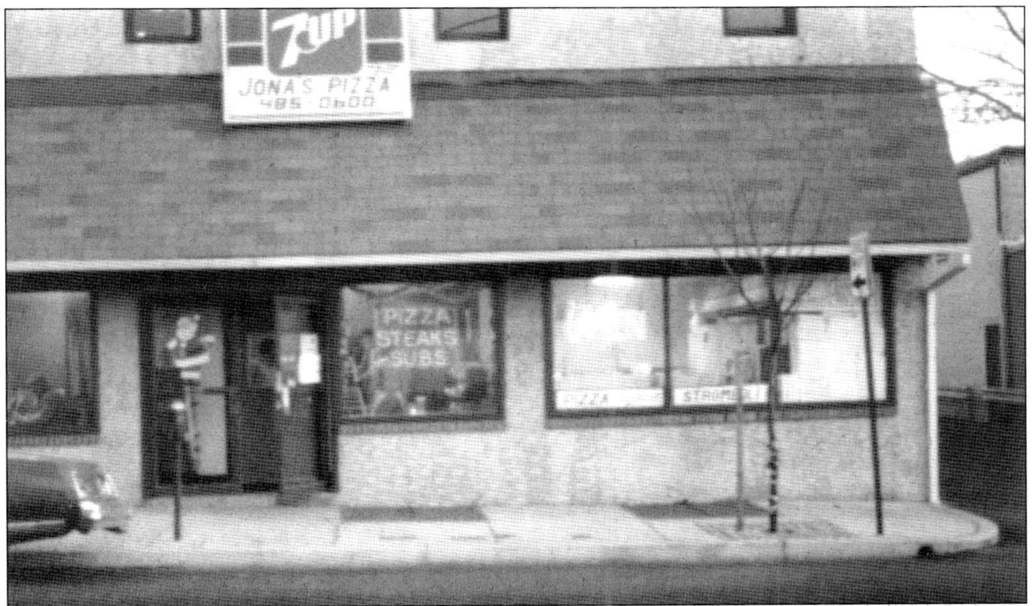

GOODFELLA'S PIZZERIA. This pizzeria was originally called Jona's Pizza, which opened in 1984. Jona's Pizza had the distinction of having the best strombolis in town. The owners of Jona's were Greek. In 2007, this pizzeria is now called Goodfella's.

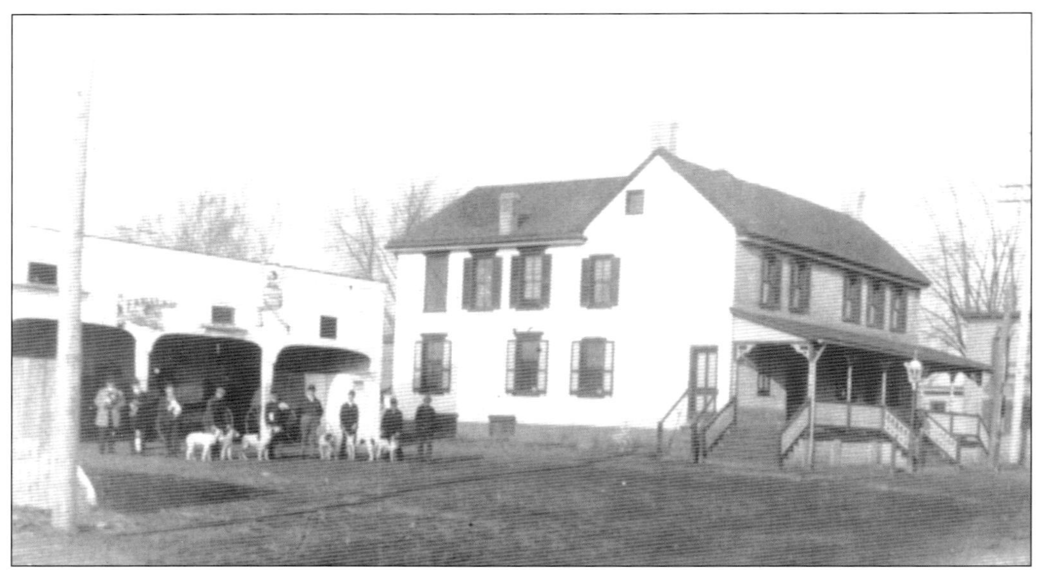

William McClure's Hotel. These nine sportsmen with man's best friend stand by the Union Hotel, originally started in 1729, which became the Marcus Hook Hotel the year this photograph was taken. William McClure, standing third from the right, was the proprietor of this hotel, which stood at the northwest corner of Tenth and Market Streets. This hotel was called the Ship Princess Amelia, the King of Prussia, the Sign of the Leopard, the United States Coat of Arms, and finally the Union Inn. Pres. George Washington and Pres. John Quincy Adams were said to have stopped at the hotel on their journeys. (Delaware County Historical Society.)

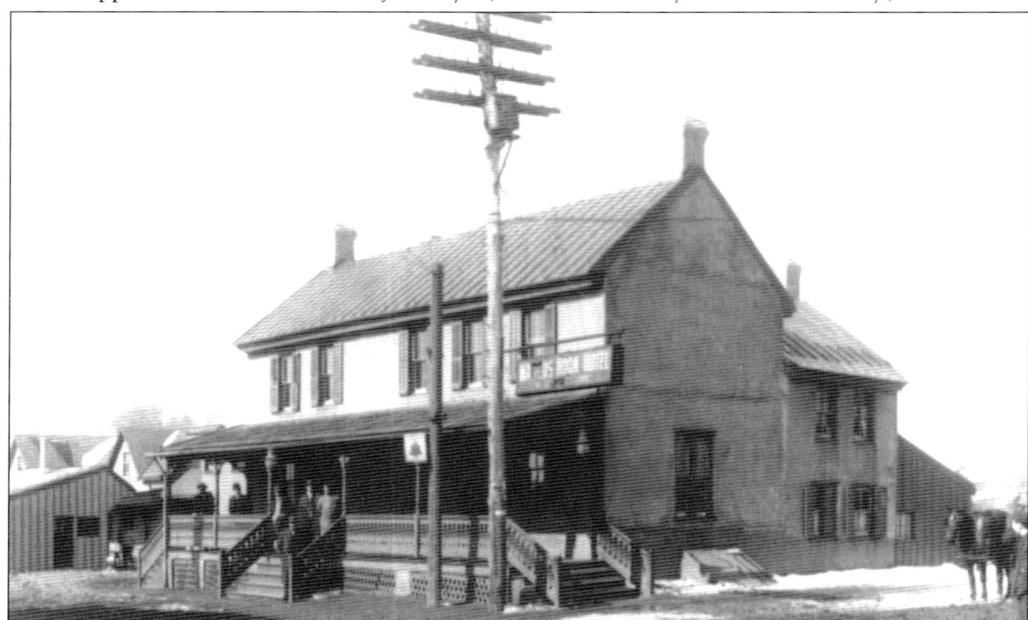

Marcus Hook Hotel. Here is the Marcus Hook Hotel with two horses and a young boy standing at the right side of the photograph. Located at Tenth and Market Streets, it was originally built in 1726, and it was later removed for the erection of the Marcus Hook National Bank. (Delaware County Historical Society.)

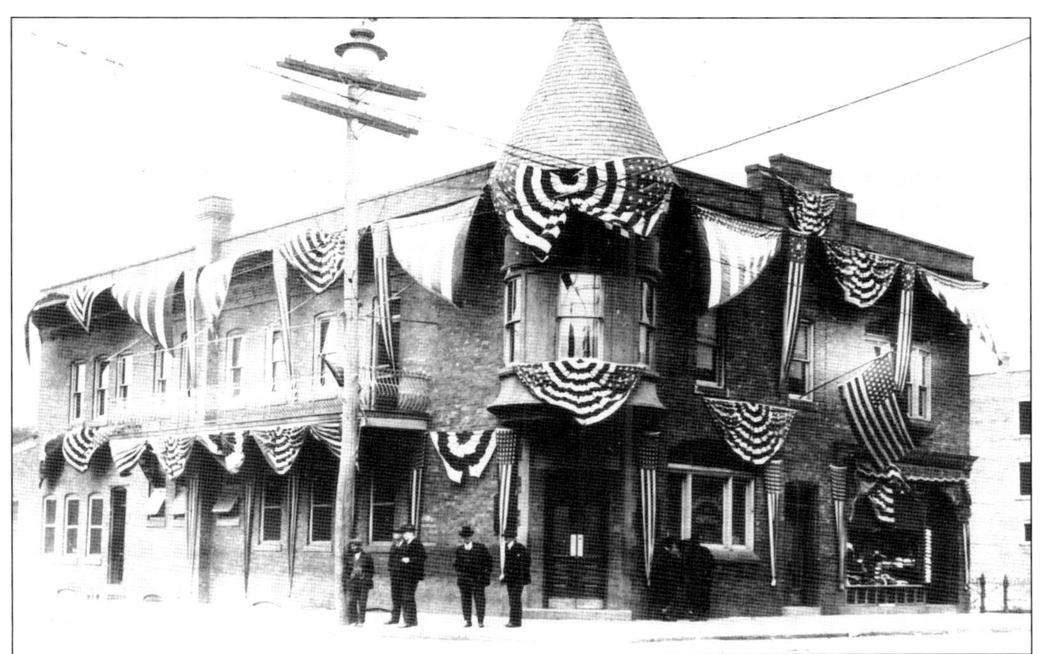

MARCUS HOOK HOTEL, C. 1911. Built in 1911, this was the later Marcus Hook Hotel at Tenth and Market Streets. The old Marcus Hook Hotel that previously occupied this site was razed. The hotel looks as if it were decorated for Memorial Day or another patriotic celebration. The photograph was taken sometime between 1911 and 1915. The hotel was a stopping point for the great and near great on trips to and from Washington, D.C. The site of the hotel later was occupied by Fidelity Bank. (Ralph Montella.)

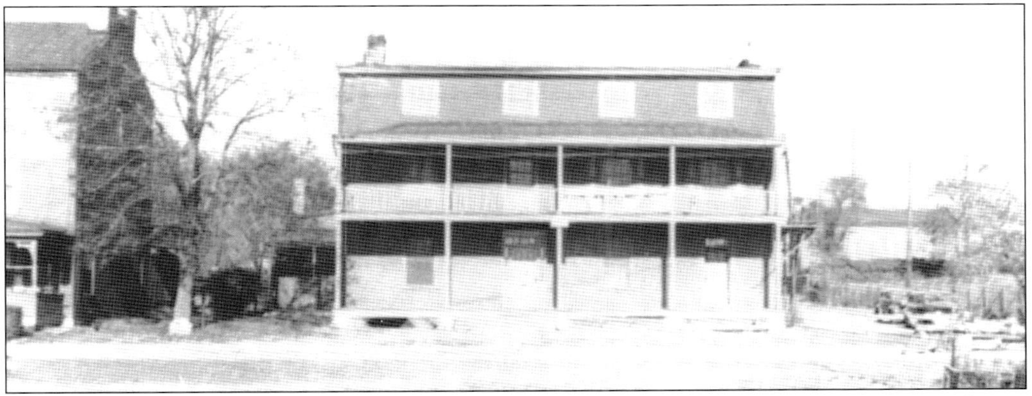

SPREAD EAGLE TAVERN. The former three-story Spread Eagle Tavern, located at the northwest corner of Delaware Avenue and Church Street, was the headquarters for sportsmen who enjoyed gunning for ducks, reed, rail birds, quail, and so on, or those interested in hook and line fishing for white perch, rock, and other fish between Pennsylvania and New Jersey. This tavern was once called the Tun and Punch Bowl, but it became the Spread Eagle Hotel in 1791. Taverns existed in Marcus Hook as far back as 1661. In 1956, it was known as the Forty-Six Hotel. The wide front porches are reminiscent of life in Marcus Hook when fishing and sailing boats were plentiful on the river. According to legend, underneath the hotel was hidden a basement room where before and during the Civil War slaves were smuggled from Marcus Hook and led through a tunnel to a wharf and shipped farther north. (Delaware County Historical Society.)

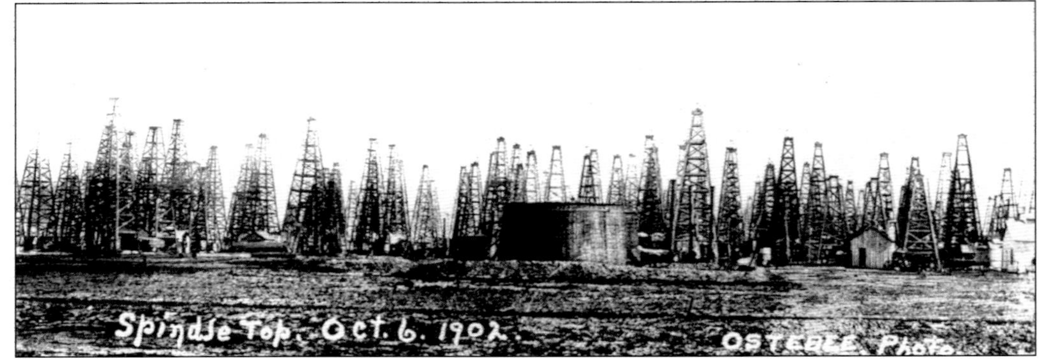

SPINDLETOP. In May 1901, Joseph N. Pew incorporated Sunoco in New Jersey and began securing leases and crude oil in the new Spindletop oil field in Beaumont, Texas. Wildcatters had struck oil on January 10, 1901. With business growing, Pew purchased 82 acres in Marcus Hook as the site for a second refinery to process crude oil shipped by tanker from Spindletop. This picture was taken on October 6, 1902. (Hagley Museum and Library.)

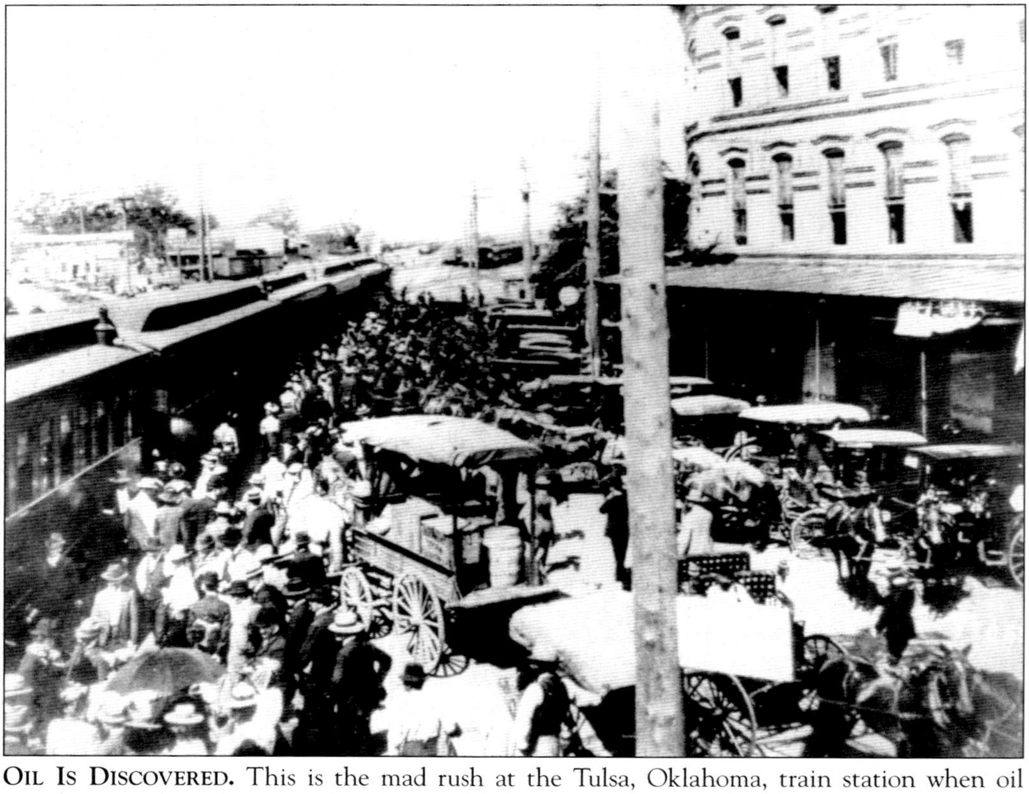

OIL IS DISCOVERED. This is the mad rush at the Tulsa, Oklahoma, train station when oil was discovered in Texas and Oklahoma. "Trains came in crowded with impatient men, who leaped off the train before the station was reached," according to a reporter from a 1901 Texas newspaper who reported about the excitement caused by the Spindletop find. (Hagley Museum and Library.)

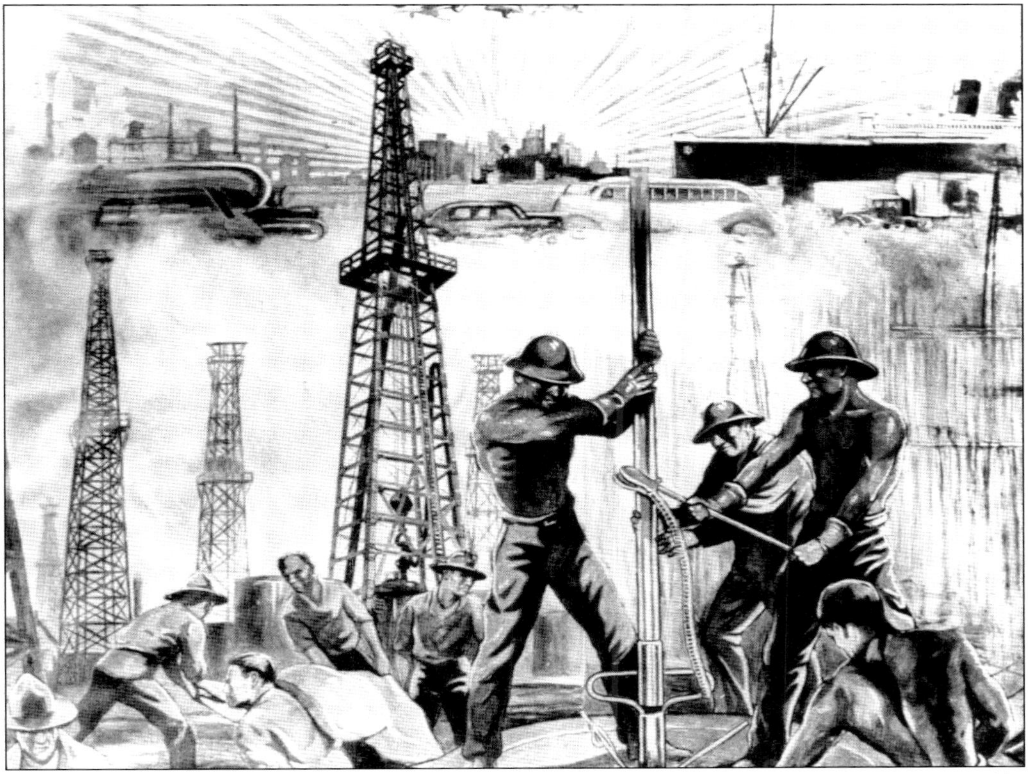

THE SEARCH FOR PETROLEUM. This drawing, which was a giant mural at the New York World's Fair in 1939, dramatizes the arduous search for petroleum. (Hagley Museum and Library.)

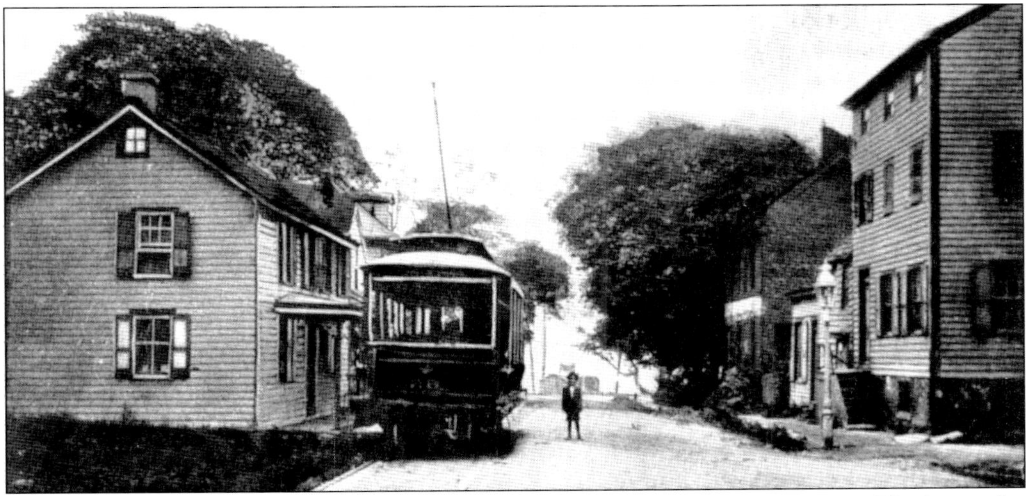

THE FOOT OF MARKET STREET. This is the foot of Market Street, Marcus Hook, in the early 1900s. On ground one block west of the spot shown, Sunoco established its Delaware River waterfront refinery in 1901. Joseph N. Pew, founder of Sunoco, purchased 82 acres and immediately began work to build refining stills. Marcus Hook was a good location because it was on the water and oil could be transported by ship and the land had access to the railroads. (Hagley Museum and Library.)

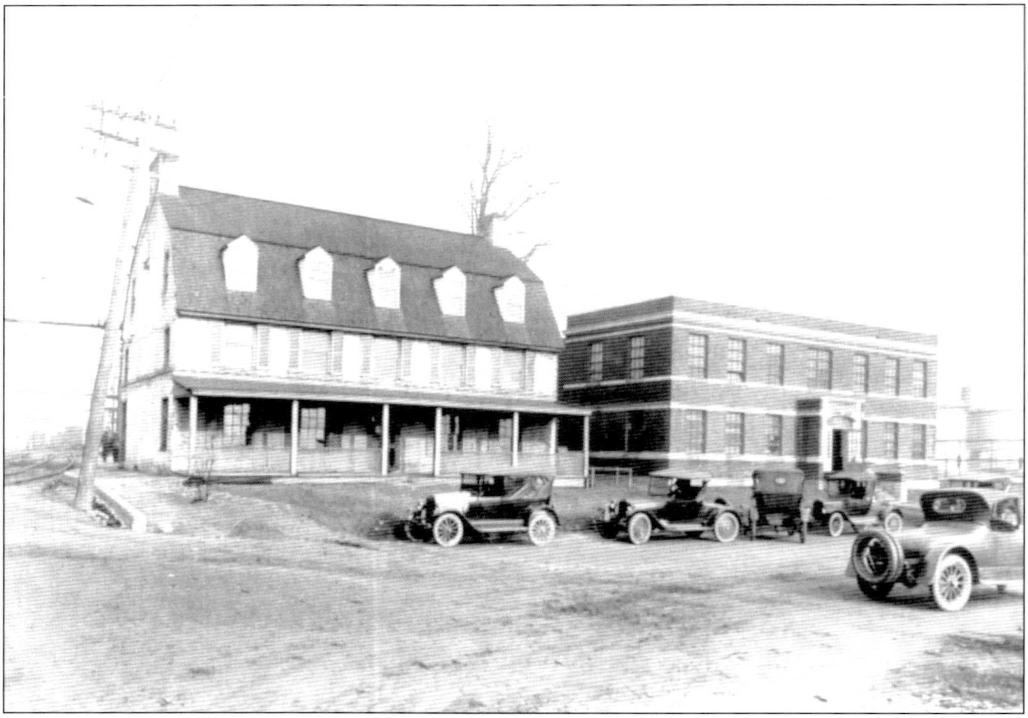

THE FIRST OFFICE OF SUNOCO. Lindenthorpe, the first office of Sunoco, is on the left, and the building on the right became Sunoco's present office in 1934. This is east of the former Hewes Avenue. This photograph was taken on February 7, 1924. (Delaware County Historical Society.)

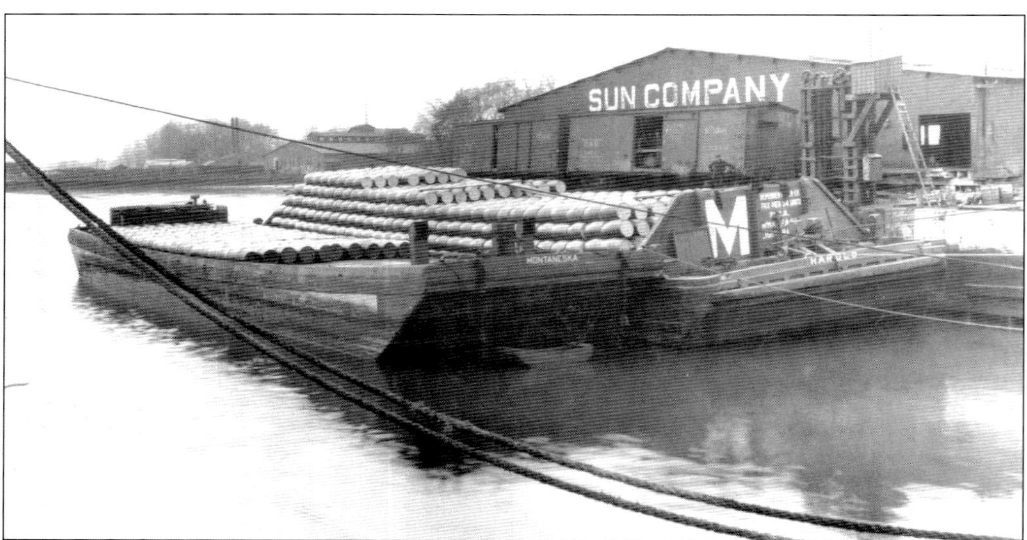

WOODEN BARRELS. In 1915, Sunoco shipped its Red Stock lubricating oil from Marcus Hook to customers in wooden drums. A total of 25 grades of Sunoco oil were shipped in wooden barrels. These were barrels from the Hardwood Packaging Company, a business in the borough that had its start in 1912 making wooden barrels. Shipments of Sunoco oil were replaced by steel drums due to the scarcity of wooden packages during World War I.

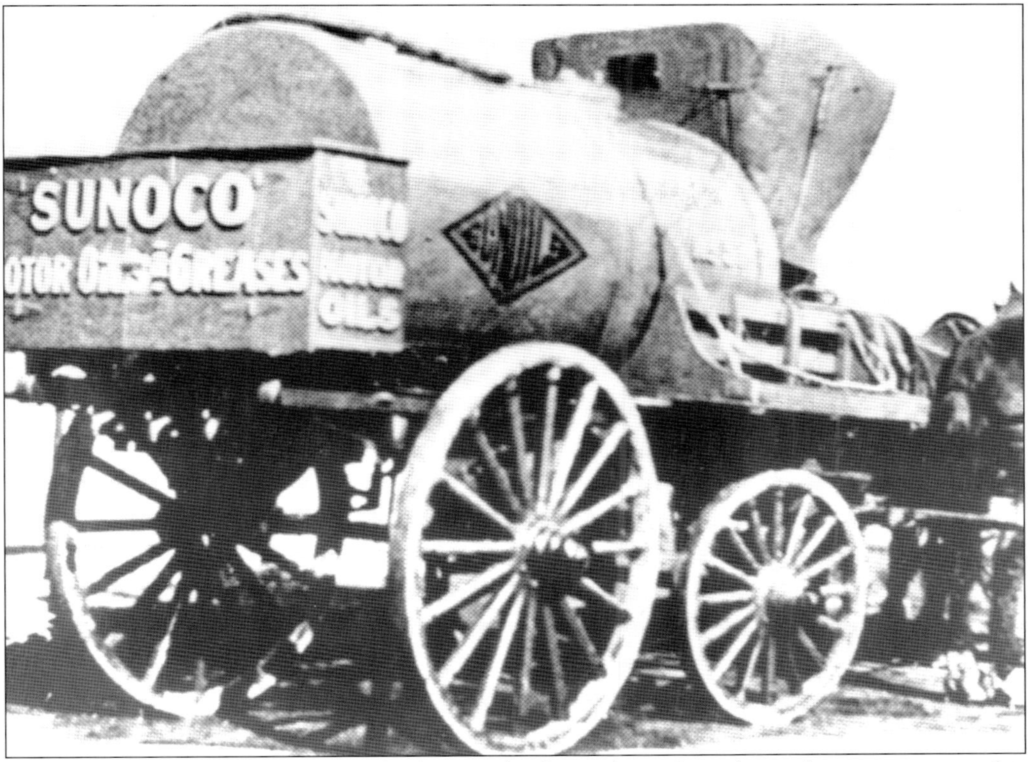

SUNOCO TANK TRUCK. Think of the big 18-wheeler tank trucks today and imagine seeing this horse-drawn carriage delivering oil before the 1920s. This was one of the Sunoco tank wagons used in the distribution of Sunoco products at Detroit in 1907.

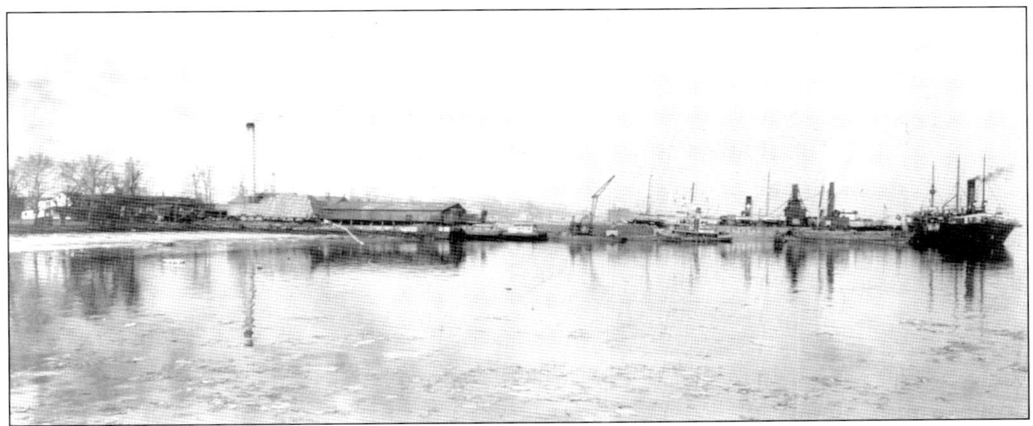

SUNOCO REFINERY ON THE DELAWARE RIVER. This photograph taken during World War I shows the vessels, dock, and old barrelhouse at Sunoco's Marcus Hook refinery. (Hagley Museum and Library.)

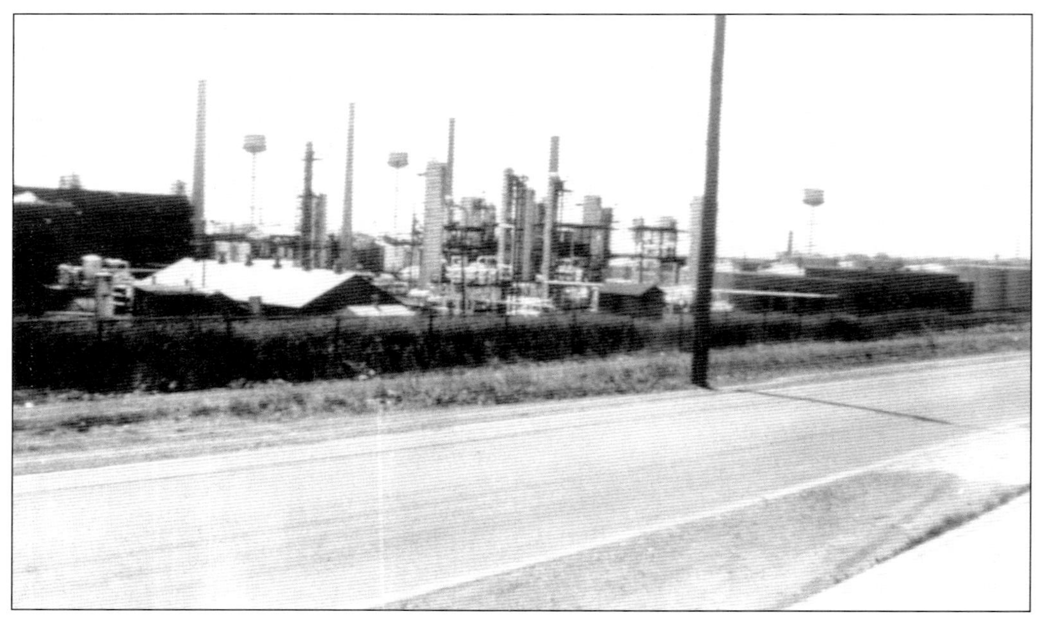

SUNOCO REFINERY, 1938. Here is an old photograph of the Sunoco refinery on Green Street in 1938. Sunoco was a major contributor in the Allied victory of World War II. It processed more aviation fuel than any other refinery during World War II. (Delaware County Historical Society.)

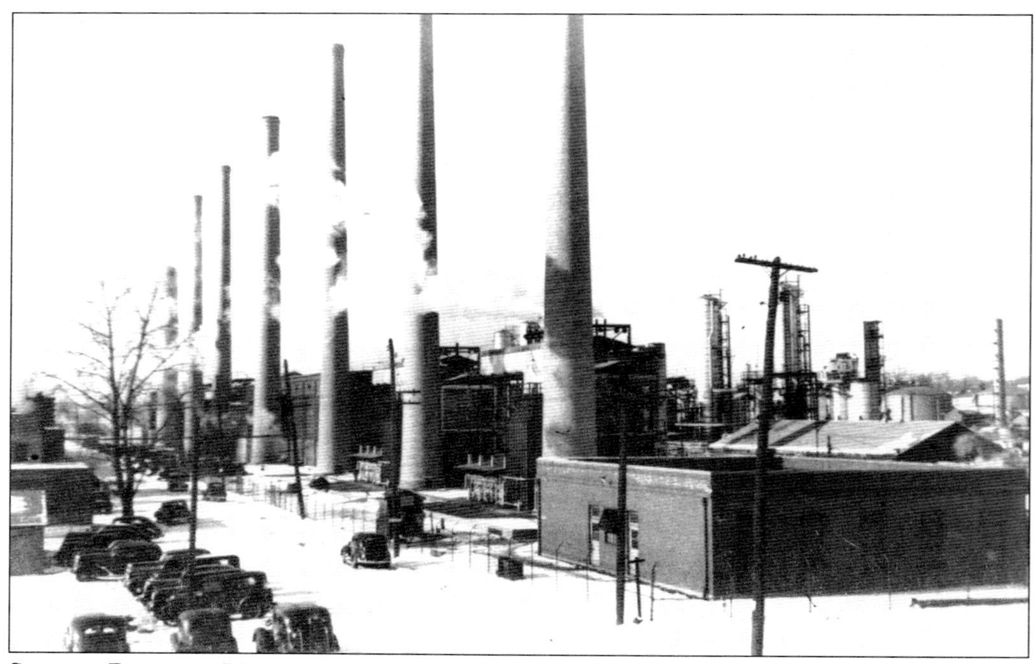

SUNOCO REFINERY UNITS. Here are Sunoco units one, two, and three looking west from Green Street in the late 1930s; they were built between 1902 and 1914.

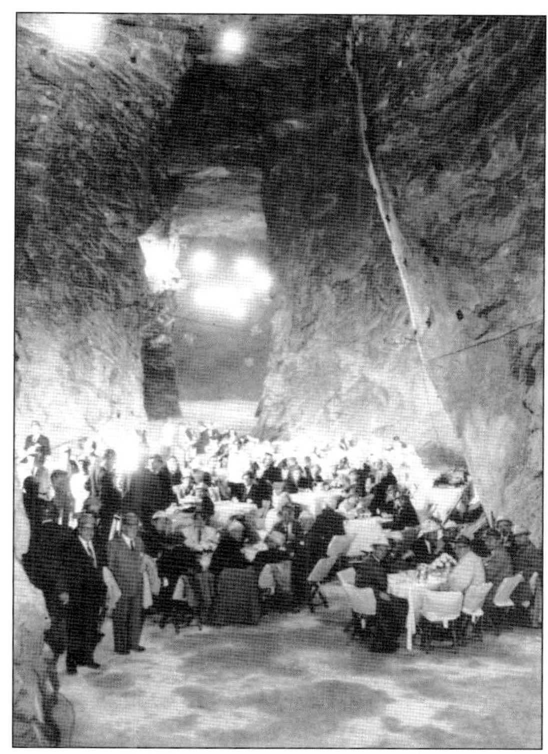

EATING IN AN UNDERGROUND CAVERN. Within the Sunoco Marcus Hook refinery footprint are located five underground caverns. Beginning in 1958, Sunoco pioneered the use of underground caverns to store butane, propane, and propylene, since they were cheaper to maintain and considered safer than the conventional network of pipes and tanks in aboveground storage. The Sunoco employees in this 1961 photograph are enjoying lunch in cavern No. 5, which holds 1.035 million barrels of product. Its construction took 22 months beginning with one man and a pneumatic drill working from a 72-inch shaft 425 feet down to the bottom of the cavern. Power equipment was disassembled, lowered piece by piece, and reerected in the cavern. The granite was mined with columns of granite left in place to maintain support.

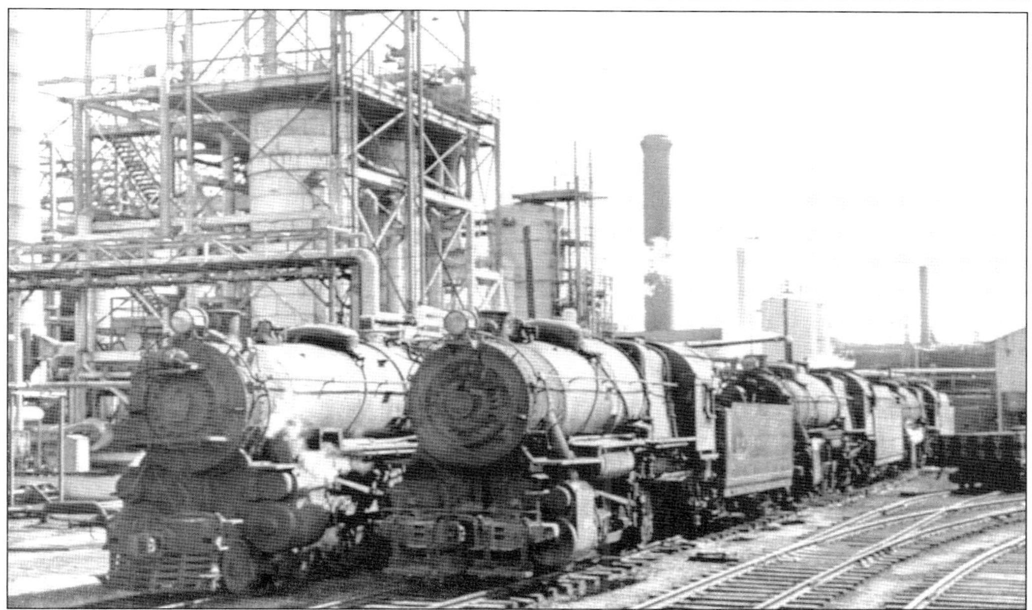

OLD STEAM LOCOMOTIVES. Here is a photograph of the old locomotives at the Sunoco refinery. They produced steam from waste gas. The photograph was taken on February 24, 1951. The old iron horses produced steam to make high-test aviation gas at the Sunoco refinery. At this time in the 1950s, they were renting for $17 a day, and they produced steam from waste gas produced in the plant. (Urban Archives of Temple University.)

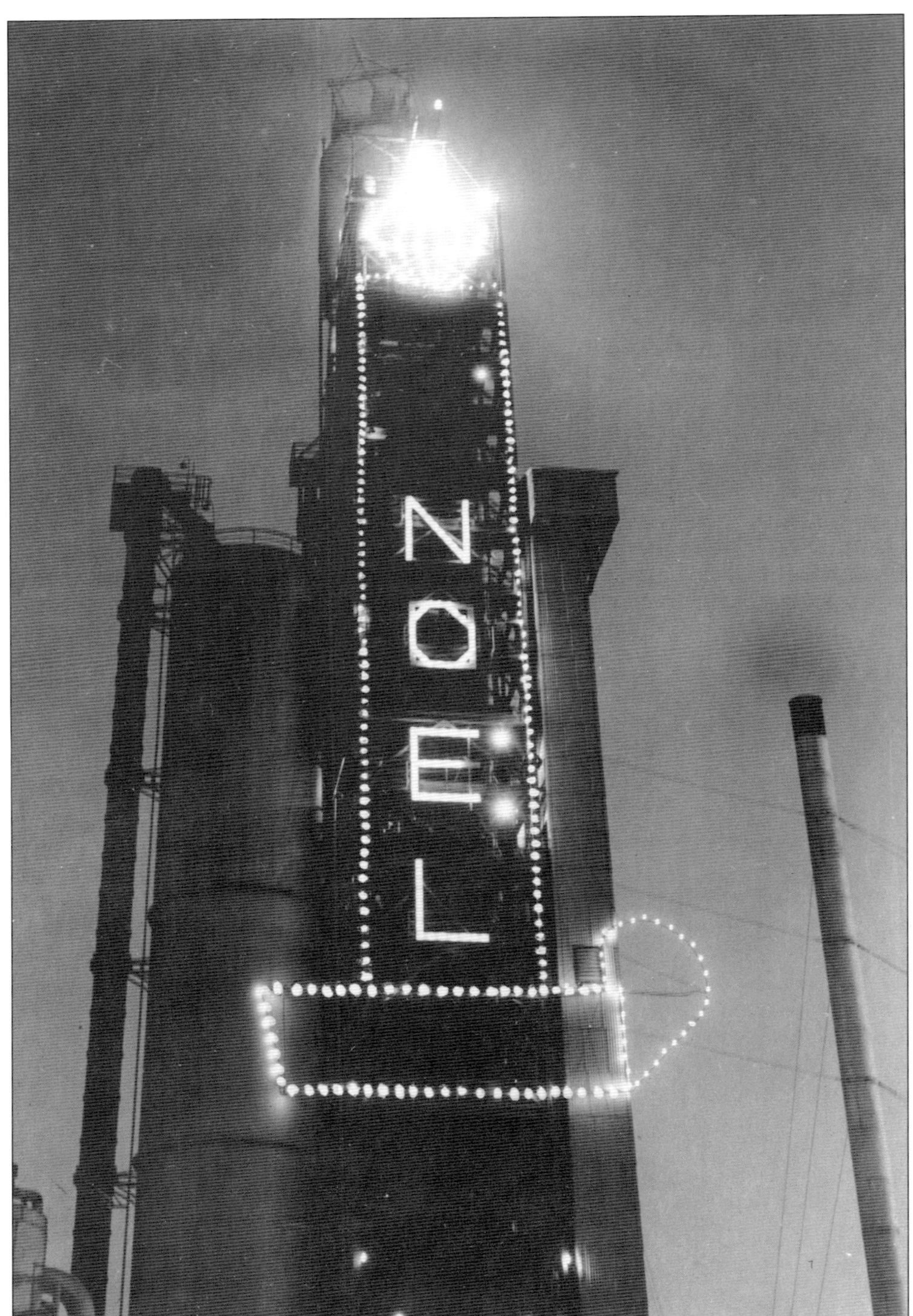

CHRISTMAS DECORATION. During Christmas in 1959 this is how the Sunoco refinery decorated the 12-3 plant in the area of Seventh and Green Streets. The giant 150-foot candle was 25 feet wide with a 60-foot base. It was outlined by red lights and had a 30-foot flame with yellow lights and a base of green lights.

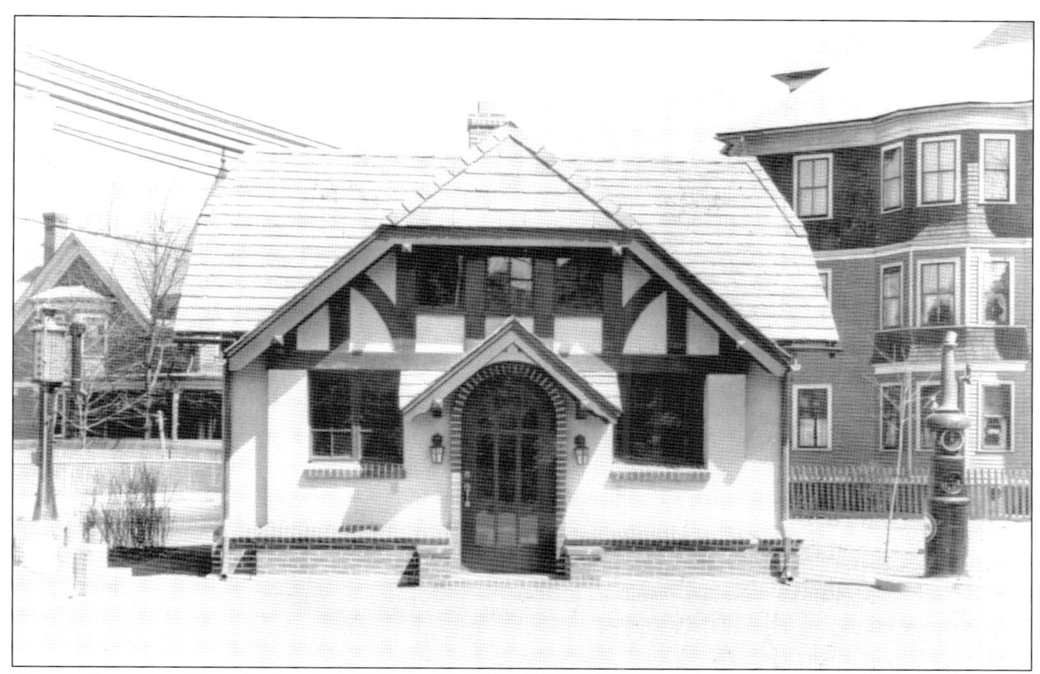

Early Sunoco Gas Station. Here is a very early Sunoco gas station with an old gas pump at the right. This station was constructed to look similar to a house. (Hagley Museum and Library.)

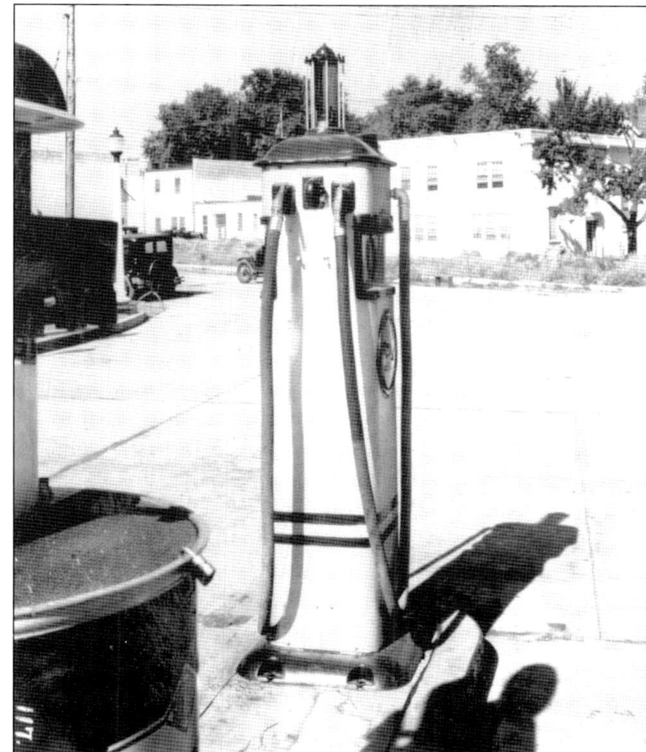

An Old Sunoco Gas Pump. This is a close-up shot of what the early Sunoco gas pumps looked like. Sunoco concentrated on improving the thermal cracking process, which produced gasoline by breaking apart crude oil molecules using high temperature and pressure. This resulted in Blue Sunoco, a high-test gasoline offered at regular gasoline prices. (Hagley Museum and Library.)

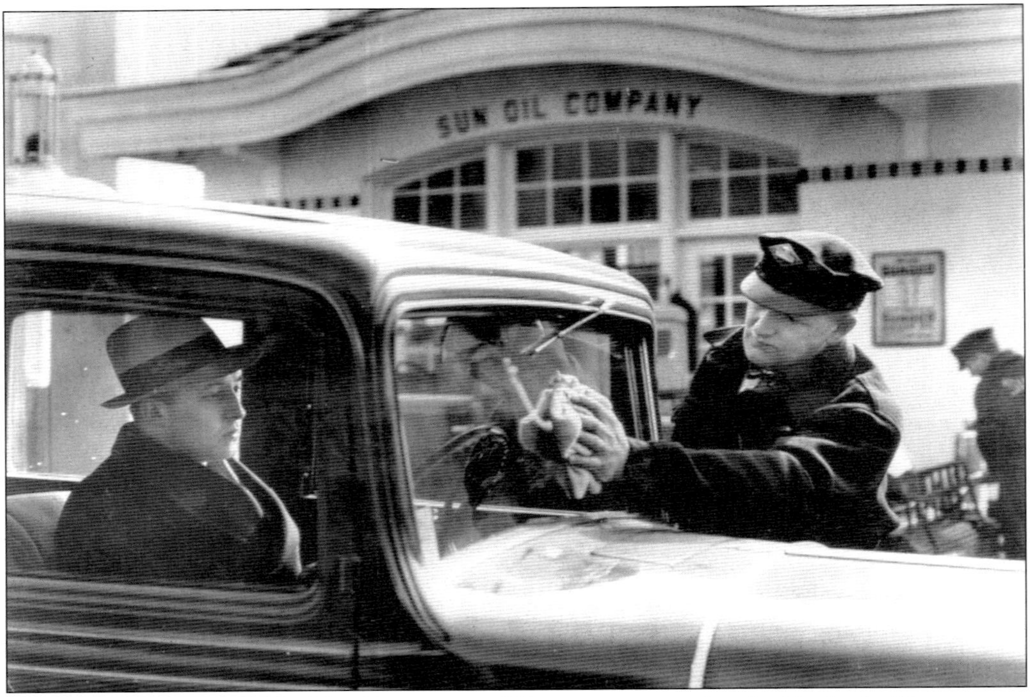

WINDSHIELD SERVICE. Windshield service, sir? This service is rarely asked for in the 21st century, but it was asked for at the Bywood Station in Bywood in 1934. This was the "thoughtfulness of the dealer" motto that Sunoco's history has been famous for. (Hagley Museum and Library.)

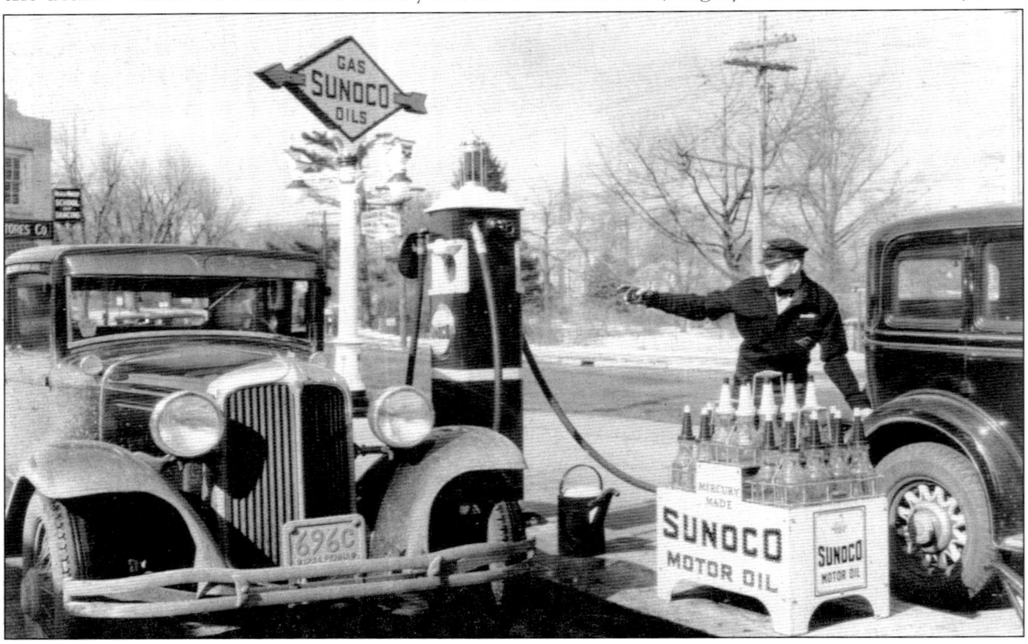

OLD MERCURY-MADE SUNOCO MOTOR OIL. Fill 'er up? The attendant stands by the old mercury-made Sunoco motor oil at the Bywood service station in Bywood in 1934. (Hagley Museum and Library.)

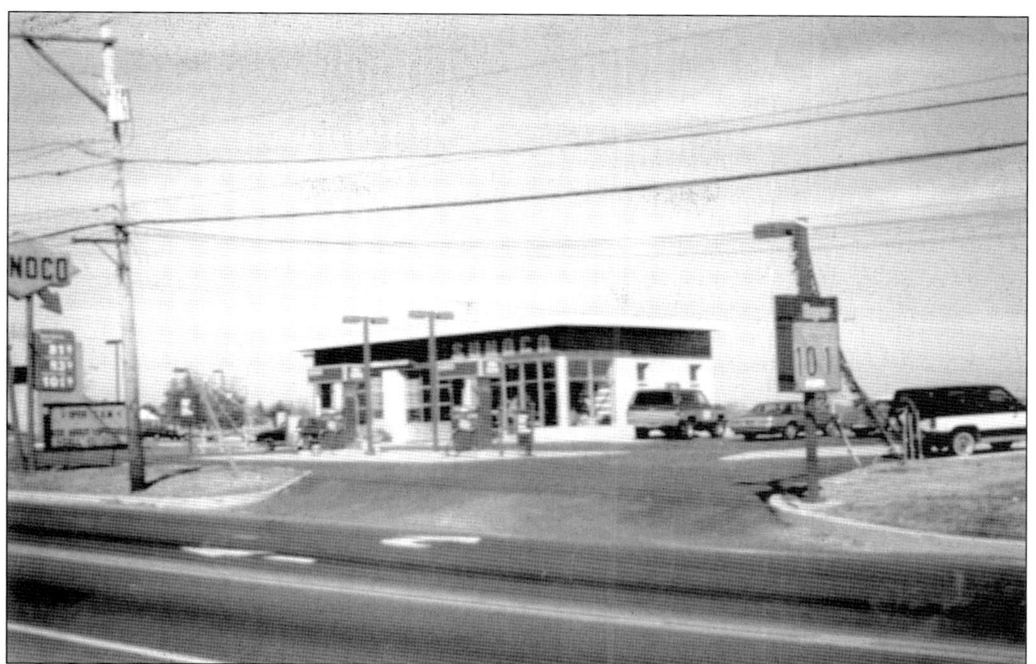

MODERN SERVICE STATION. This is a Sunoco service station of the 1980s. Notice the price of gasoline—$1.01 per gallon. Since the 1980s, the price of gasoline has steadily climbed to prices over $2 a gallon, which Americans are paying in the first decade of the 21st century.

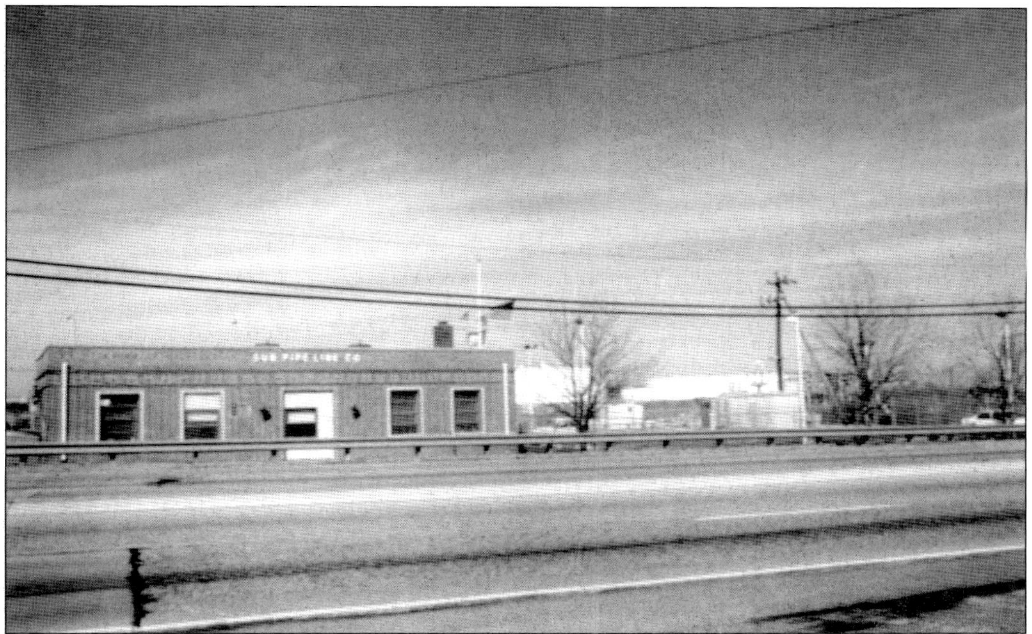

SUN PIPE LINE COMPANY. The Sun Pipe Line Company on Route 322 is shown here in March 1988. This company came into operation in 1951. The company operates a system that delivers refined petroleum products from Marcus Hook to terminals at Newark, New Jersey; Syracuse, New York; Cleveland, Ohio, and intermediate points.

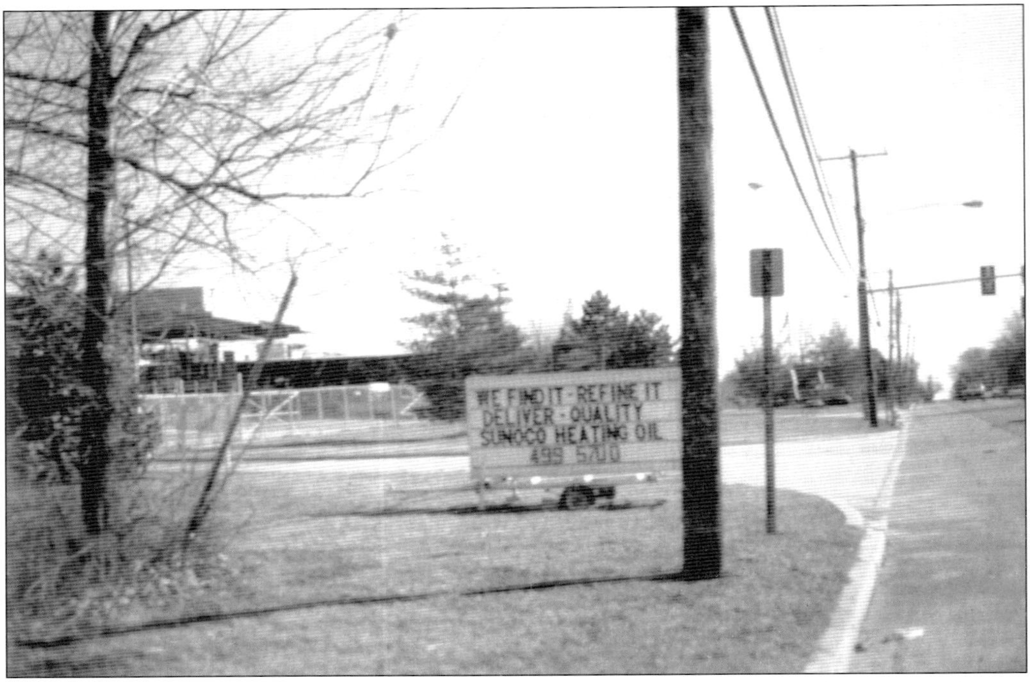

SUNOCO HEATING OIL. Here is a sign of the times in the Delaware County Marcus Hook area, a sign advertising Sunoco heating oil.

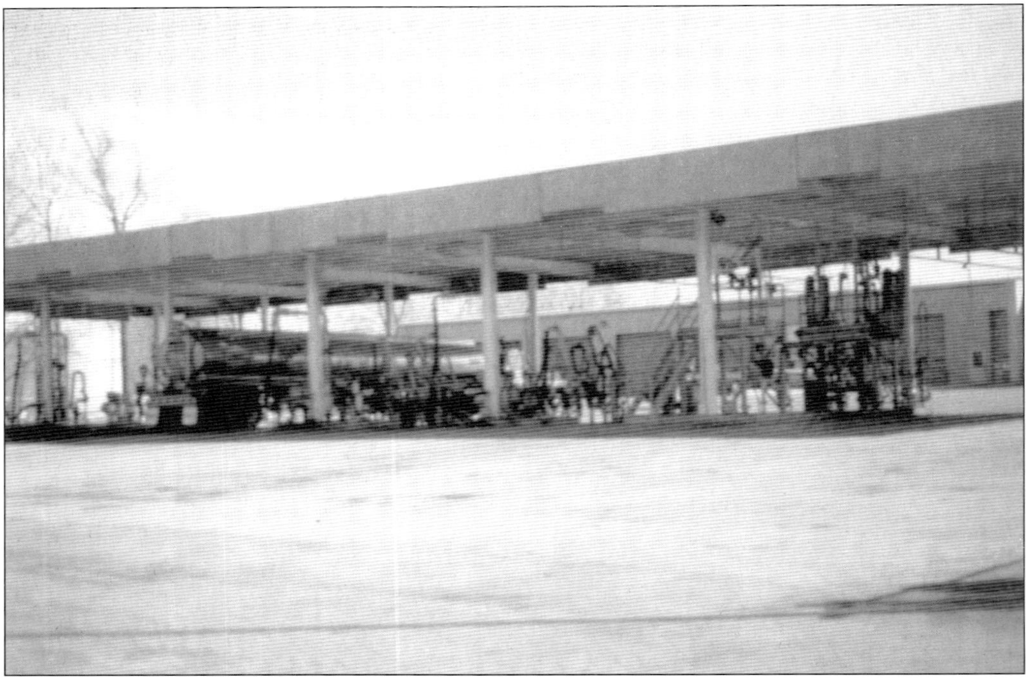

SUNOCO'S TWIN OAKS TERMINAL PUMPING STATION. This is Sunoco's Twin Oaks Terminal pumping station in Aston. Oil is being pumped into a huge tanker at the station.

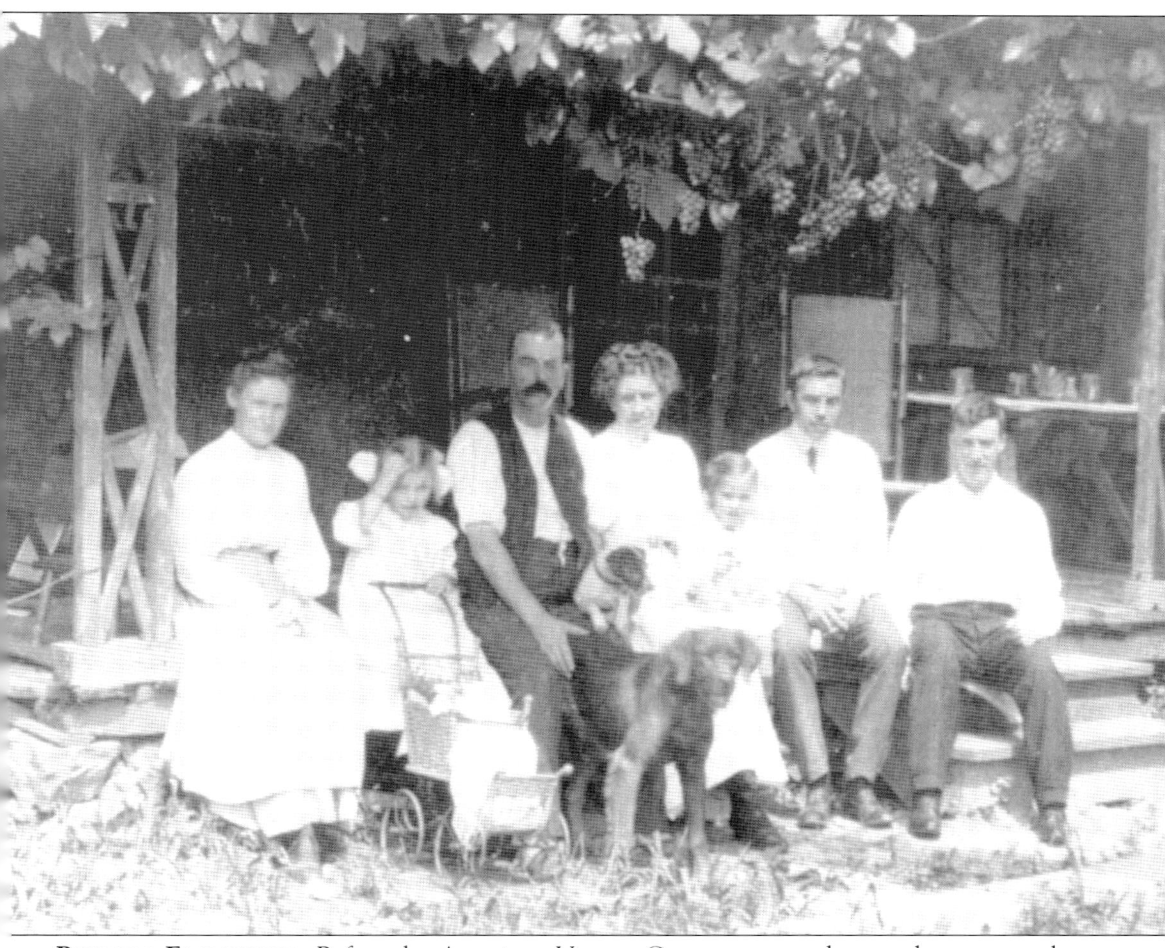

PENNELL FARMHOUSE. Before the American Viscose Company started to produce rayon, the Pennell farmhouse stood at its present site on Tenth Street near Marcus Hook Creek. At right of this 1911 photograph are Ernest Copson and James Oakes. In 1912, the farm was taken over by the American Viscose Company, which had begun its production of rayon in Marcus Hook in 1910. Samuel Agar Salvage, an Englishman, opened the business at the suggestion of an English textile firm. Rayon thread, or "artificial silk" as it once was called, was originally made from the cellulose plant, and its success was owed to continuing research. (Delaware County Historical Society.)

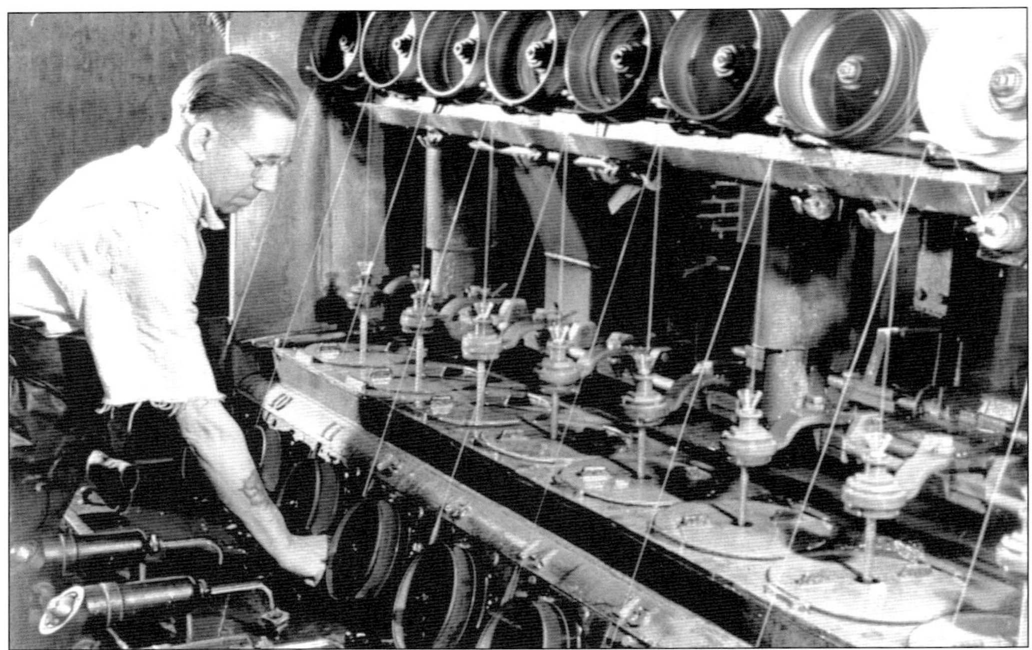

SPINNING RAYON. The artificial silk did not begin to be called *rayon* (a derivation of *ray* and *cotton*) until 1924. By the 1940s, spinning rayon in the Marcus Hook plant of the American Viscose Company was one of the nation's most advanced industries. The plant was composed of several buildings on 38 acres. This photograph was taken in July 1946.

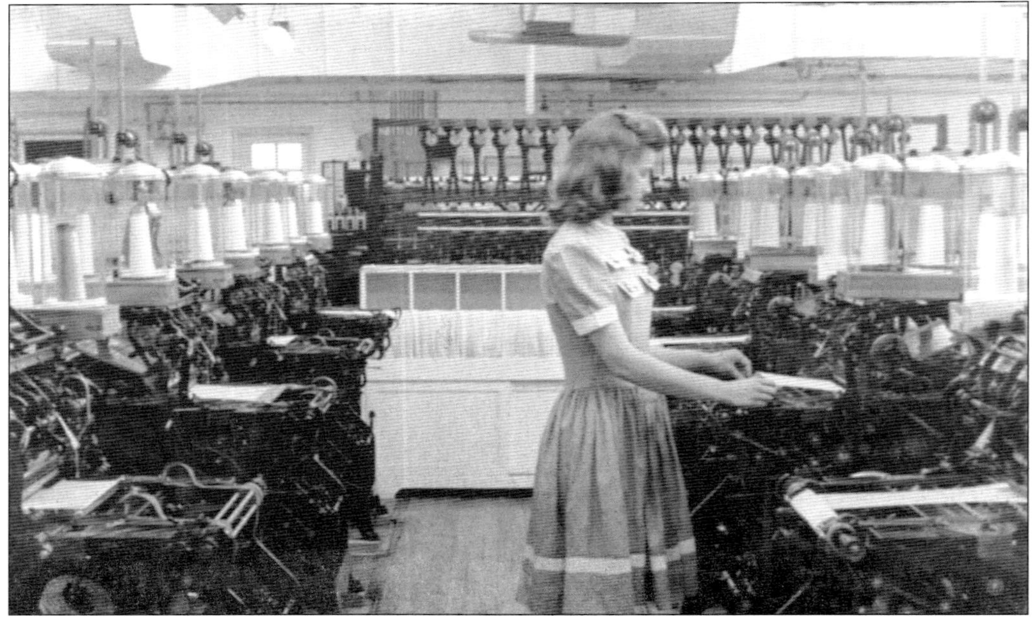

HOSIERY KNITTING MACHINES. This 1946 photograph shows full-fashioned hosiery knitting machines, installed in the hosiery section of the American Viscose Company's textile unit at Marcus Hook. Here rayon hosiery is made under commercial conditions, and numerous tests are under way to improve the quality and wear of the new rayon stockings.

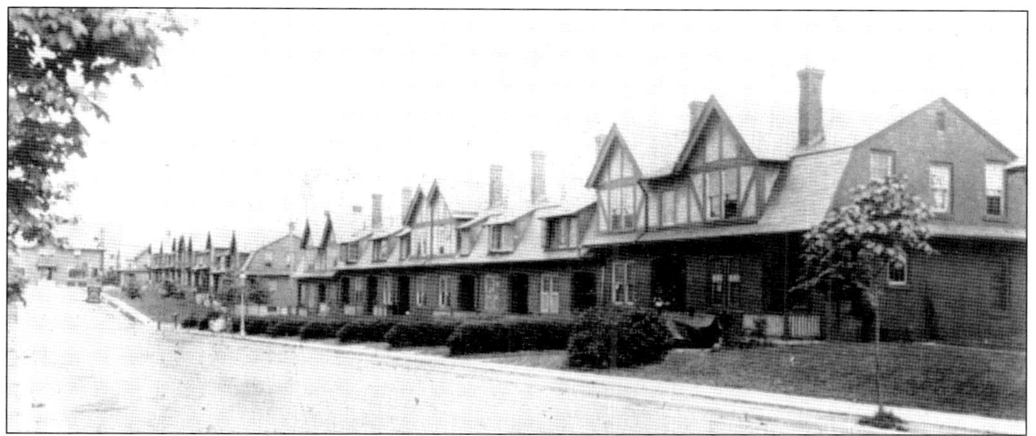

HOUSES BUILT FOR TEXTILE WORKERS. Here are some of the 261 houses built opposite the plant of the American Viscose Company. Built for the textile workers, they rented for $12 to $18 a month in the 1940s when these photographs were taken. (Urban Archives of Temple University.)

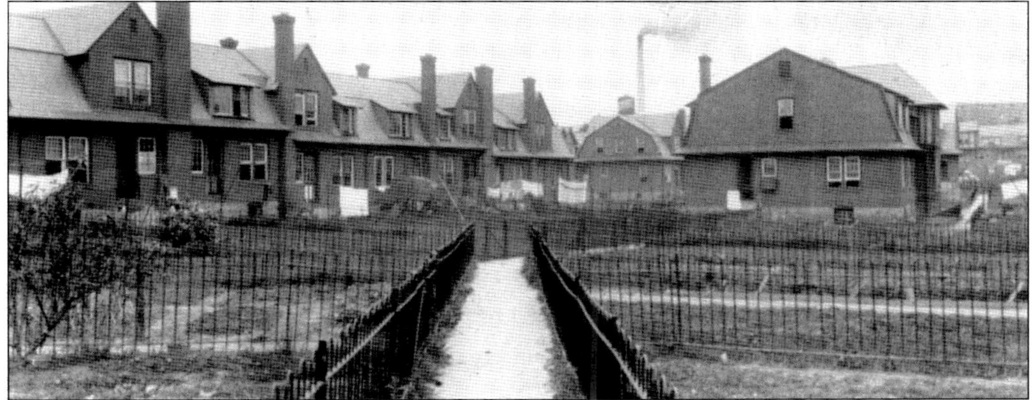

HOUSES BUILT FOR TEXTILE WORKERS, 1949. In 1949, the homes were sold, with employees given the first right to purchase them. (Urban Archives of Temple University.)

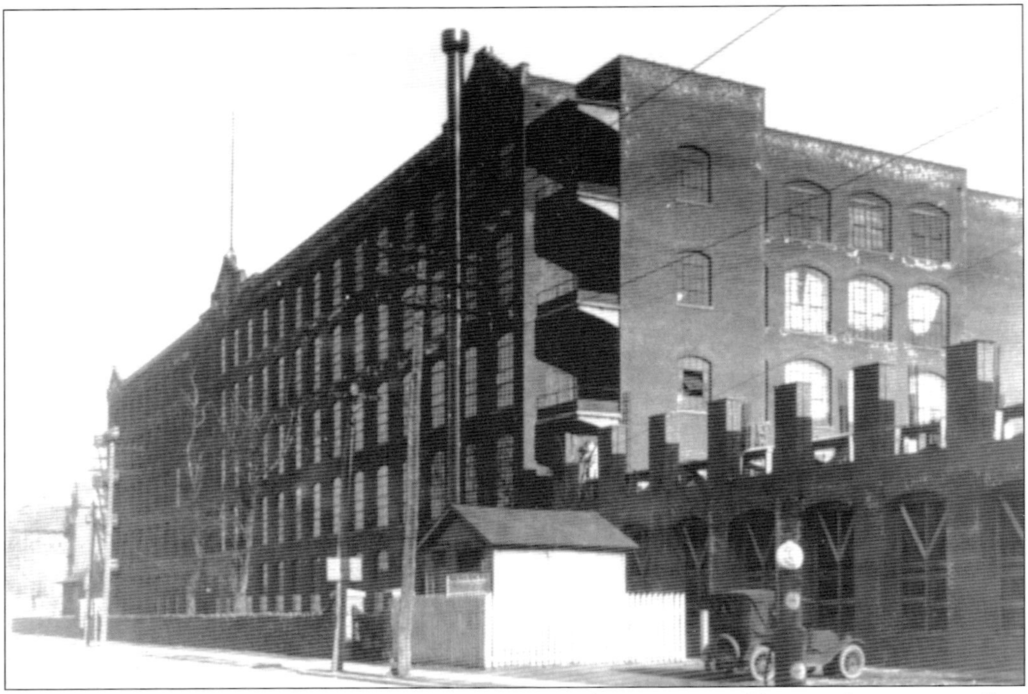

THE AMERICAN VISCOSE FACTORY, 1920S. Here is the American Viscose Company at East Tenth Street, opposite Yates Avenue. Looking at the parked car, one can only guess this photograph is from the 1920s. (Delaware County Historical Society.)

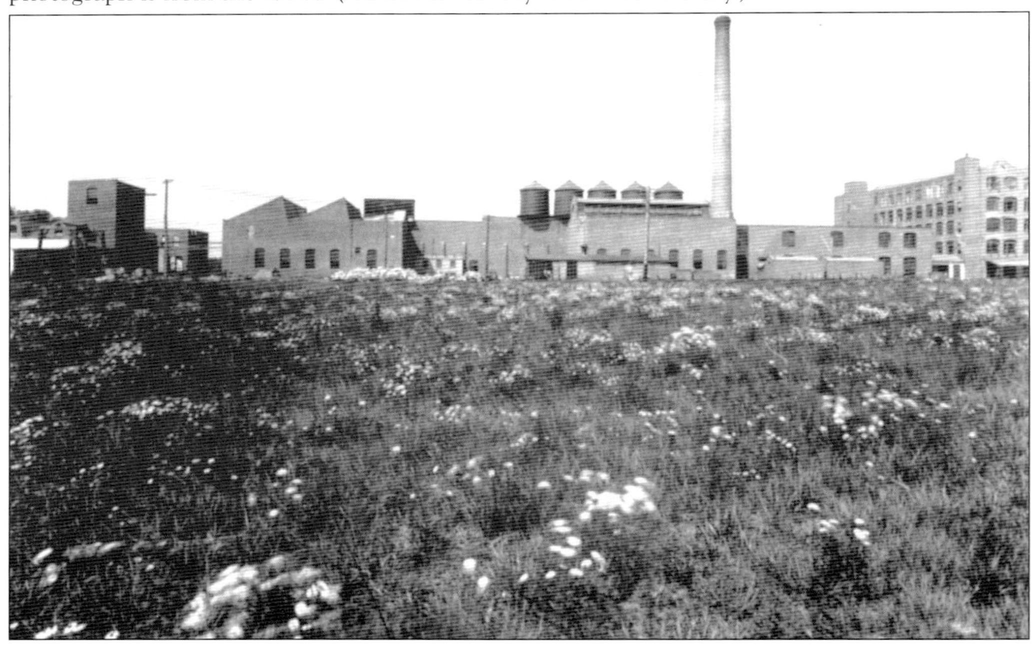

AMERICAN VISCOSE COMPANY FACTORY. Here is an antiquated photograph of the American Viscose Company on Tenth Street just west of Marcus Hook Creek. The view was taken through a field of flowers. (Delaware County Historical Society.)

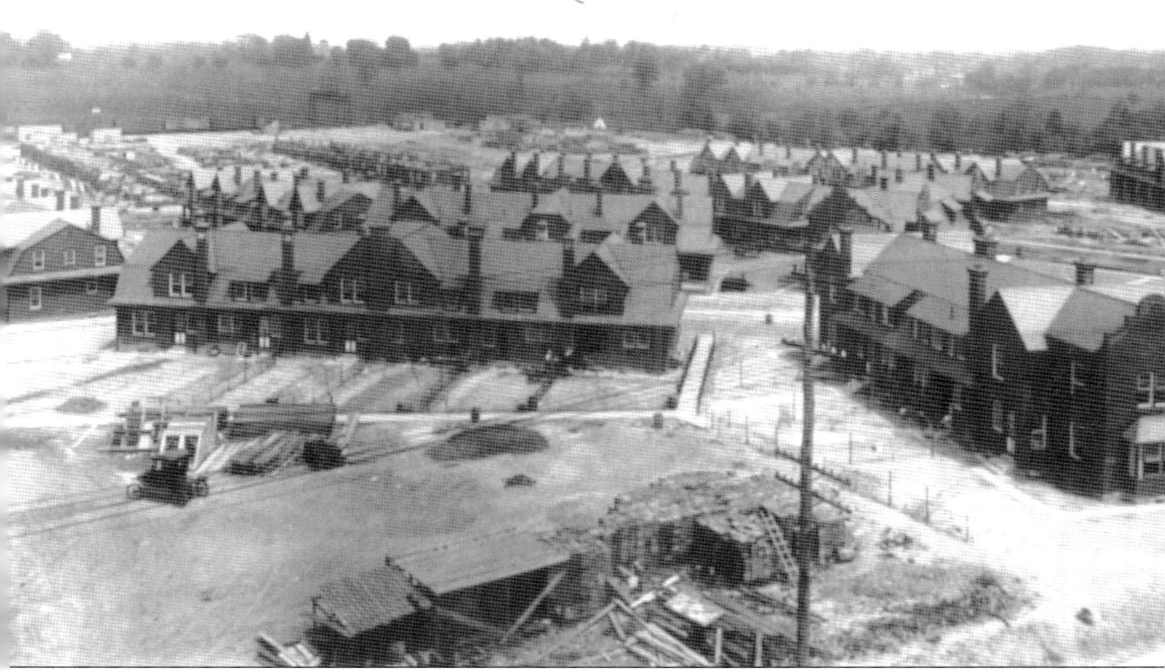

Aerial View of Model Village. Here is an aerial view of the model village of the American Viscose Company, west of Marcus Hook Creek. The village sits on a tract of 20 acres on East Tenth Street. Originally built in 1912, the village contained 261 homes, two boardinghouses, a village store, a dining hall, and a recreation building. William Provost Jr., H. I. Taylor, and the Nolan brothers were among the contractors, and Ballinger and Perot were the architects and engineers. The village has streets diverging from a central plaza, with beautiful vistas. All village homes are two-story brick structures attached in groups of as many as 14, and most are placed on rectangular lots along perpendicular streets. In the original village, every household was required to have at least one American Viscose employee. (Delaware County Historical Society)

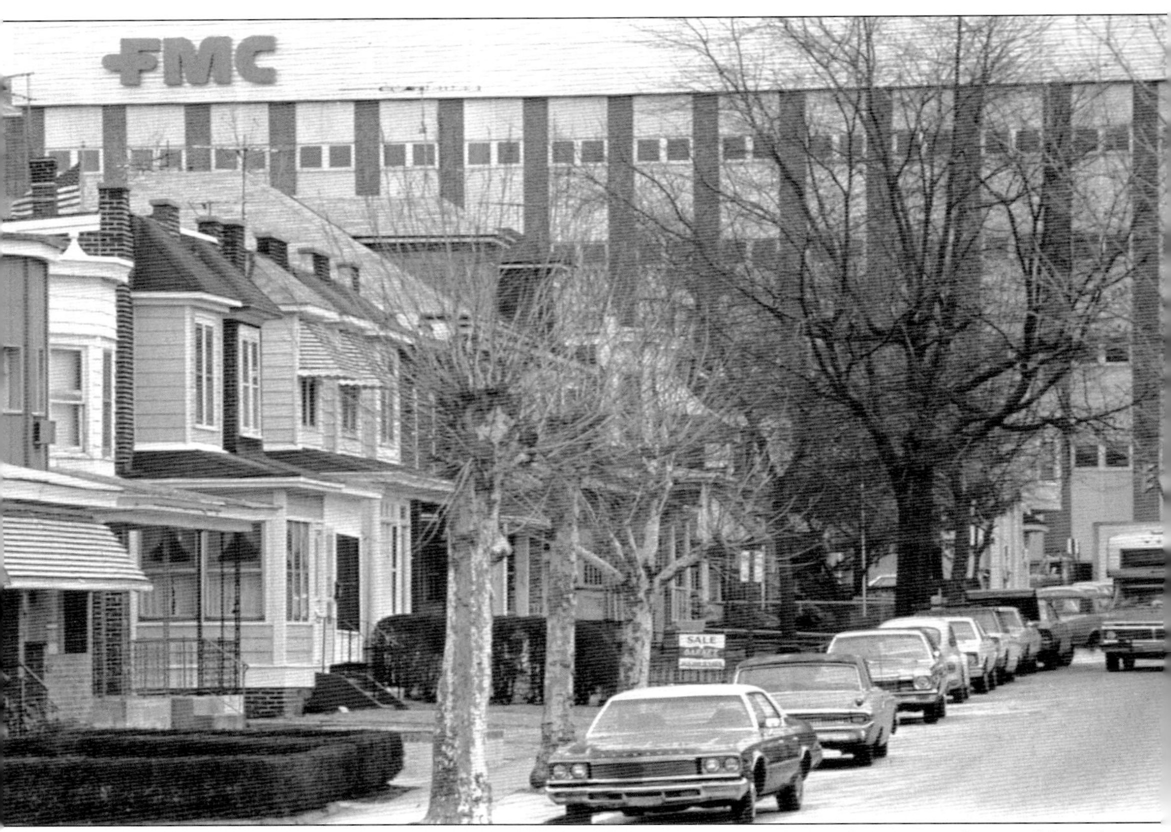

THE FOOD AND MACHINERY CORPORATION. The American Viscose Company changed hands and became FMC (Food and Machinery Corporation) on August 5, 1963, becoming one of the nation's largest makers of the packaging material cellophane. This view taken on January 3, 1977, down Yates Avenue toward the FMC research and development building, shows where many retired FMC employees lived. When the plant was shut down in 1977, 580 jobs were lost. Starting in 1974, due to a recession and the development of new packaging products, the demand for cellophane dropped. (Urban Archives of Temple University.)

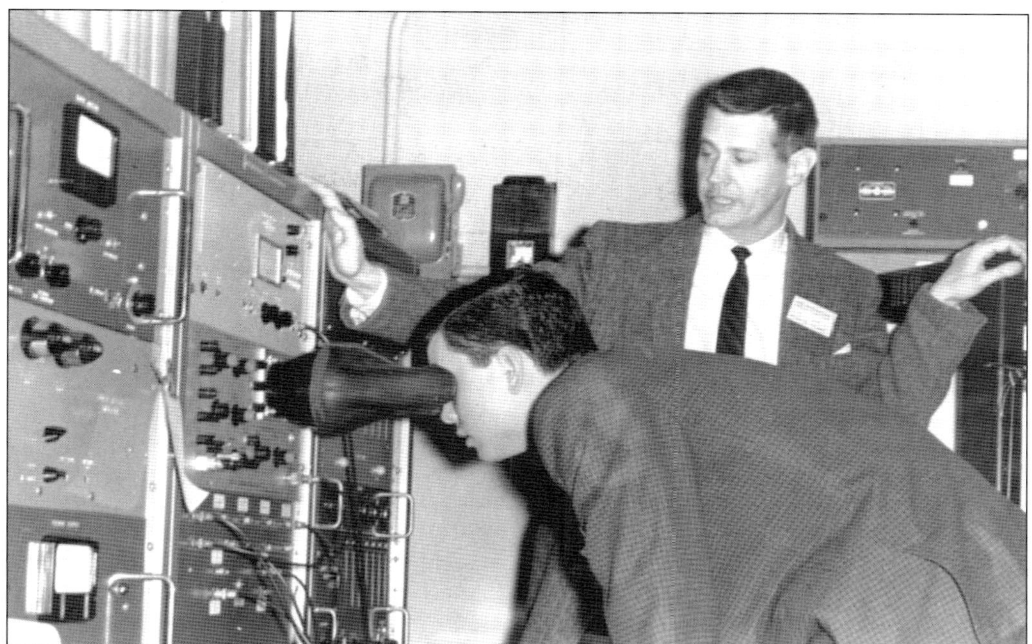

THE X-RAY DIFFRACTION DEVICE. The X-ray diffraction device interests Michael Guthrie of Episcopal Academy during a science career guidance tour of the American Viscose Research and Development Center at Marcus Hook. Norman M. Walter of American Viscose explains its operation. This photograph was taken on December 30, 1963.

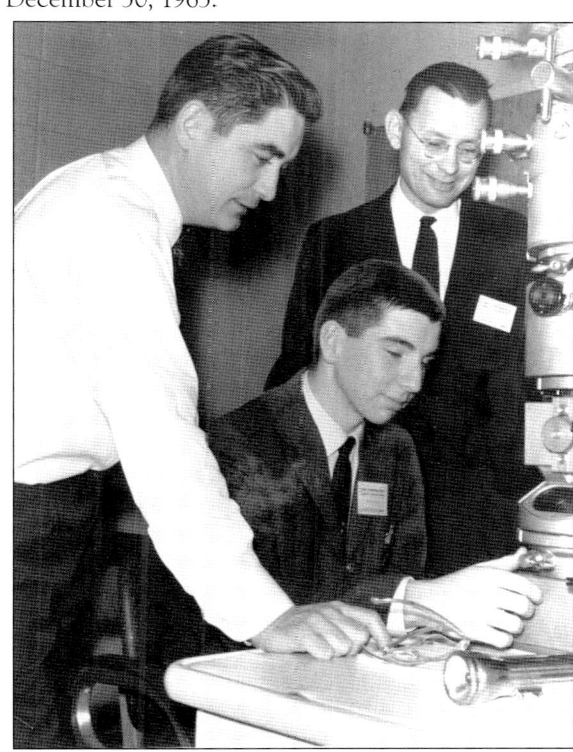

THE ELECTRON MICROSCOPE. The electron microscope is explained by Clinton D. Felton, of Avisco's special instruments group, to William Crielly of St. James Catholic High School for Boys in Chester and his teacher Brother L. Dwyer. This photograph was taken on December 30, 1963.

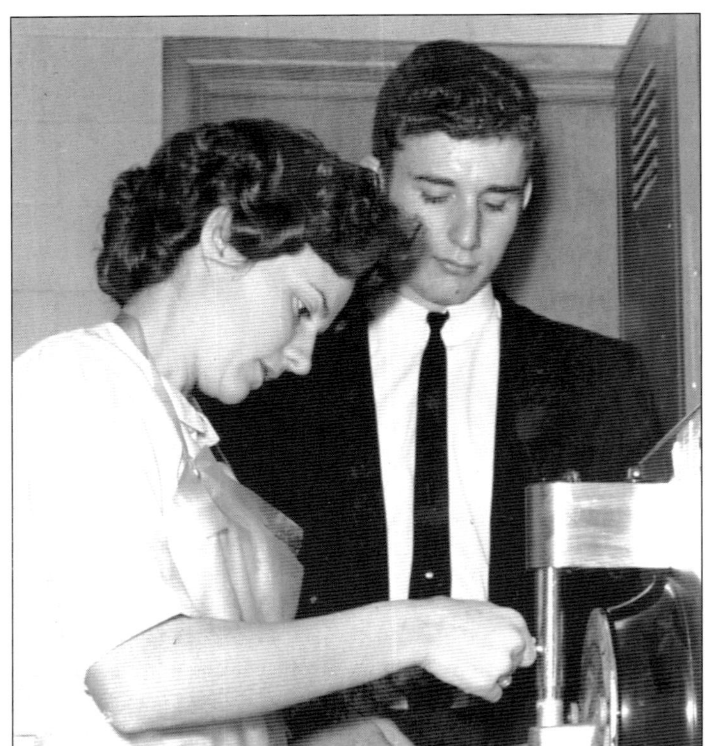

A Product of Cellulose. Trudy Keeney, of the Avisco research group, draws some frozen dessert made with Avicel microcrystalline cellulose for George Daniel of Chichester High School in Boothwyn. This photograph was taken on December 30, 1963.

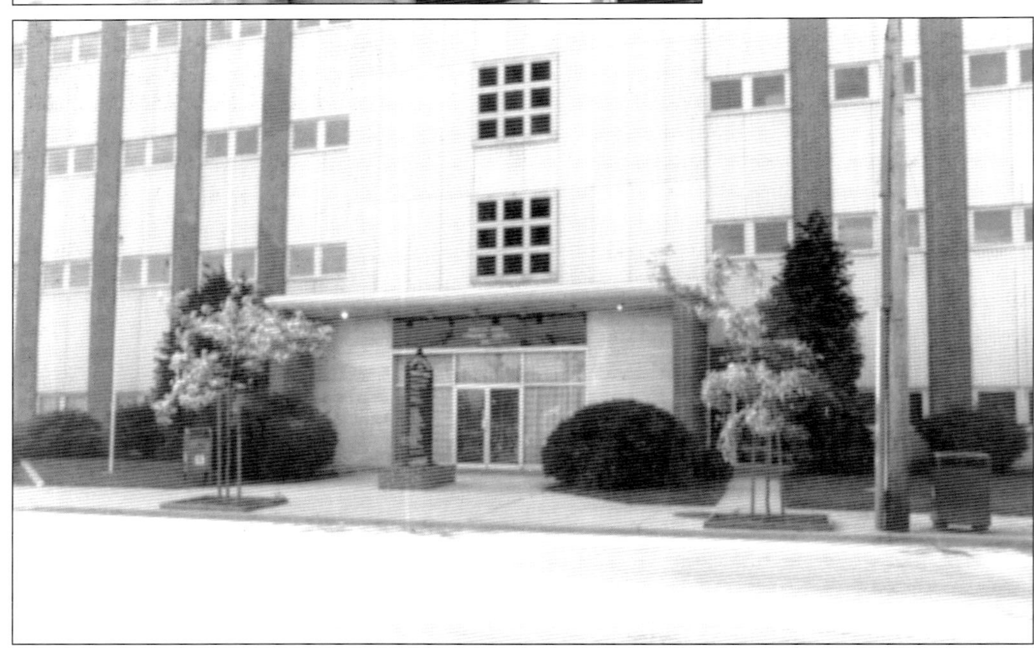

Marcus Hook Community Center. In 1980, the Marcus Hook Community Development Corporation began renovations to the first floor of the former FMC research and development building. The west half of the first floor would house business tenants, and the east side provided space for senior citizens and a recreation hall. This photograph was taken in August 1984.

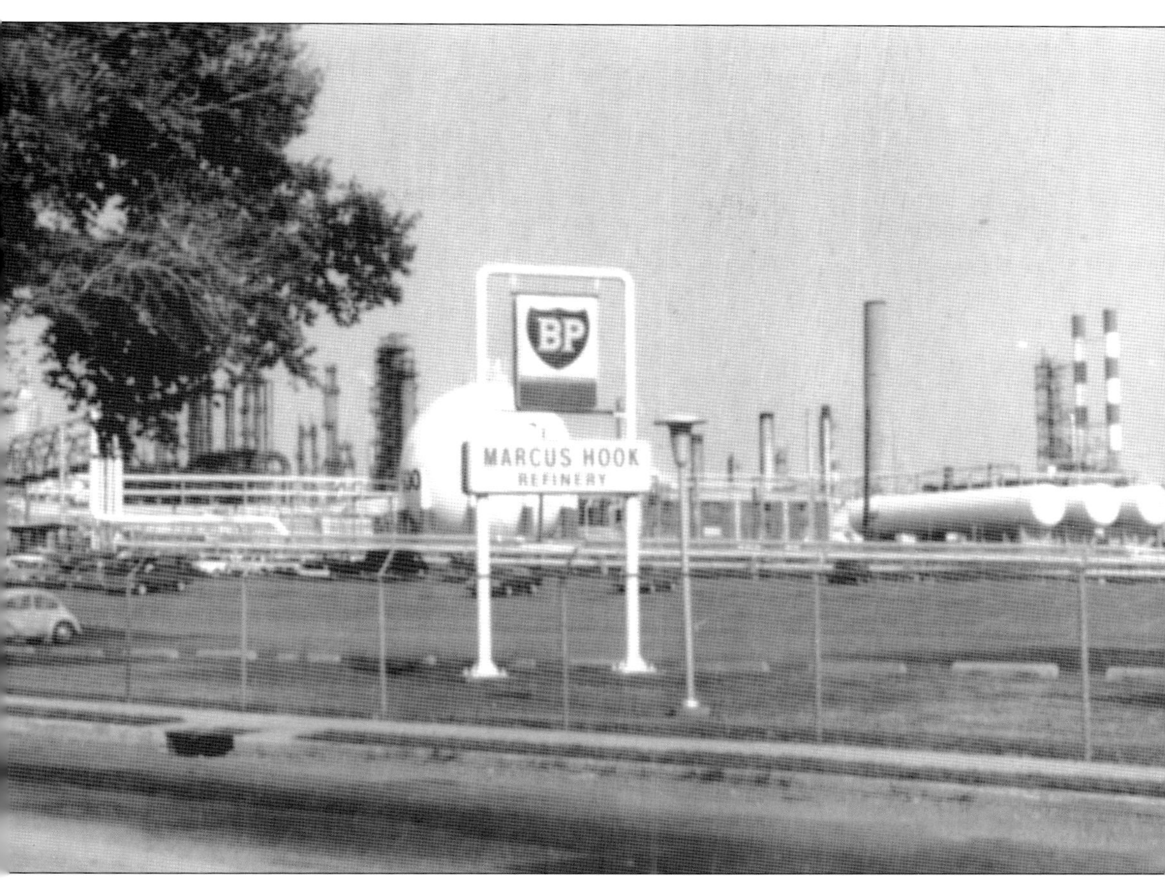

British Petroleum. In 1900, the Reading Railroad Company leased some ground to the Union Petroleum Company, and a refinery was built along the Delaware River. In 1916, the Union Petroleum Company bought the ground and was by then giving support to the Sinclair Refining Company, whose symbol in service stations was once a dinosaur. The Sinclair Refining Company leased 17 acres in Marcus Hook and added 242 acres in Trainer in 1921, expanding from a 10,000- to 160,000-barrel-a-day production capacity. The business has had several subsequent owners—BP Oil Company, Tosco Corporation in 1996, and ConocoPhillips in 2001. The deepwater harbor allows inexpensive delivery of crude oil by tanker and efficient export to domestic overseas markets.

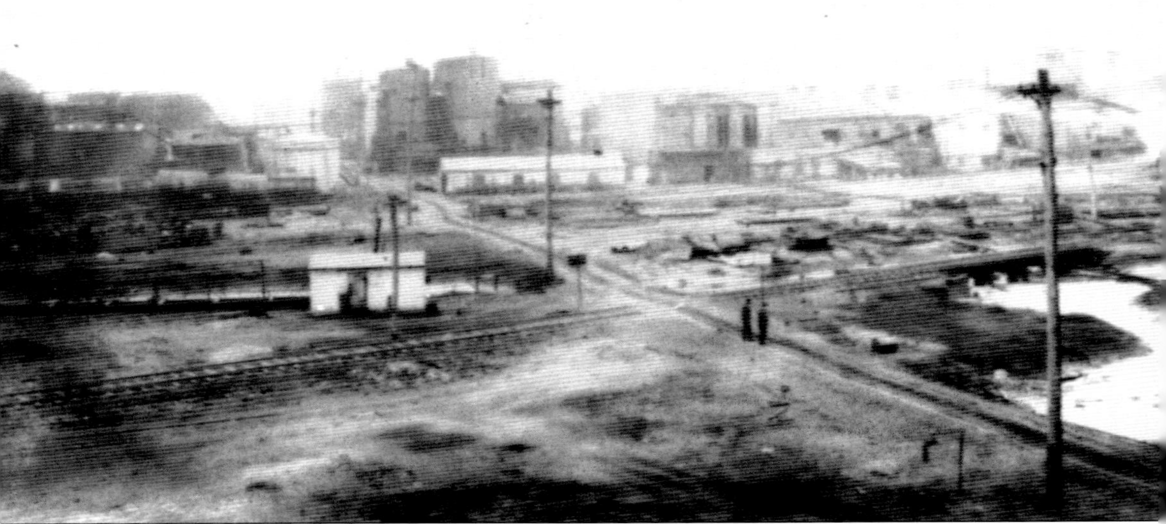

Pure Oil Company. Another oil refinery in Marcus Hook was Pure Oil Company. This view is southeast toward the Delaware River. In 1902, this refinery was erected, and when it was completed, it was one of the largest in the United States. It was supplied with oil from the United States Pipe Line, the longest pipeline in the world. Other early refineries were the Bear Creek Refining Company and the Crescent Oil Company. (Delaware County Historical Society.)

Four

Shipping

During Colonial times, Marcus Hook served as the first port of call for Philadelphia shipping and rivaled Chester in size. The principal industry in the early days was boatbuilding. Peter Kalm, a Swedish naturalist who often visited the town, recorded that "they build here every year a number of small ships for sale, and from an iron work which lies higher up in the country, they carry iron bars to this place and ship them."

Few people know about the growth or existence of shipbuilding at Marcus Hook. Many have heard of Sun Shipyard in Chester, but few have ever heard of the shipyards that once existed in Marcus Hook. In 1890, Houston and Woodbridge operated a shipyard, building a number of iron vessels, including the steamboat *Sarah Jenks*. There was also a quarantine station and pier, erected in 1893, in Marcus Hook.

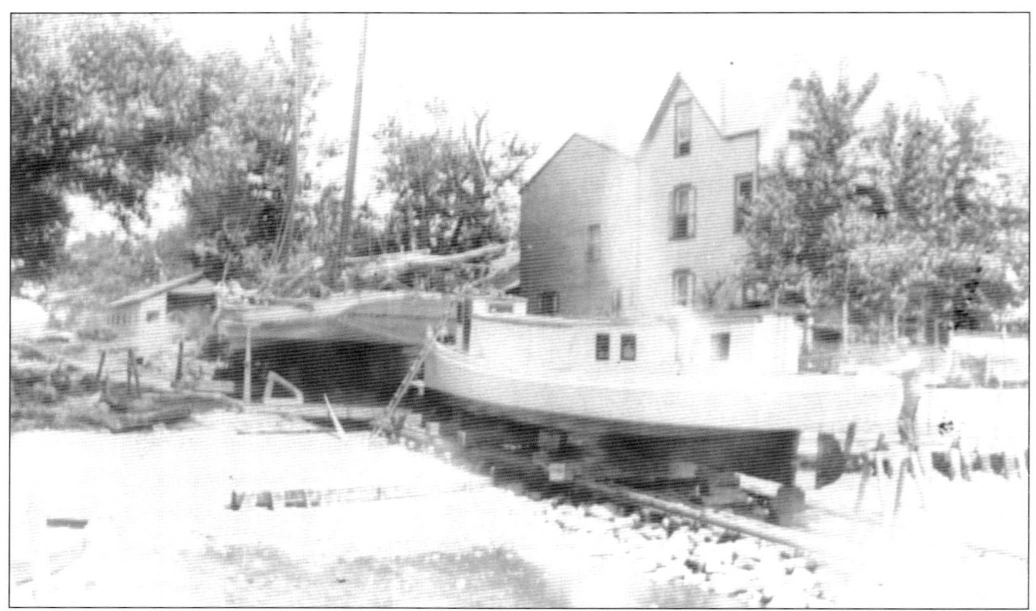

BURTON'S SHIPYARD. For over 200 years, Philadelphia had one of the finest shipyards in the southeastern Pennsylvania area—the Philadelphia Naval Shipyard. It closed in the 1990s and was reopened a decade later. However, farther south on the Delaware River was Marcus Hook's own Burton's Shipyard. Pictured in 1902 is the schooner *Juanita*, a motor yacht angler owned by Job Green of Marcus Hook. The view is east of Blueball Avenue. (Delaware County Historical Society.)

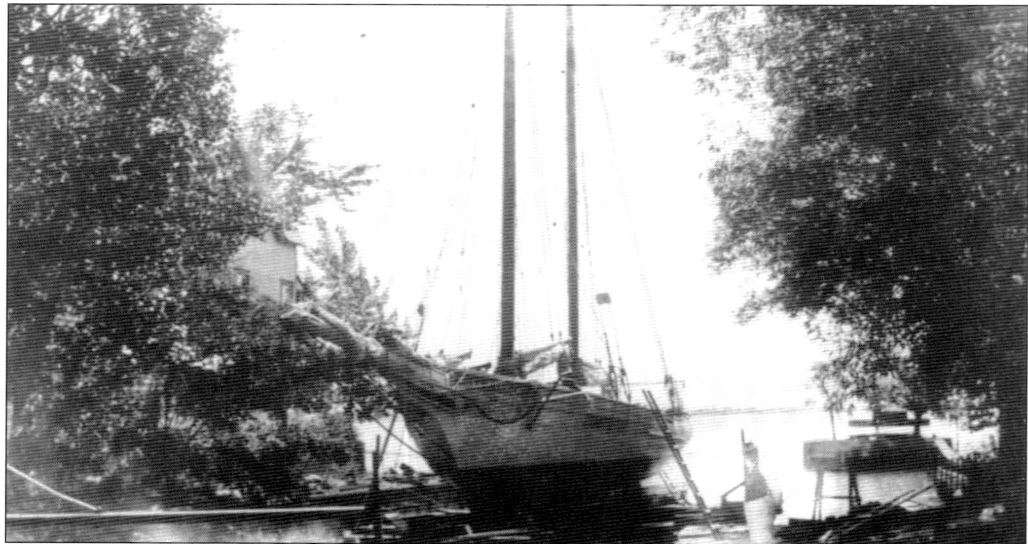

SAMUEL J. BURTON. Samuel J. Burton is looking at the camera in this view of the shipyard on the Delaware River east of Blueball Avenue. He stands next to the *Rosa Lambert*, one of many large schooners over 100 feet in length built at this shipyard. Many of the schooners built were oyster schooners with some three-masters. Some of the boats were given the names of Burton's family, such as Sarah J. Burton, Katie Burton, Edward C. Burton, and Samuel Lee Burton. (Delaware County Historical Society.)

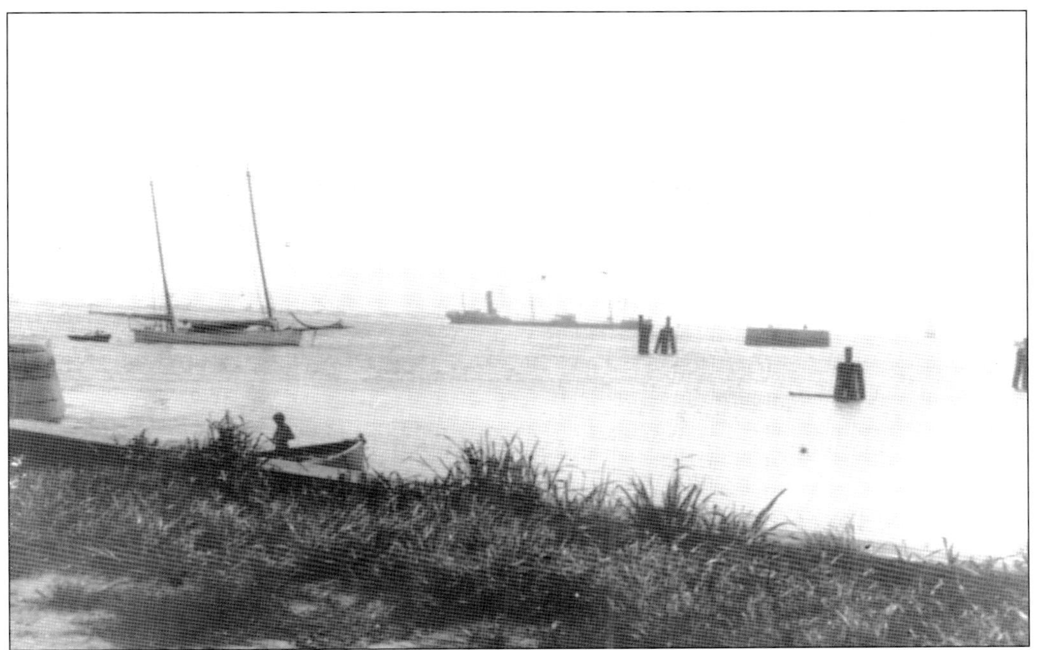

Yacht Garden. Believe it or not, this is a *c.* 1900 yacht garden, owned by a Mr. Rudder of Philadelphia. This 1905 view from the Middle Wharf shows the *Javelin*, the last of the yachts to use the Marcus Hook Anchorage. One can also get a glimpse of the fine sandy beach that once extended to the Delaware state line. (Delaware County Historical Society.)

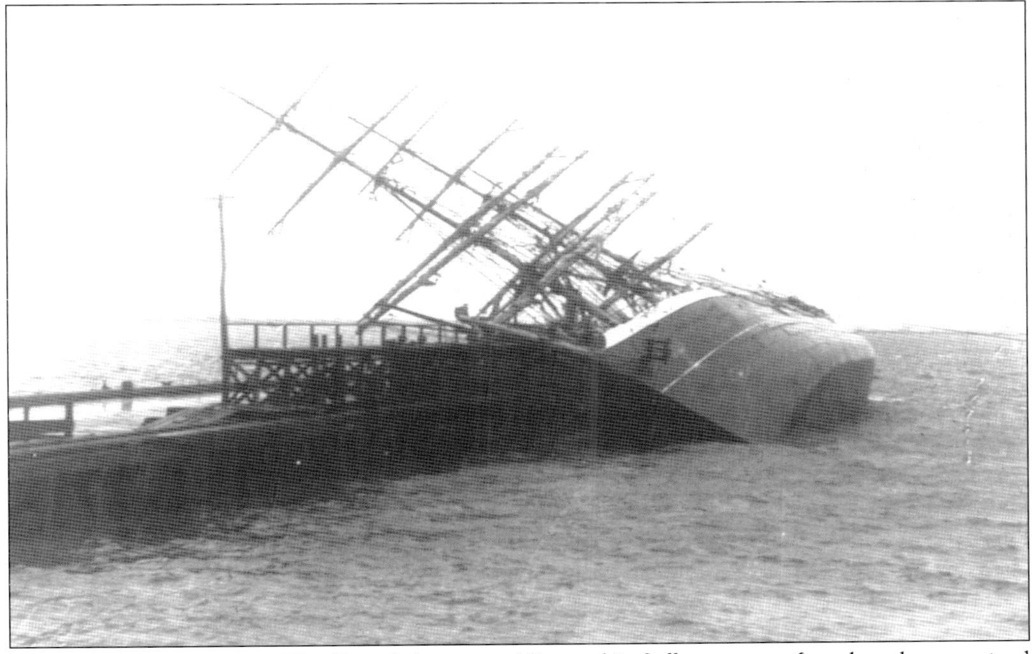

Capsized Oil Tanker. The French baroque *Alice and Isabelle* was an oil tanker that capsized upon being overloaded at the Bear Creek Refining Company wharf on April 4, 1903. The vessel was righted by Harry Hueber of 302 Market Street in 1938. (Delaware County Historical Society.)

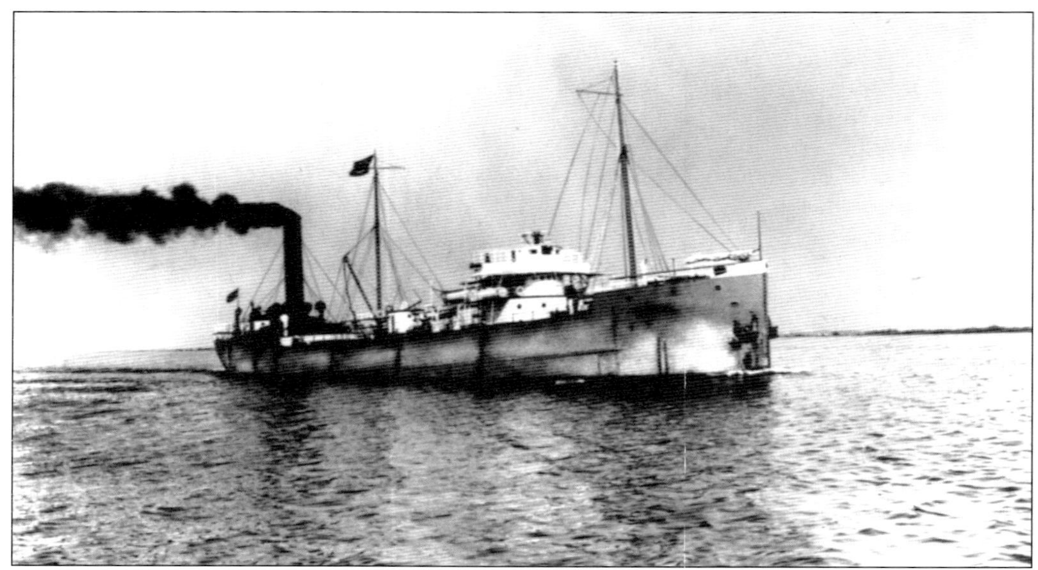

SS PARAGUAY. The first shipment of crude oil arrived in Marcus Hook in March 1902 in Sunoco's first tanker, the SS *Paraguay*, a converted ore carrier. The ship, converted to transport oil, was 242 feet long and had a capacity of 18,000 barrels. In 1909, its capacity was increased to 25,000. It was in service until 1923, when it was berthed at the Marcus Hook dock and used for storage purposes. (Hagley Museum and Library.)

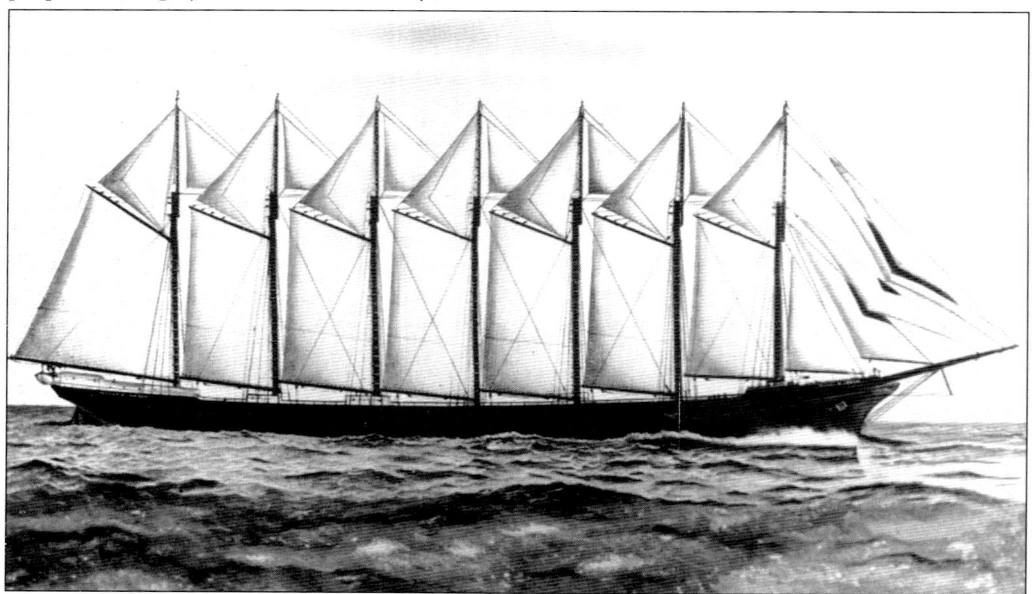

THE THOMAS W. LAWSON. Sunoco converted this seven-masted tanker, the *Thomas W. Lawson*, in 1905 and it made several voyages. Originally it was built at Newcastle-upon-Tyne, England, and was named the *British Sun*. This tanker had a capacity of 51,600 barrels and an overall length of 395 feet. It was the only seven-masted sailing vessel ever built. Its fate came in 1907 after a voyage to England. Lying at anchor on the Isles of Scilly off the entrance to the English Channel, the *Lawson* was driven into a reef during a severe gale and sunk. (Urban Archives of Temple University.)

THE *BIDWELL*. The tank ship *Bidwell*, which was in service of Sunoco, steams into port after a German submarine attack off Cape Hatteras on the night of April 6, 1942. The photograph, taken on June 4, 1942, shows one of four of Sunoco's tankers that carried oil from Marcus Hook that were sunk by Nazi torpedoes. The *Bidwell* was one of 222 tankers that were built by Sun Shipbuilding and Dry Dock Company of Chester. (Urban Archives of Temple University.)

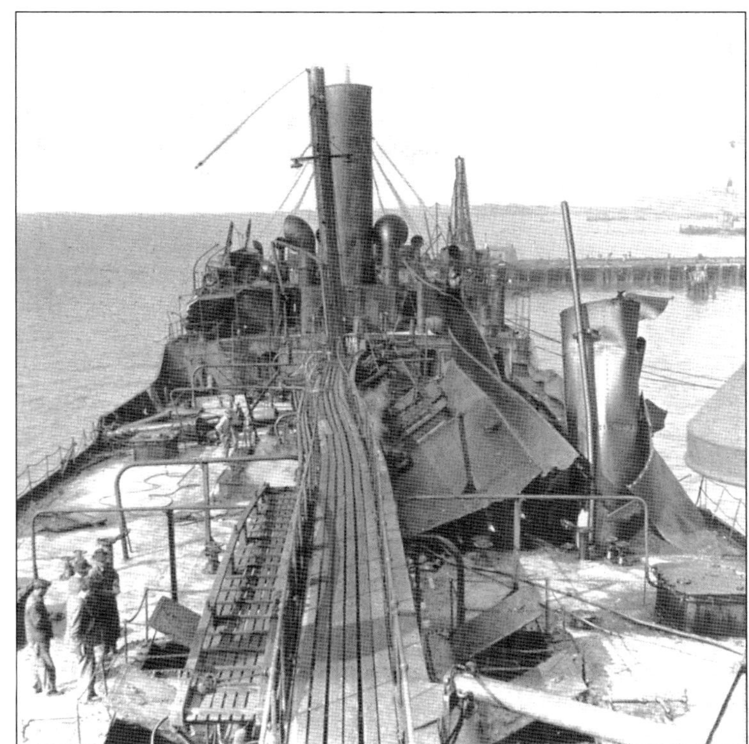

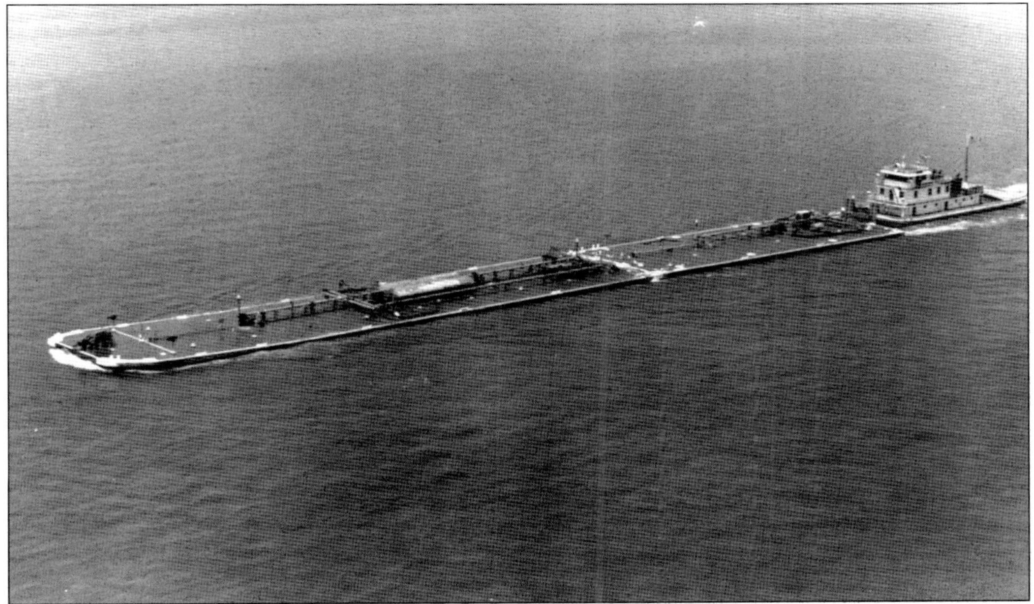

MB *CHESAPEAKE SUN*. The MB *Chesapeake Sun*, a 101-foot Mississippi towboat, moves crude oil and finished products on the Delaware River. It was powered by 900-horsepower engines. It was used with three barges to supply Sunoco's main markets in Baltimore, Maryland, and Norfolk and Richmond, Virginia, and they had a combined capacity of 2.2 million gallons of oil. The ship is seen here in July 1964. (Sun Oil Company.)

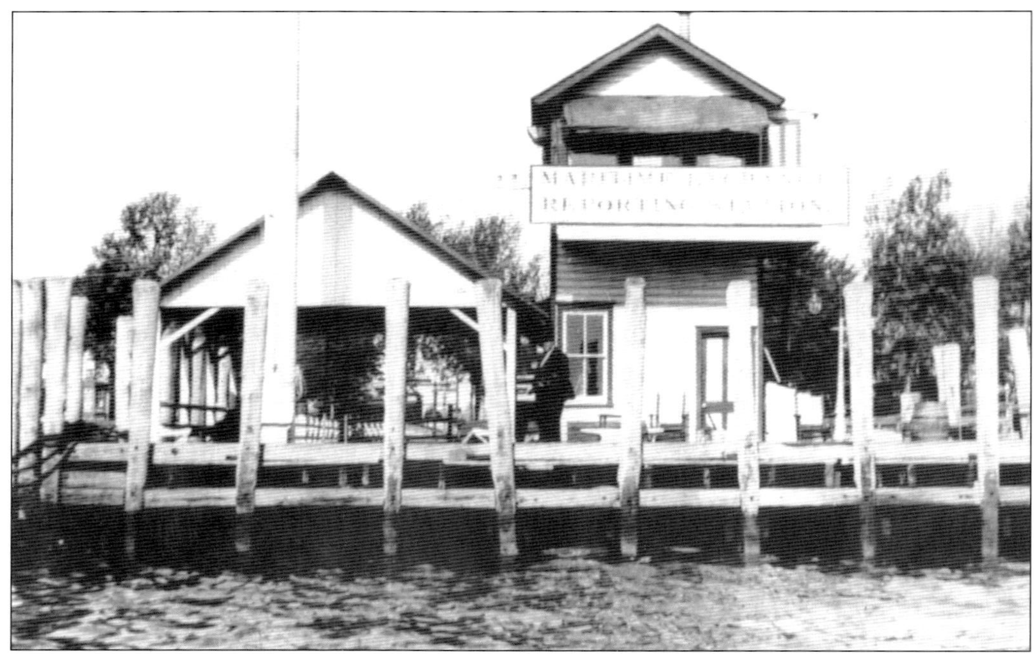

MARITIME EXCHANGE REPORTING STATION. The Maritime Exchange Reporting Station, founded in 1898, had a 24-hour observation service equipped with radio and blinker-type communication systems. This service supplied data on the movement of all incoming ships bound for Philadelphia. It notified in advance of the vessel's arrival to some 300 agencies such as tugboat companies, ship chandlers, stevedoring firms, and the ship's owners or agents. This photograph was taken in 1910, when the town hall was still in the gaslight era. In 1955, the station was moved to New Castle County, Delaware. (Delaware County Historical Society.)

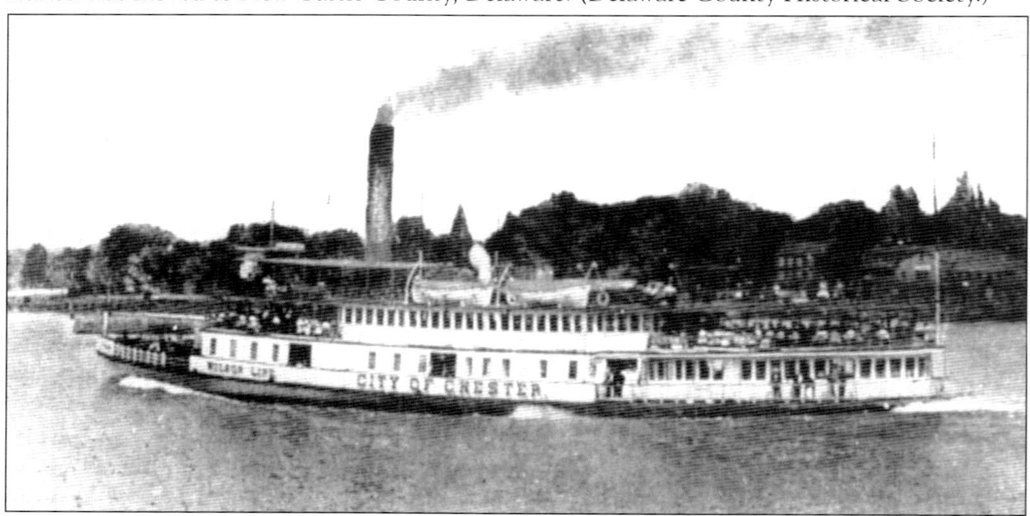

CITY OF CHESTER. The old Philadelphia Naval Shipyard terminal has been used in recent years as a cruise terminal for huge cruise ships like the *Freedom of the Seas* of Celebrity cruise lines, but go back in time for an instant and imagine sailing on a famous cruise ship of the Wilson Line, the *City of Chester*, a steamboat that left from Marcus Hook and sailed to Philadelphia at a cost of only 15¢. This photograph was taken in 1904. (Delaware County Historical Society.)

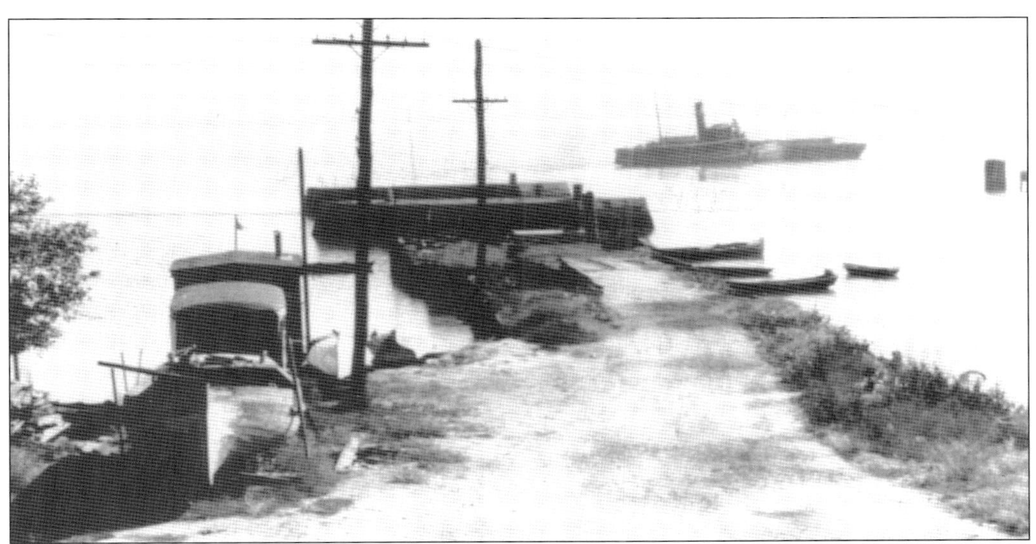

LOWER GOVERNMENT WHARF, 1930. Why were these stone piers built at Lower Government Wharf? They were constructed for ships to find safety from the drifting ice floes at one time on the Delaware River. The piers are shown in this photograph taken on October 15, 1930. This is the present site of Hueber's Boat Launch and shore shop, which has been run by the Moran family for the past 17 years. For years, Henry Hueber hauled supplies by launch to ships in midstream after receiving prearranged signals and aided in the rescue of crews whose ships had met disaster on the Delaware River. Hueber spoke seven different languages and received orders for many weird things, including one of the straightjackets used by Harry Houdini. (Delaware County Historical Society.)

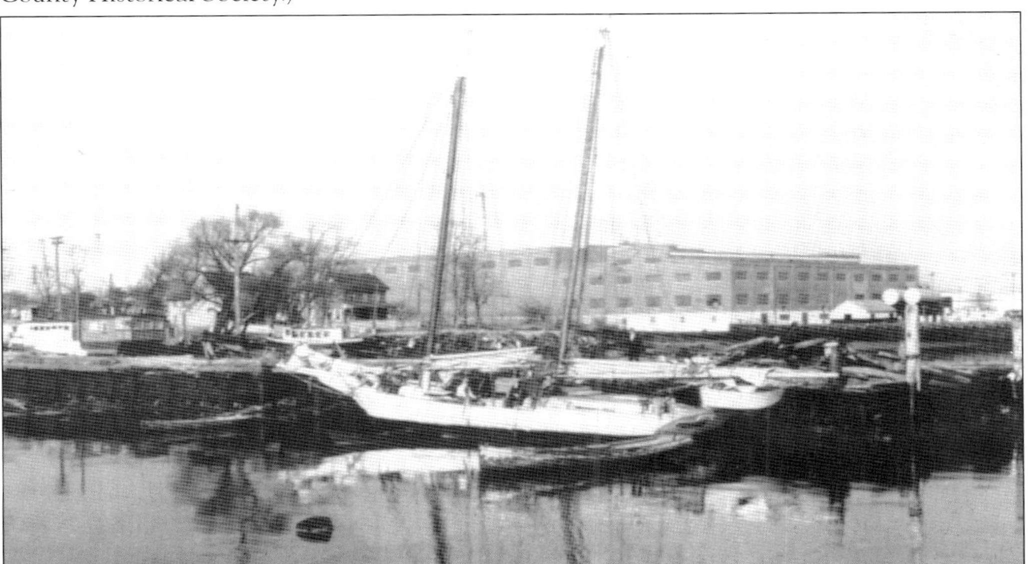

DOCKED BOATS OF THE BUSH LINE. Looking north, seen in Church Street Wharf in Marcus Hook are docked boats of the Bush Line Wharf. Clara Young, a noted personality of Marcus Hook, said one could get oysters for 50¢ a bushel off a boat that came into the wharf every Thursday night. A plant of Sinclair Refining Company (now ConocoPhillips) is in the background of this 1932 photograph. (Delaware County Historical Society.)

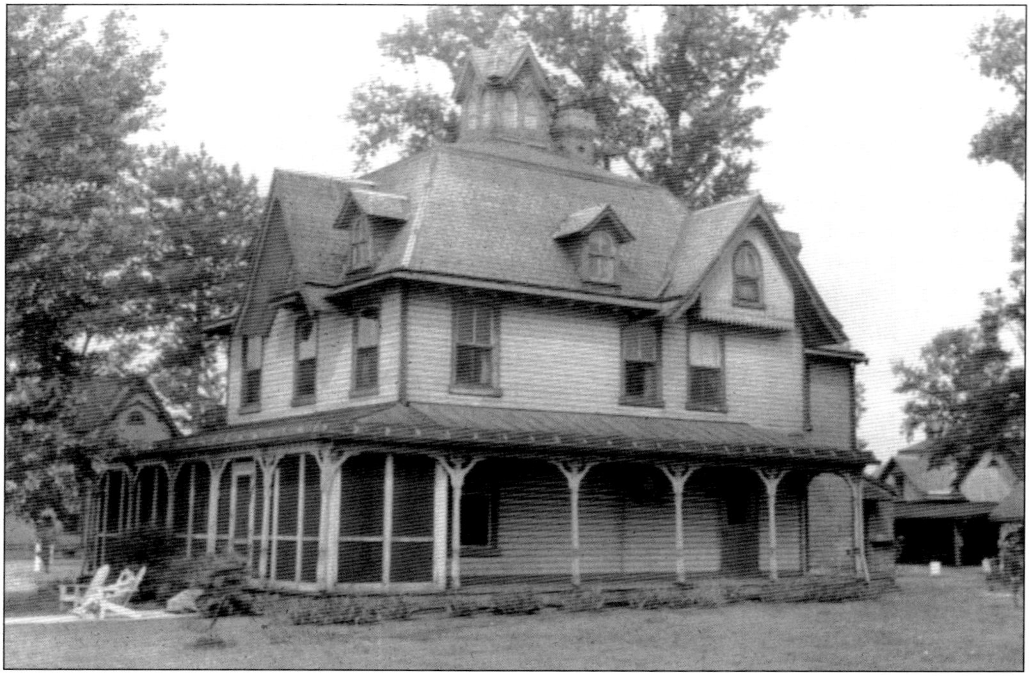

QUARANTINE STATION. The Marcus Hook Quarantine Station, which began operation in 1898, was an important branch of governmental service where a doctor and one or more inspectors boarded every ship coming from a foreign port to examine it for evidence of dangerous diseases. The primary purpose of the inspection was to detect the presence of rats, which carry the bubonic plague. A rat-infested ship was fumigated before it was allowed to make port.

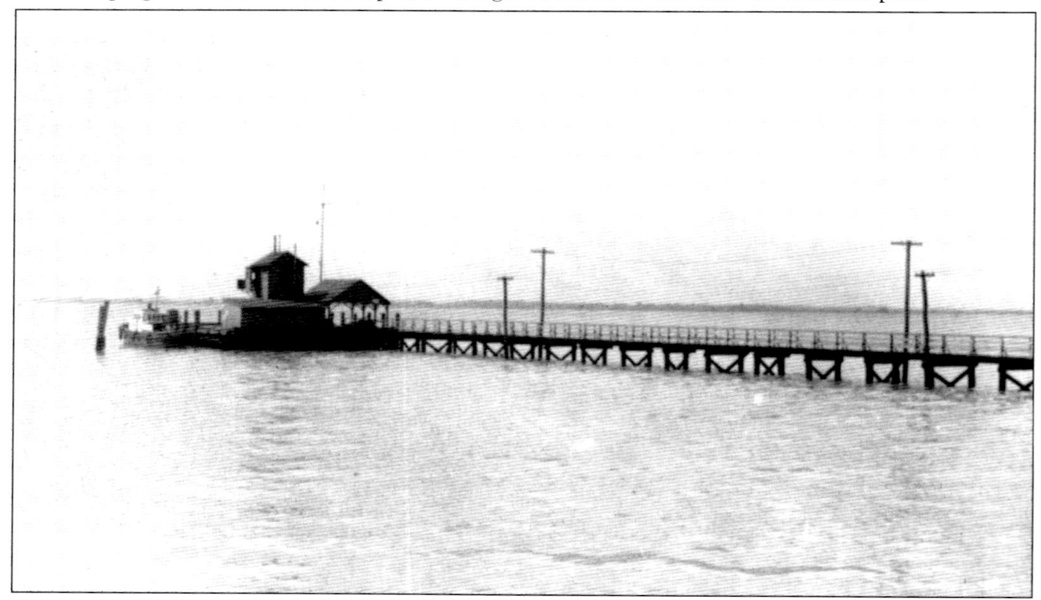

QUARANTINE PIER. The old Marcus Hook Quarantine Station pier was located 215 feet west of Blueball Avenue in the borough of Marcus Hook. The quarantine station was moved to Delaware Avenue in the mid-1950s.

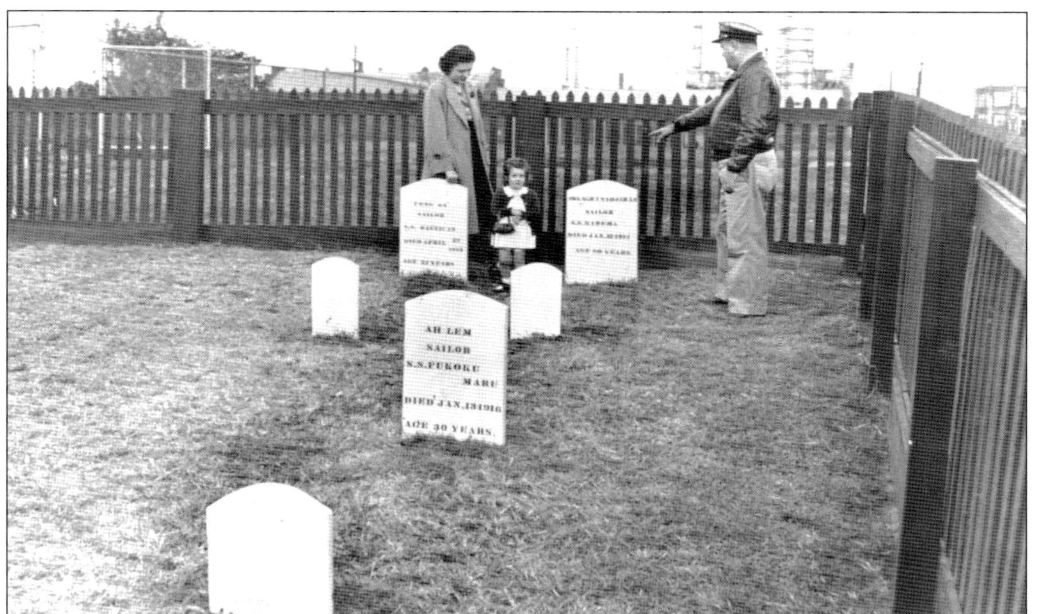

QUARANTINE STATION GRAVES. This photograph, taken on October 20, 1948, shows a cemetery at the U.S. quarantine station. This was the country's smallest cemetery. A Public Health Service employee points out the graves of three foreign seamen buried in the station's cemetery between 1912 and 1916. These foreign seamen died of contagious diseases while their ships were en route to the quarantine anchorage there. Enclosed by a picket fence in the burial plot are the graves of two Chinese seamen, a Hindu sailor, and an unidentified child. The amity of Japan and China is reflected on the legend of the 1916 tombstone of Ah Lem, a Chinese cook who was employed on the *Fukoku Maru*, a Japanese ship. (Urban Archives of Temple University.)

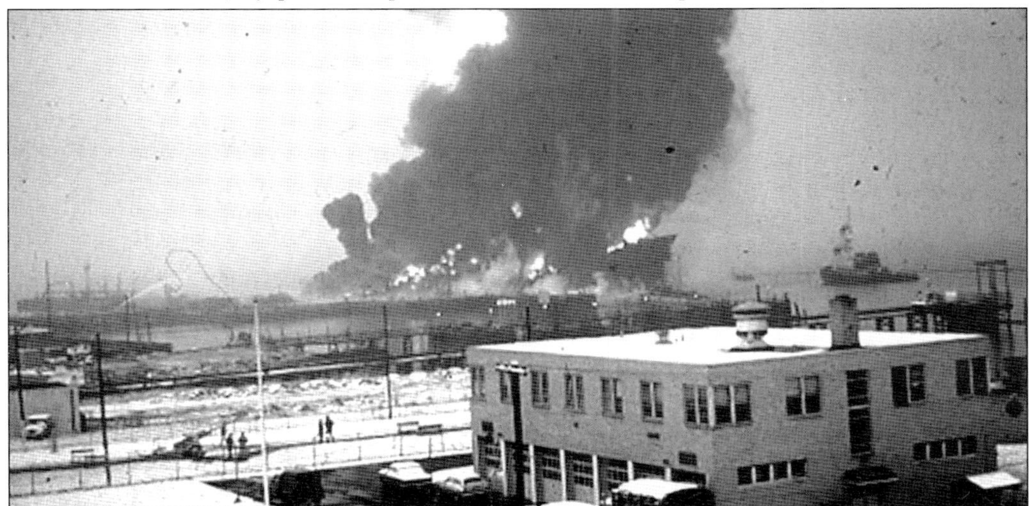

CORINTHOS DISASTER. The *Edgar M. Queeny* left the Monsanto Company dock at Bridgeport, New Jersey, at 12:06 a.m. on January 31, 1975. At 12:26 a.m., the *Edgar M. Queeny* made contact with the tanker *Corinthos* docked at the British Petroleum refinery in Marcus Hook. The resulting series of explosions rocked the town and the *Corinthos* became a raging inferno. At the time of impact, it was estimated that the *Corinthos* had 300,000 barrels of crude oil in its tanks.

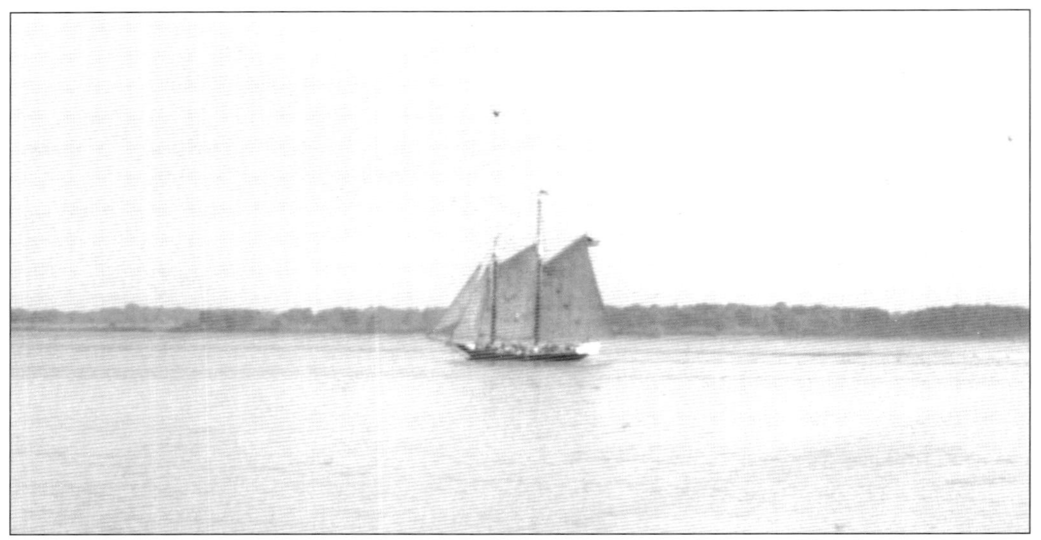

THE *PIONEER*. The *Pioneer*, a schooner built in Marcus Hook in 1885 by the Pioneer Iron Company, has had 16 different owners, four major changes of rig, worn out five engines, and been rebuilt at least twice. This series of six photographs was taken during a fall celebration at the new Market Square Memorial Park in October 1987. The *Pioneer* was docked at the U.S. Army pier next to the park. The pier and adjoining U.S. Army property was conveyed to the borough in October 2000.

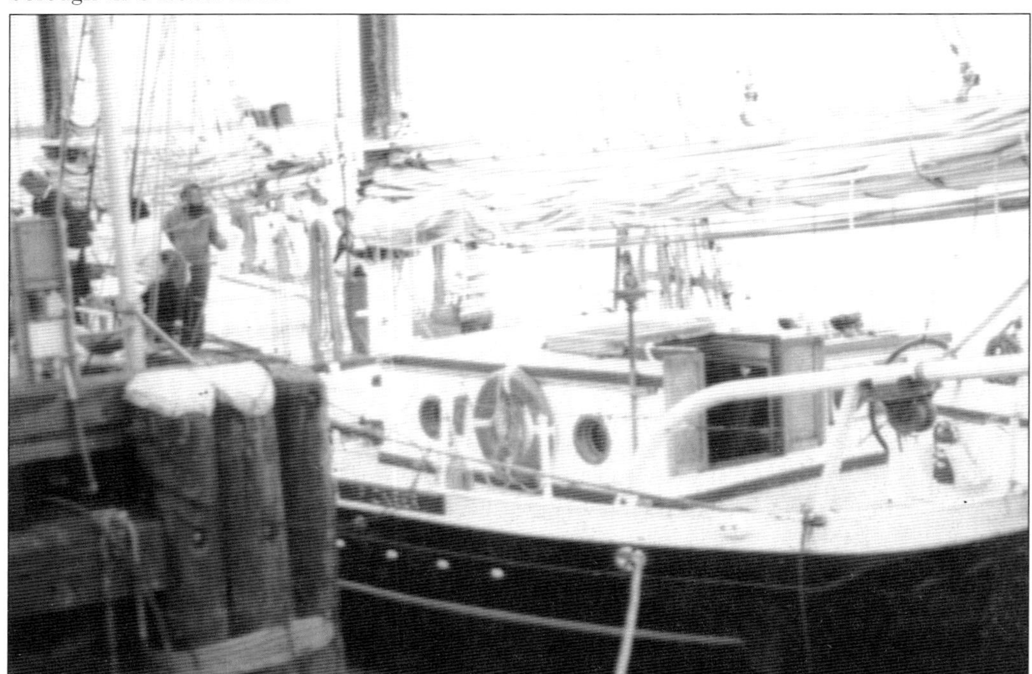

RIDING THE *PIONEER*. The *Pioneer* was built to carry sand mined near the mouth of the Delaware Bay to an iron foundry in Chester and was originally built as an iron sloop. It was the first iron sloop built in the United States and is the only surviving American iron-hulled sailing vessel. It originally had a length of 65 feet, beam of 22 feet, depth of 5 feet, and a capacity of 90 tons.

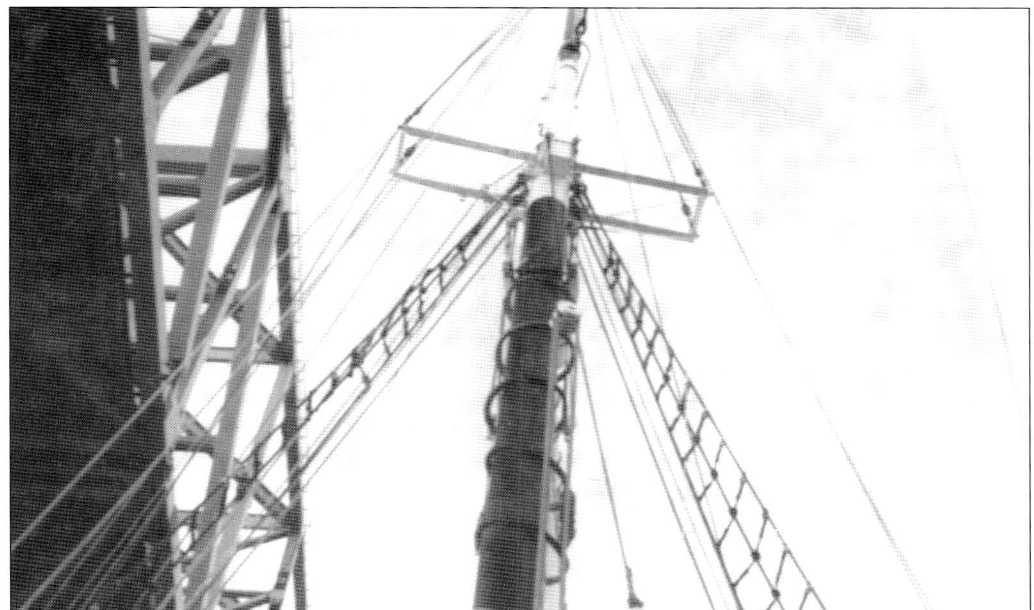

Early Delivery Vehicles. In 1895, the *Pioneer* was sold to J. C. Fender of Philadelphia and rerigged as a schooner. In the days before paved roads, schooners were the delivery trucks of their era, carrying various cargoes between coastal communities. The *Pioneer*'s masts were removed in 1907, and its next half century of service was as a motor barge. In 1956, it found its way to New Bedford, Massachusetts, and when its wrought iron plates gave way, it was beached and abandoned to rust.

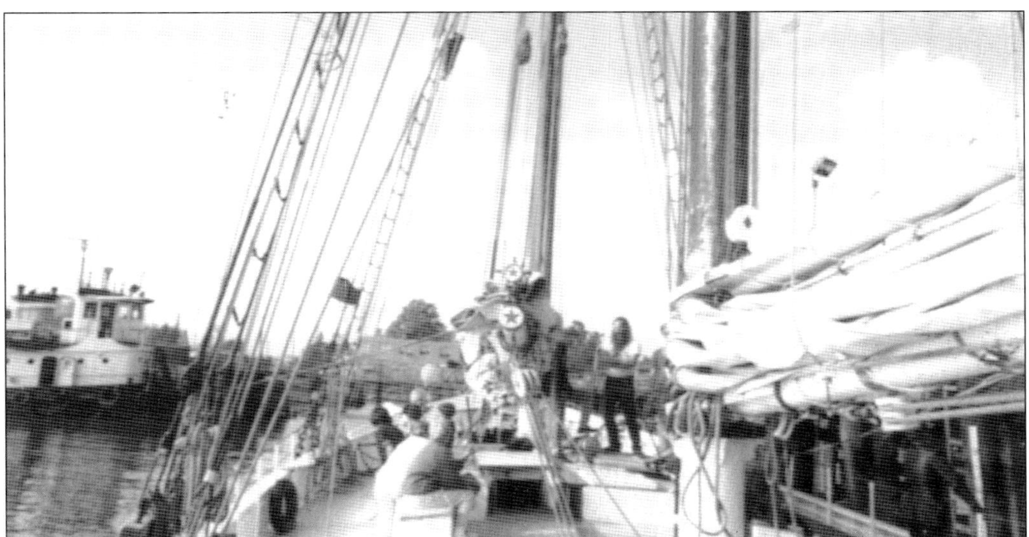

Ride On. A dock builder from Gloucester, Massachusetts, Russell Grinnel Jr. had the *Pioneer* completely rebuilt, replacing the steel and rerigging it as a schooner. After Grinnel's death in 1970, the family donated the ship to the South Street Seaport Museum in New York City in his memory. Subsequently the renovated 102-foot-long *Pioneer* became available from April to October for short passenger cruises around New York Harbor and for longer sails to other destinations.

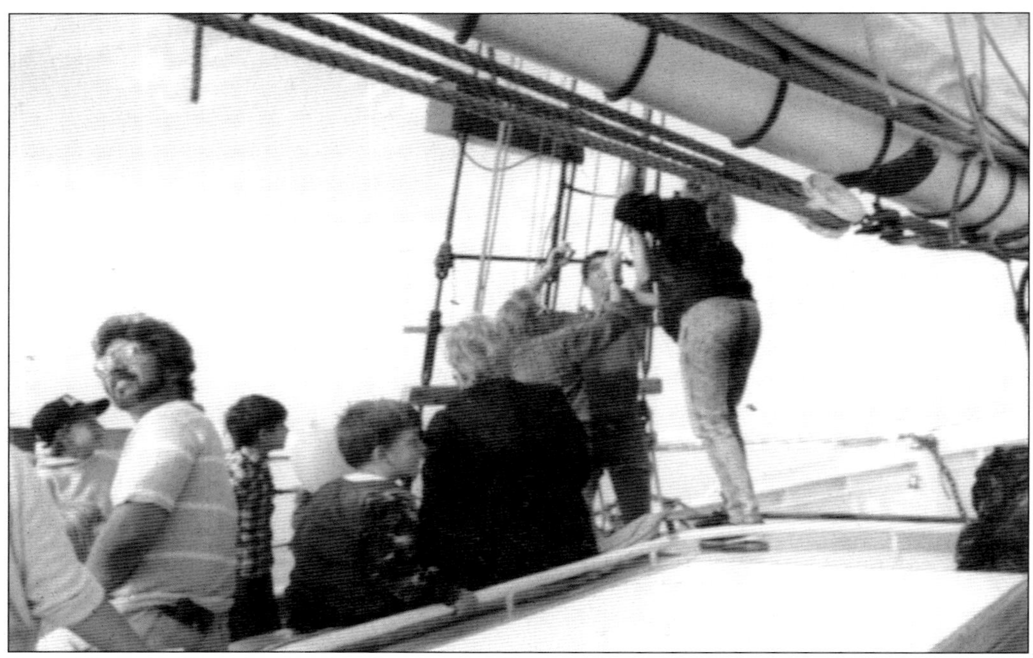

See a Piece of History. In this fall celebration, the *Pioneer* is available for a dockside tour and public sailing in Marcus Hook. The *Pioneer* is now dedicated to re-creating 19th-century sailing for the public. Besides sailing to Marcus Hook, it tours the Chesapeake and Delaware Bays, the Long Island Sound, and the Hudson River on a coastwide itinerary of port visits.

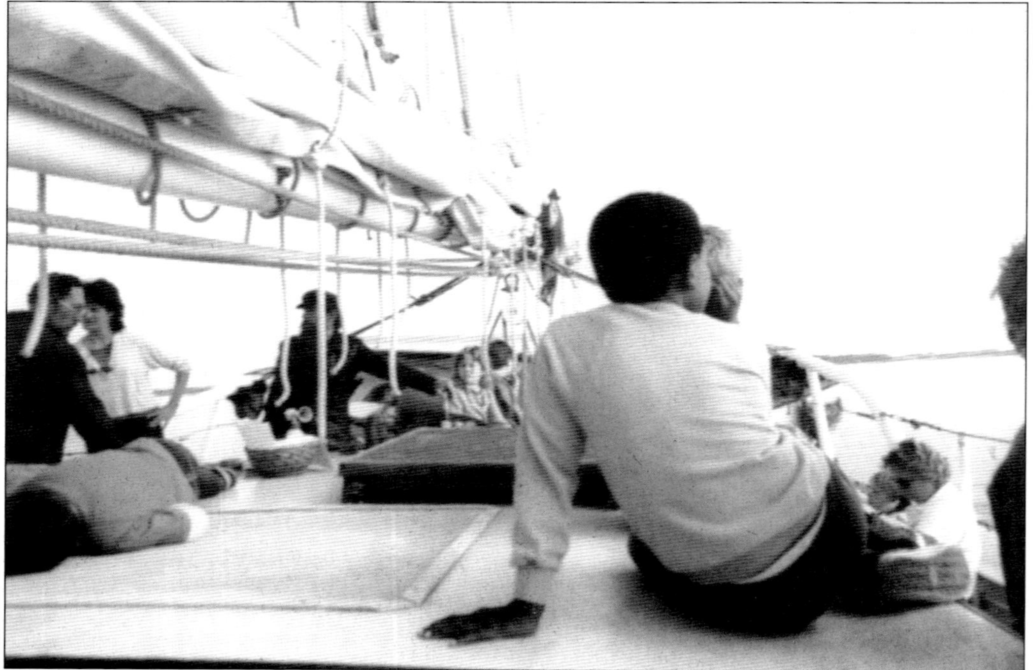

Annual Visits. The *Pioneer* has been making visits to the borough since its 100th anniversary celebration in 1985.

Five

Paths and Means of Travel

Marcus Hook had dirt roads until 1897 when loads of crushed oyster shells were purchased for the roads and carloads of cinders from the Pennsylvania Railroad were used for sidewalks. Market Street was actually paved with 10 inches of oyster shells. In 1911, brick gutters were placed in the streets, cement sidewalks were constructed, and the streets were macadamized or covered with small broken stones.

Although the growth of Marcus Hook was gradual, it was stimulated by repeated improvement to the Queen's Highway (Route 13 from Chester to Darby) and the King's Highway (Route 13 from Chester to New Castle). Along this famous highway the mail was carried from Philadelphia southward, and highwaymen infested the wilderness between Marcus Hook and Philadelphia. The whole area was overgrown with woods, and robbers made their homes in the forests. Often the mail coaches were held up by bandits in open daylight and the mails rifled. Old stagecoaches, attached with six horses, carried mail and passengers. Nearly all travelers over this route carried arms. Often there were exchanges of shots between passengers on the stagecoaches and the highwaymen that resulted in death.

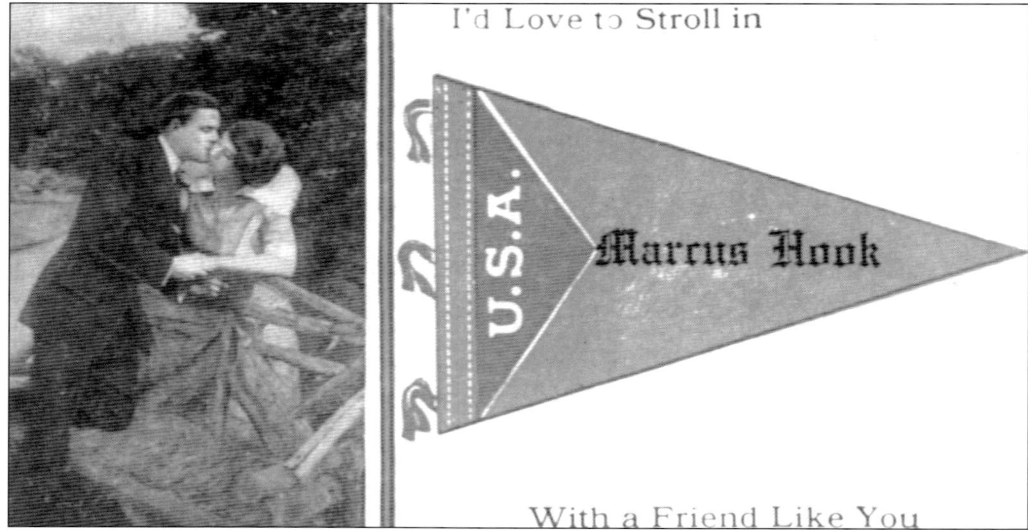

EARLY POSTCARDS. These early postcards, from around 1918, reflect a time in Marcus Hook before the age of the automobile when love letters and postcards were sent. This man sent a postcard to his lover, a Miss Hickman, requesting a stroll down a path in Marcus Hook. The opportunities were certainly great for love, as shown in the second postcard. According to Frank Sill of the Chichester Historical Society, these postcards depict a leisurely early-20th-century time. (Chichester Historical Society.)

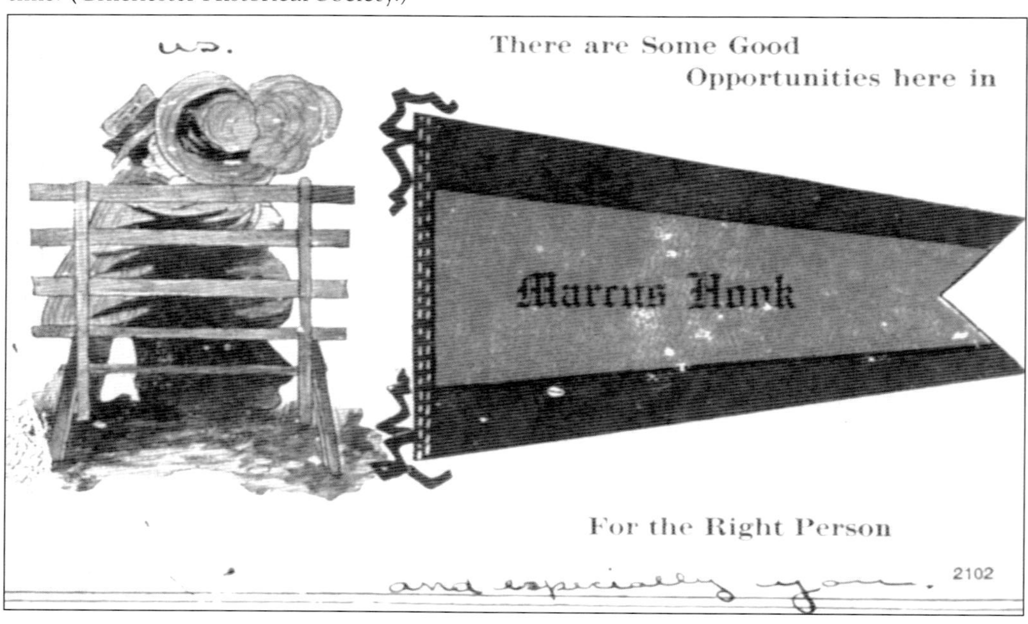

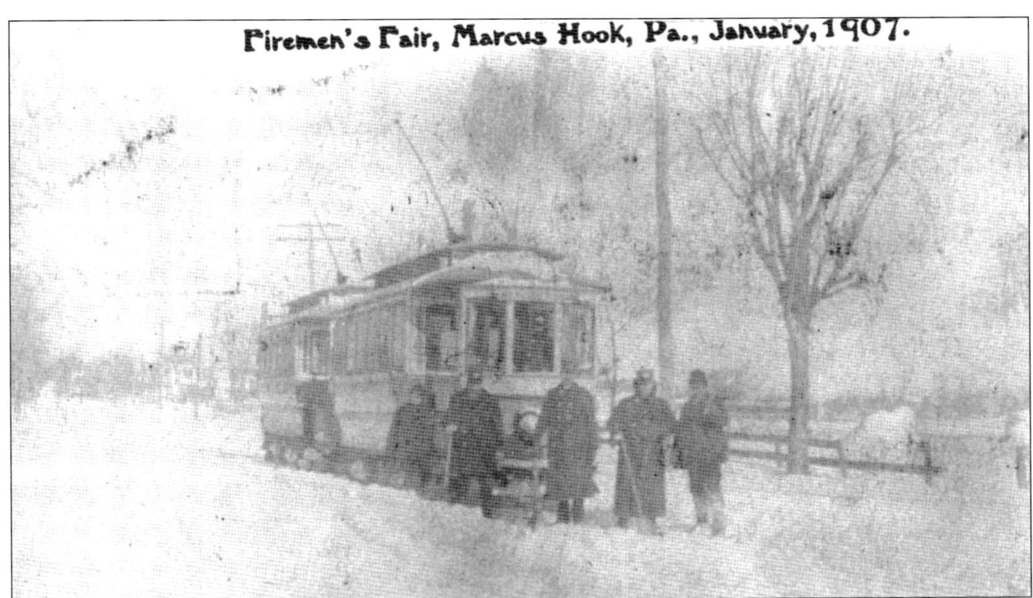

FIREMEN'S FAIR. This old photograph of a trolley and four men in uniform in the snow was taken in Marcus Hook over 100 years ago in January 1907. The Firemen's Fair was an early type of parade in the borough. In later years it was called the Firemen's Day parade, where firemen from several companies and their members joined in a parade. (Hagley Museum and Library.)

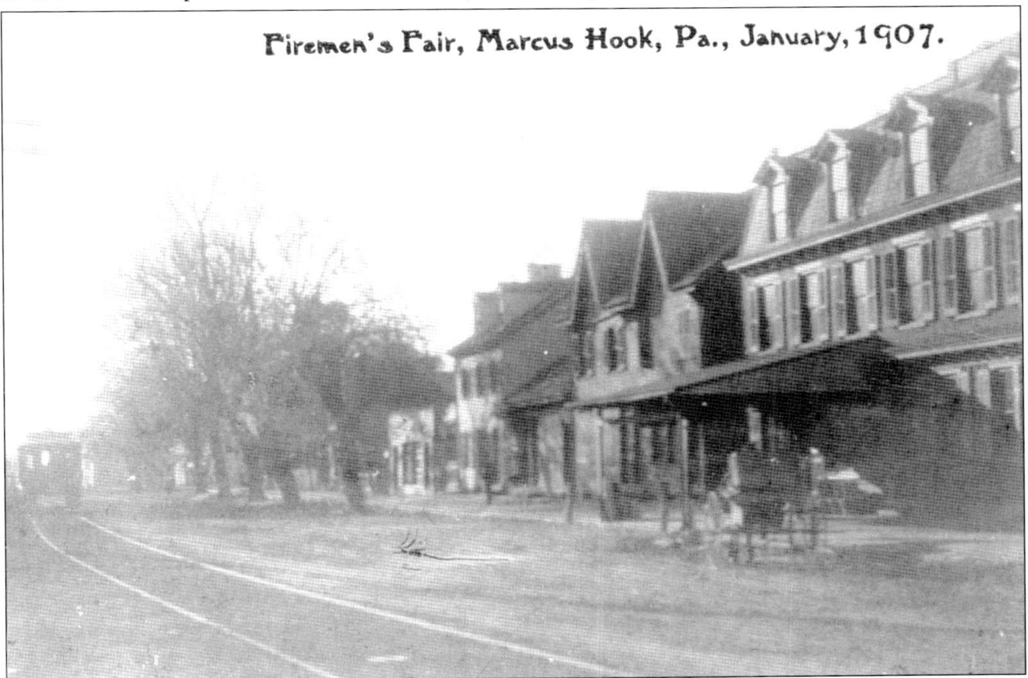

FIREMEN'S FAIR, 1907. This is the Firemen's Fair in January 1907 on Market Street at Fourth Street looking south when the roads were dirt roads. In the photograph one can see the trolley and tracks and a horseless carriage. The early trolley lines were constructed by the Chester Traction Company.

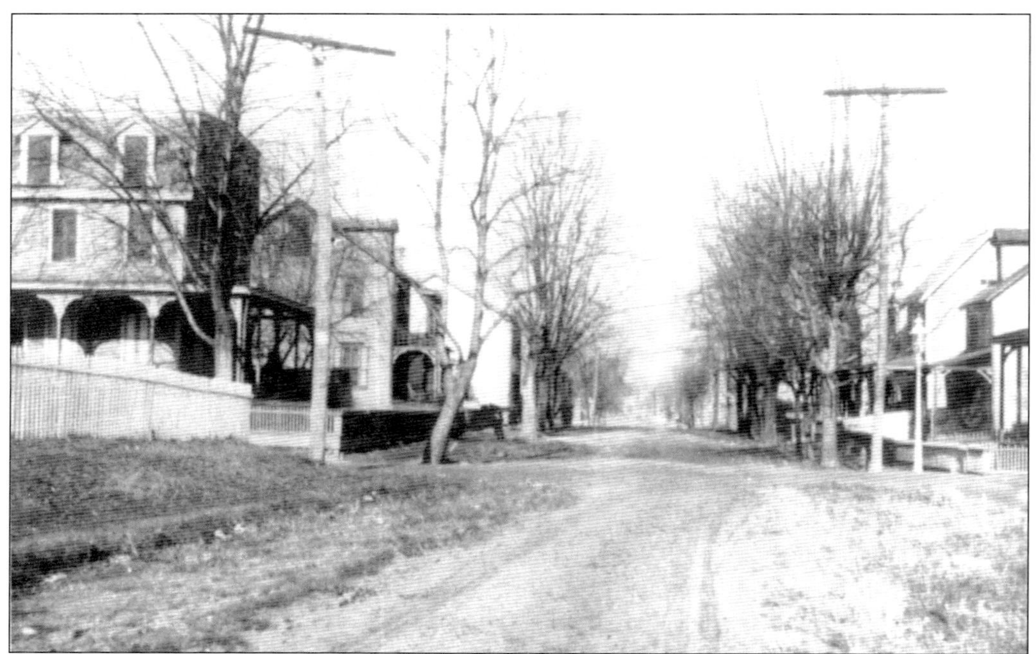

Green Street at Second Street, Looking Toward Third Street. This picture was taken by Harry Hueber in February 1903. The houses on the left are no longer standing. This ground was incorporated into the Sunoco refinery. The first two houses on the right remain. (Delaware County Historical Society.)

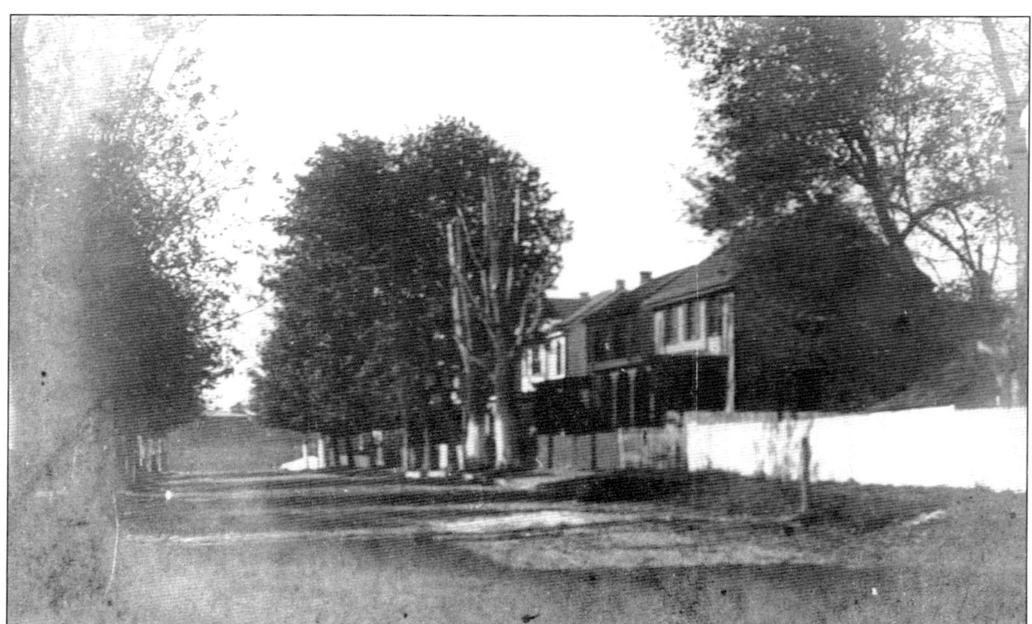

Dirt Road. This photograph depicts the dirt roads that existed before macadamizing of the roads on Ninth Street, looking west from Market Street, in 1907. Market Street was once surrounded by deep woods.

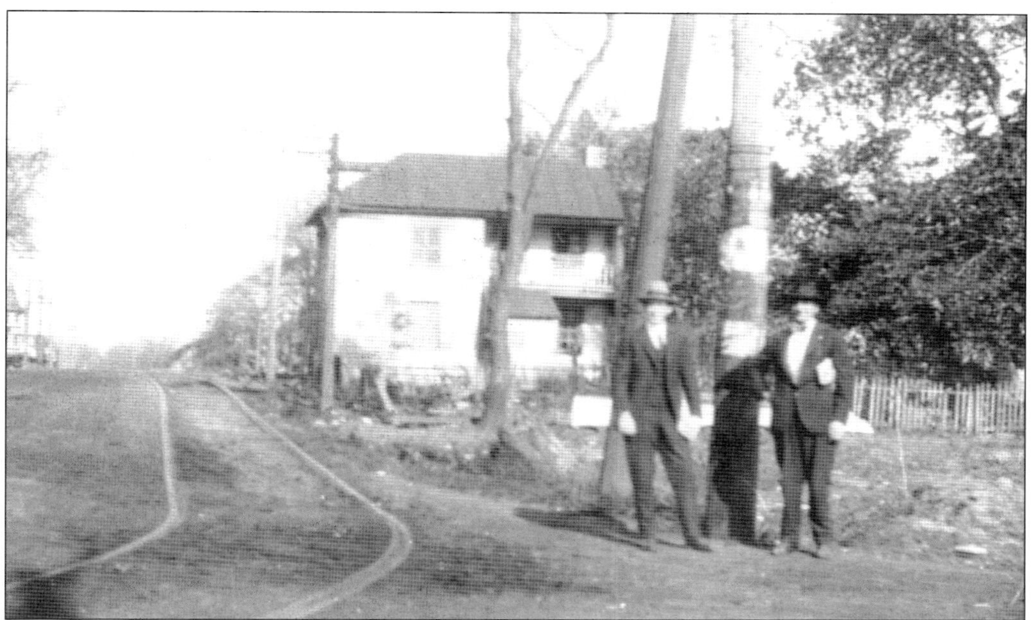

WAITING FOR THE TROLLEY. From this photograph one sees a hint of a popular mode of transportation of the day. Perhaps these prominent men, Greenwald and Pennypacker, were waiting for a trolley at Market Street north from Delaware Avenue in 1916. (Delaware County Historical Society.)

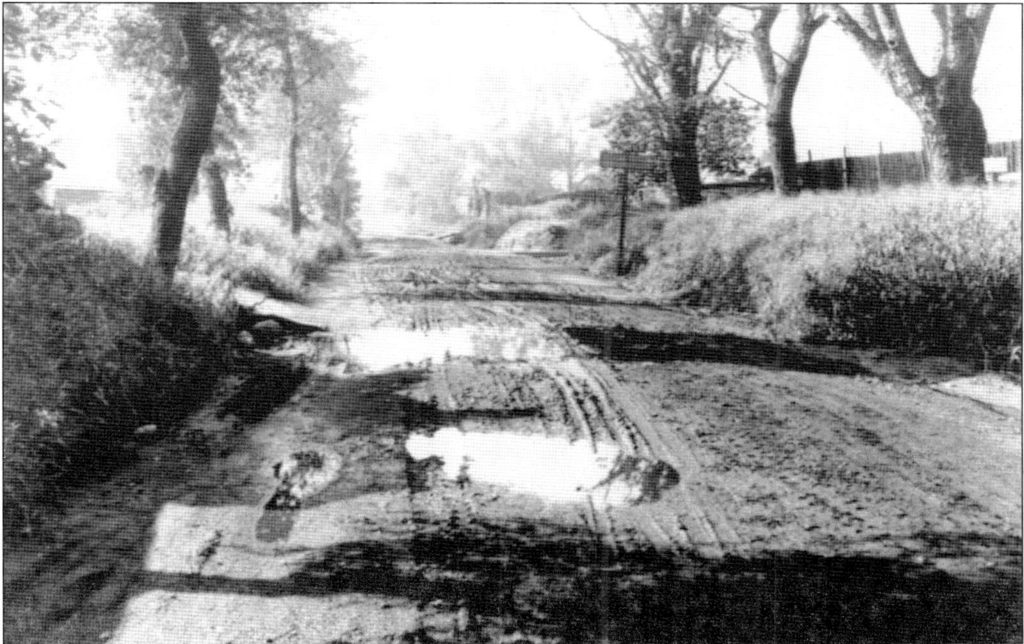

PENN AVENUE THROUGH AMERICAN VISCOSE COMPANY. This photograph is of Penn Avenue through the American Viscose Company property south of Post Road or Tenth Street. Paving had not reached this small street yet. Penn Avenue is shown on September 13, 1922. (Delaware County Historical Society.)

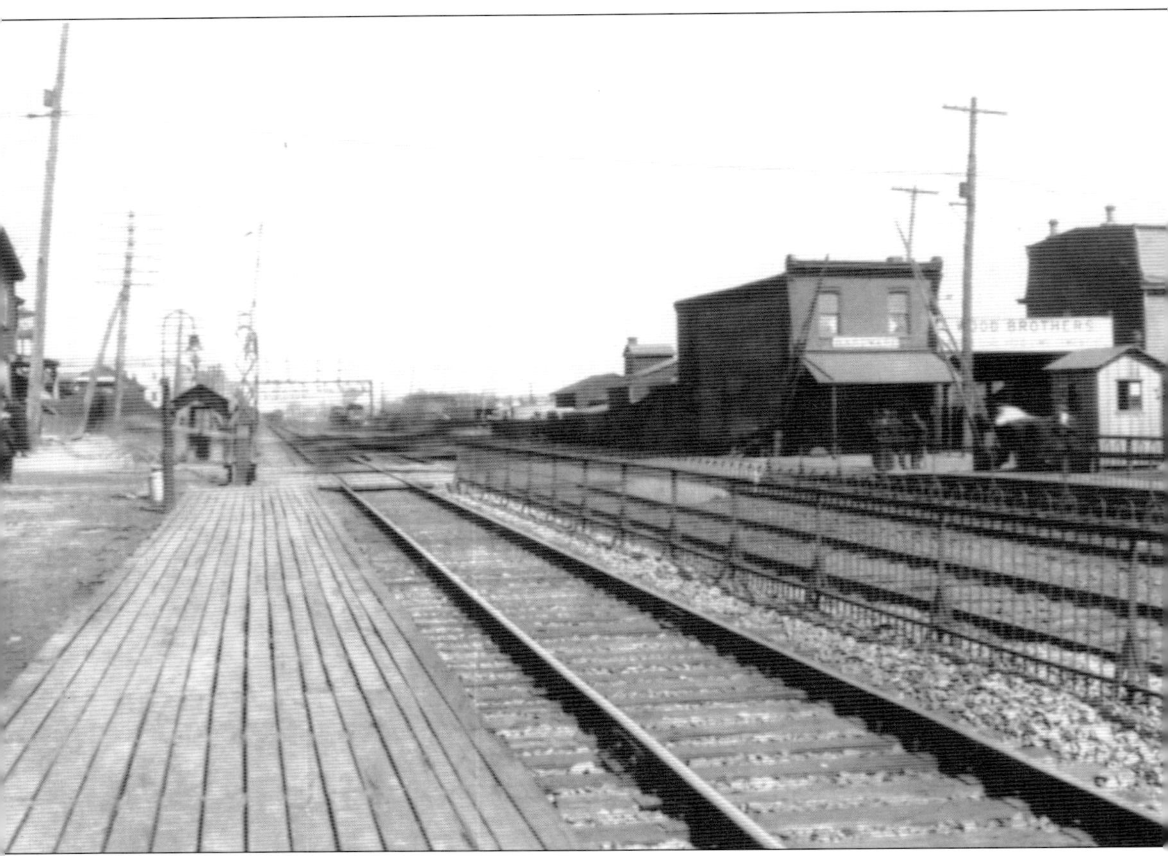

MARKET STREET CROSSING. Here is a Market Street railroad crossing. Several gentlemen seem to be waiting for the train on both sides. Notice the two small businesses on the right-hand side of the photograph. In addition to the aboveground railroad, according to a few early residents, there was also an underground railway to transfer slaves at one time. Escaped slaves were moved through Delaware into Marcus Hook. Delaware imposed a fine for helping escaped slaves while Pennsylvania had no such fine, so Marcus Hook was a gathering place where slaves were then sent on to other safe areas. (Delaware County Historical Society.)

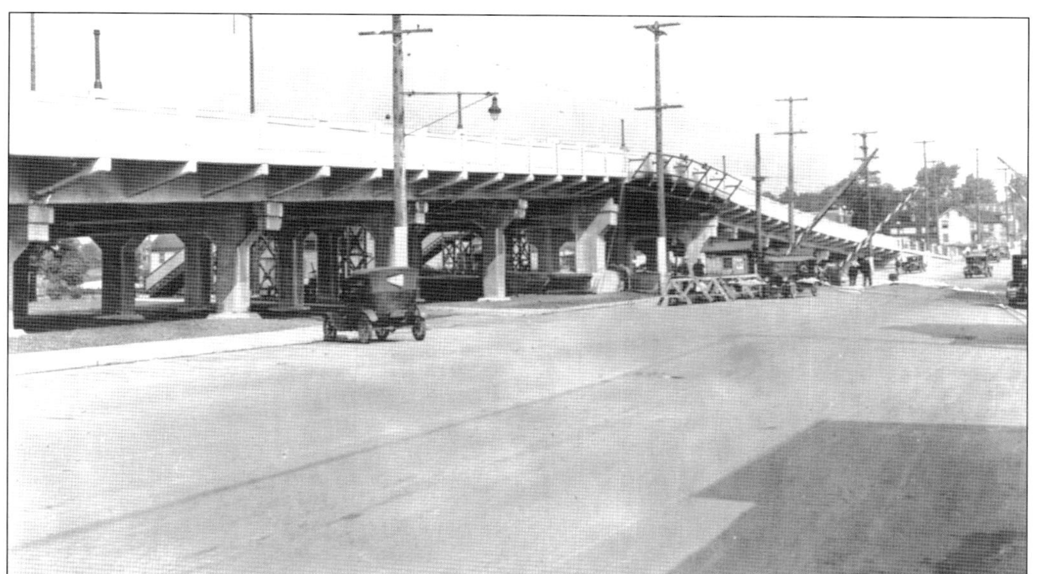

New Concrete Bridge. A new concrete bridge was built at the old Market Street grade crossing, Marcus Hook, on August 3, 1927. More than 400 automobiles stood waiting on either side of the bridge. (Urban Archives of Temple University.)

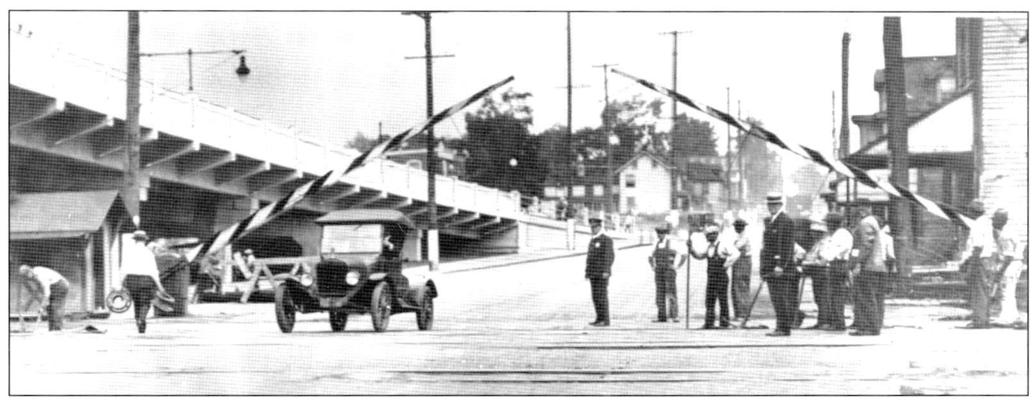

First Crossings. The first automobile to cross the new structure was a Model T and was occupied by burgess William McClure and P. J. McBride, a police sergeant, both of Marcus Hook. The bridge cost $450,000 and was designed by Pennsylvania Railroad engineers. (Urban Archives of Temple University.)

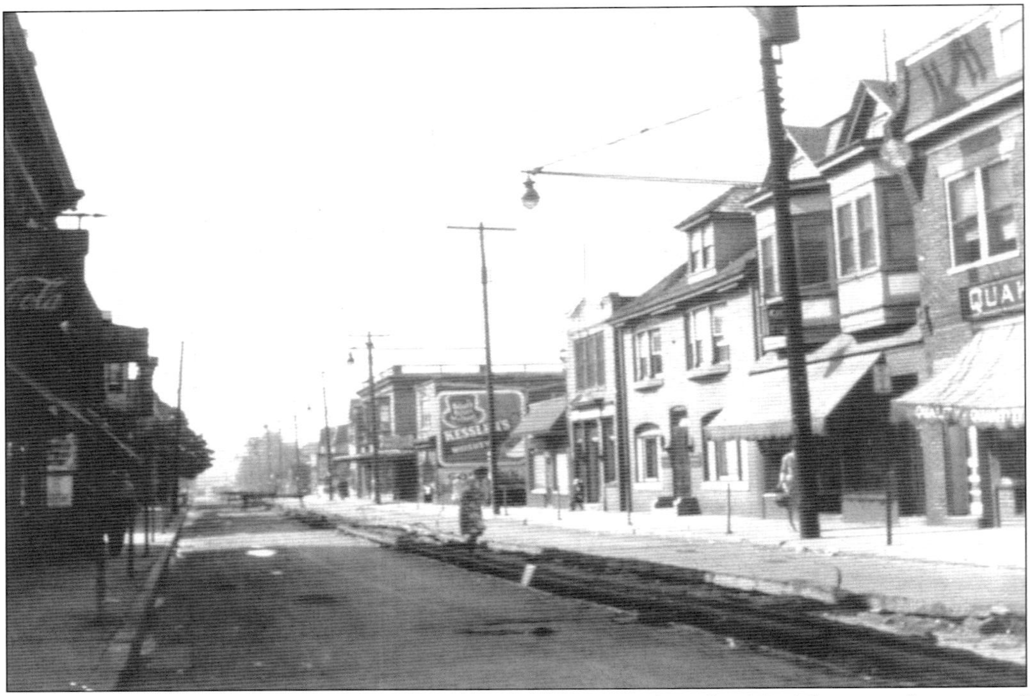

REMOVAL OF TROLLEY TRACKS. Is this damage from an earthquake? No. This was the removal of trolley tracks prior to the repaving of Market Street. The view is south from Tenth Street in 1945. (Delaware County Historical Society.)

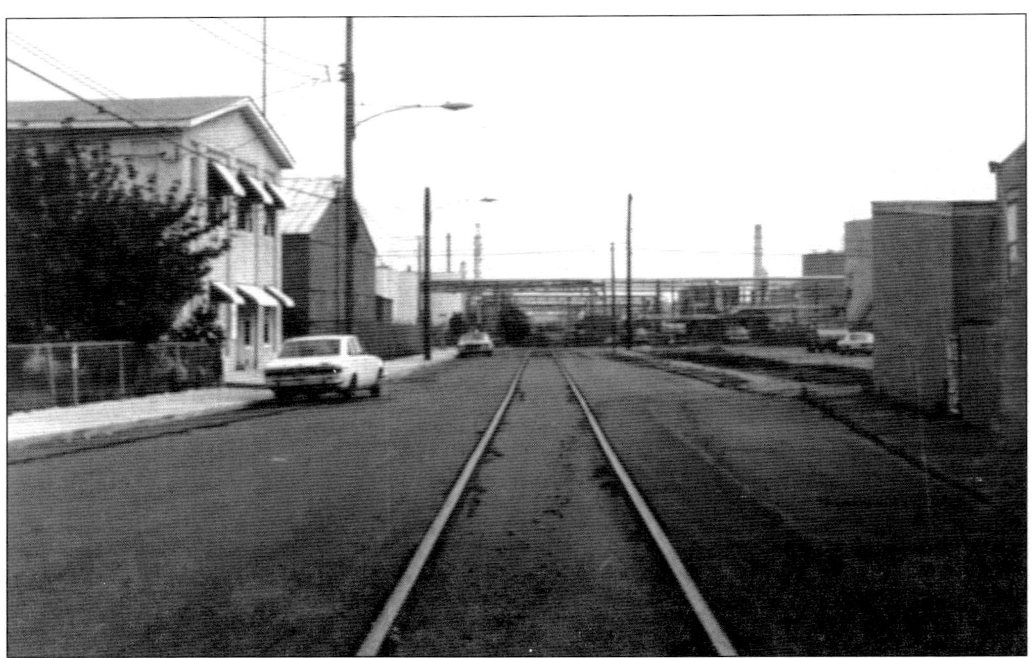

TRAIN TRACKS ON FOURTH STREET. The Conrail rail spur heading into the Sunoco Marcus Hook refinery is seen here in 1984.

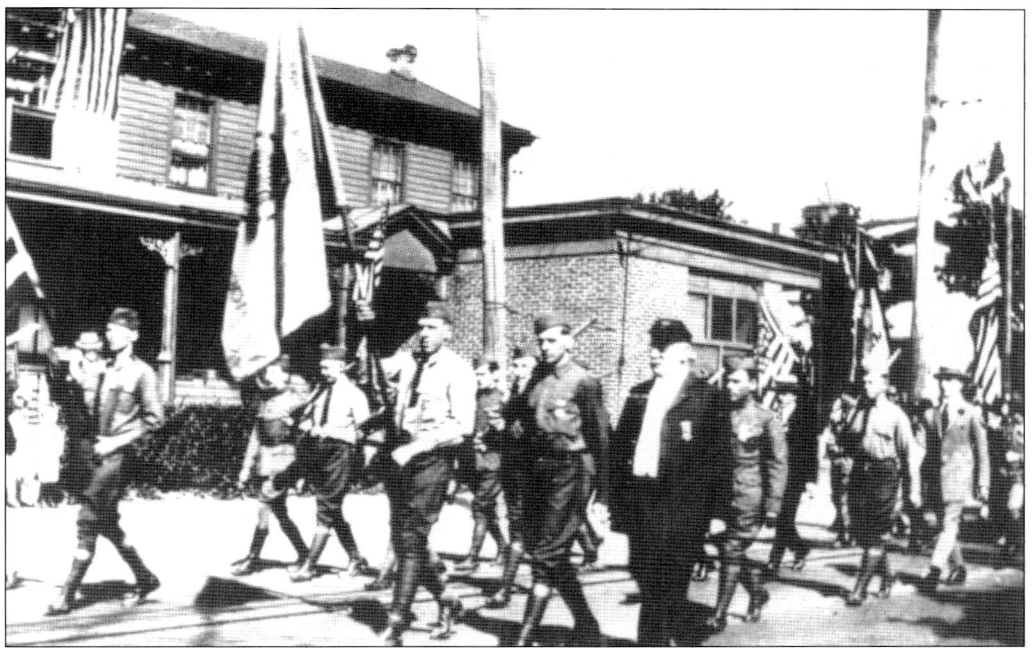

MARKET STREET PARADE. Market Street in Marcus Hook has always been the path since early times for the patriotic march on Memorial Day. Here is a 1923 shot of the first appearance of McKenna's Post in the Memorial Day parade. (Delaware County Historical Society.)

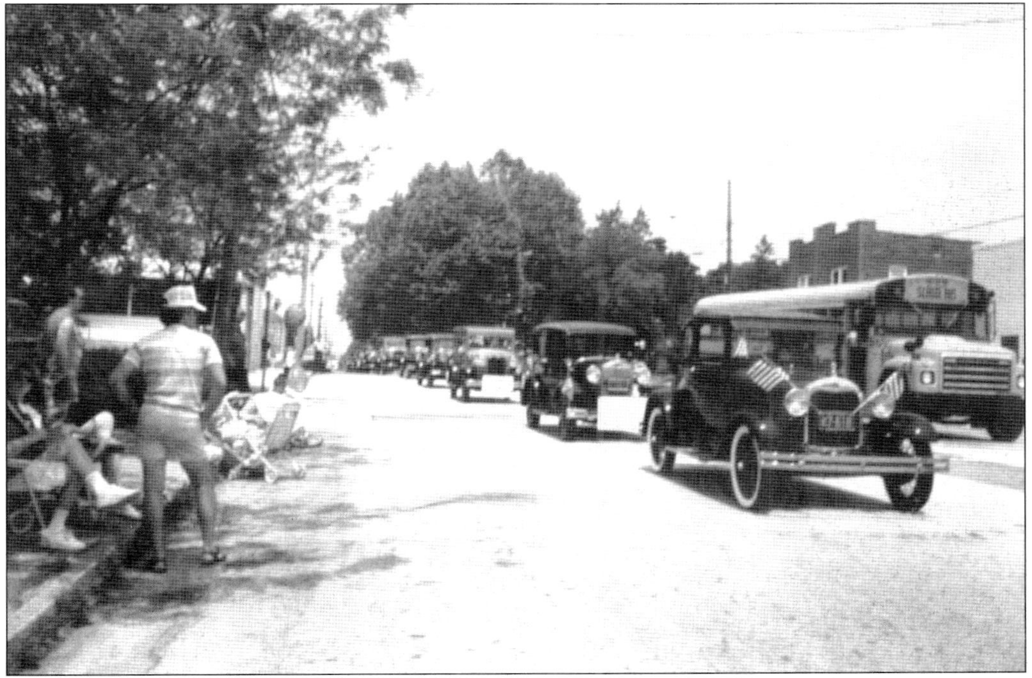

MARKET STREET PARADE, 1988. Here is a modern-day version of the march on Memorial Day down that same path, Market Street. An annual tradition for the Memorial Day parade is the promenade of Model Ts, which this photograph shows.

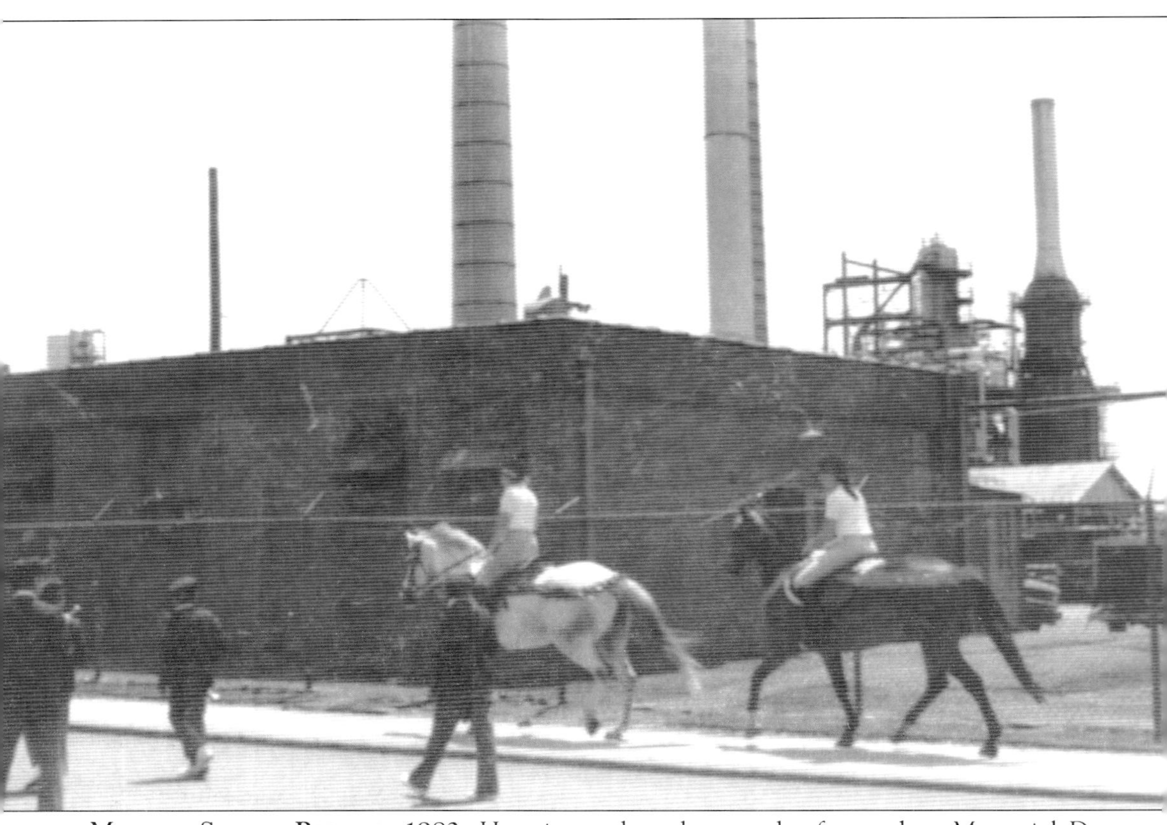

Market Street Parade, 1983. Here is another photograph of a modern Memorial Day Marcus Hook parade. These marchers and horseback riders march down Green Street against the backdrop of the Sunoco refinery. In this year, the parade route followed Green Street to Delaware Avenue and proceeded up Market Street.

Six

Schools, Churches, Parks, and Public Buildings

The first school in Marcus Hook was organized in the old frame church of St. Martin's. The Marcus Hook Baptist Church (located in 1854 on Market Street between Second and Third Streets) was used as a school between 1854 and 1890. This was followed in 1895 by the Seventh Street Grammar School at Seventh and Green Streets. The Marcus Hook Elementary School at Eighth and Market Streets was constructed in 1917. This school was actually an elementary and junior high school with industrial arts shops and home economics.

Marcus Hook over the years has welcomed many races and religions. St. Martin's Episcopal Church opened for worship in 1702. The Baptist congregation was organized in 1798 and relocated a number of times. The present church building is situated at 1345 Market Street in Linwood. The Mount Hebron African Methodist Episcopal Church had its roots in Marcus Hook and its first church building on the west side of Green Street (between Seventh and Eighth Streets). In 1926, the church property was purchased by Sunoco, and the congregation relocated to Lower Chichester Township where it remains to this day. The Cokesbury Methodist Church building dates to 1871, and the Immaculate Conception of Lourdes Roman Catholic Church was officially dedicated on August 15, 1917. In 1930, the Union Gospel Missionary Church was built on Market Street next to the Market Street bridge.

The first municipally owned park in the borough was Plaza Park (later renamed Robert E. Haebel Plaza in 1987). This property was acquired from the American Viscose Company for $1 as per the deed dated December 6, 1948. Williamson Field followed. The park was named for Charles L. Williamson, president of the Marcus Hook Recreation Board in the early 1950s. Memorial Field, now known as Mickey Vernon Park, was acquired from the Marcus Hook School District on November 23, 1965. In 1984 and 1985, adjoining land parcels next to McClure Park were purchased giving rise to the establishment of Market Square Memorial Park, the beautiful waterfront park on the Delaware River.

The Marcus Hook Municipal Building, located on the northeast corner of Tenth and Green Streets, was constructed in 1939. It is an imposing building built in a classical Egyptian-Greek Revival style set upon a high podium entered by symmetrical formal staircases. The overall quality of design and construction and the fine sequence of interior spaces and finishes contribute to this architecturally unique building. The municipal building was a Federal Works Agency, Public Works Administration project.

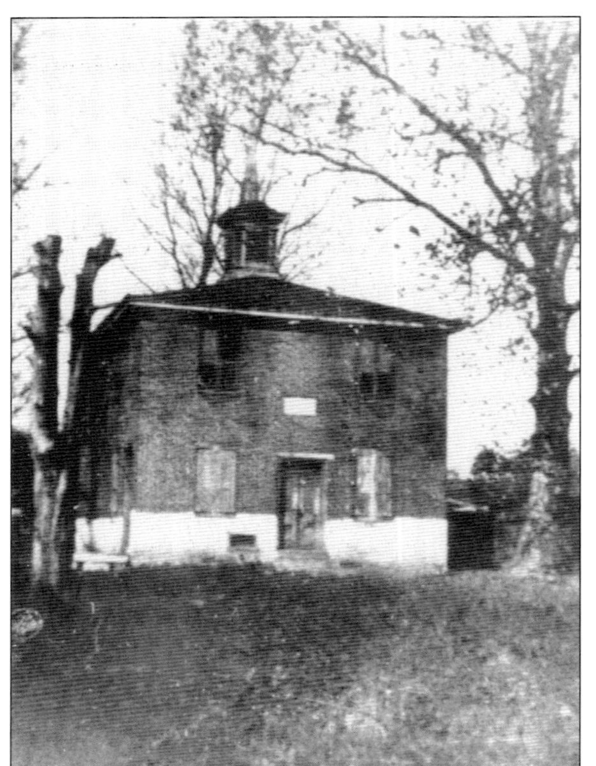

Cedar Grove School. Cedar Grove School, on Penn Avenue in Marcus Hook, is so called because it was situated in a clump of cedar trees. According to a 1936 article in the *Delaware County Democrat*, a Mr. Ferguson (or "Fergy") taught older pupils on the first floor, and Maggie Dunn taught younger ones in the upper room in the 1870s, when corporal punishment was in vogue and four hickory switches were used. On the blackboard Fergy would write "Broom Brigade," and names would be written under it for infractions of discipline. In 1908, the property was bought by the American Viscose Company. (Delaware County Historical Society.)

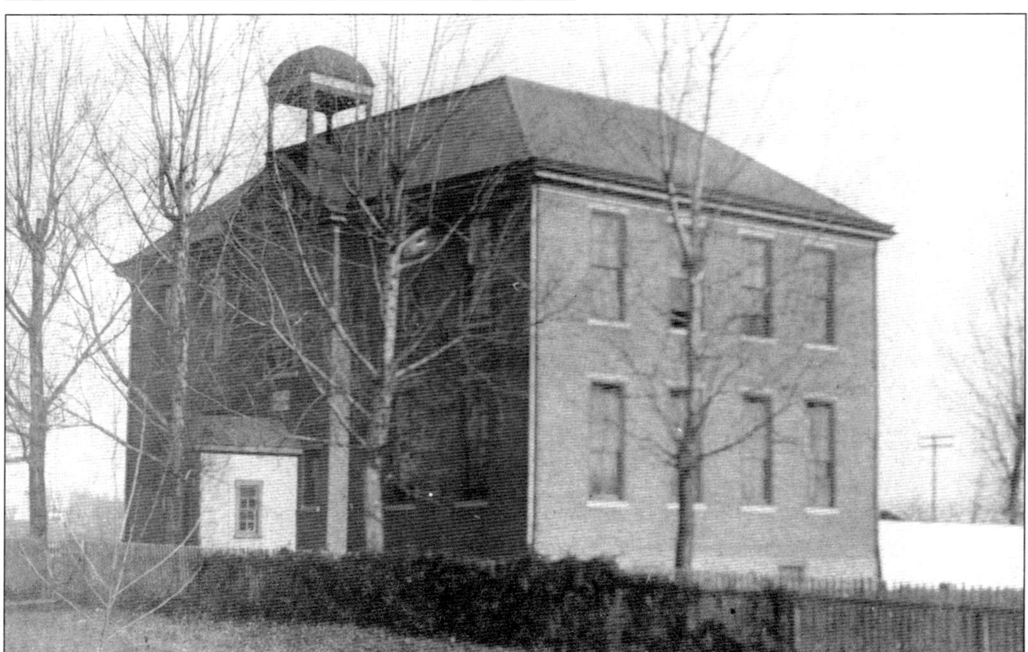

Central School. This is a photograph of Central School, which stood at Tenth and Church Streets. The building was demolished in 1921. On the same site, the Congress Theater was later built.

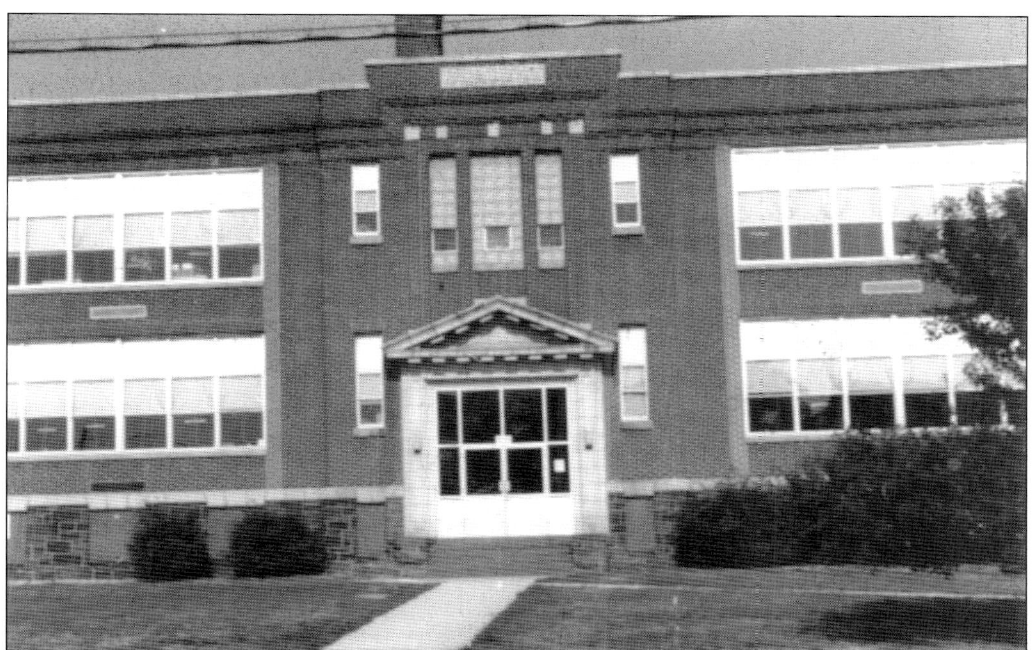

MARCUS HOOK ELEMENTARY SCHOOL, 1984. The Marcus Hook Elementary School was first built in 1917. The school is shown here in April 1984.

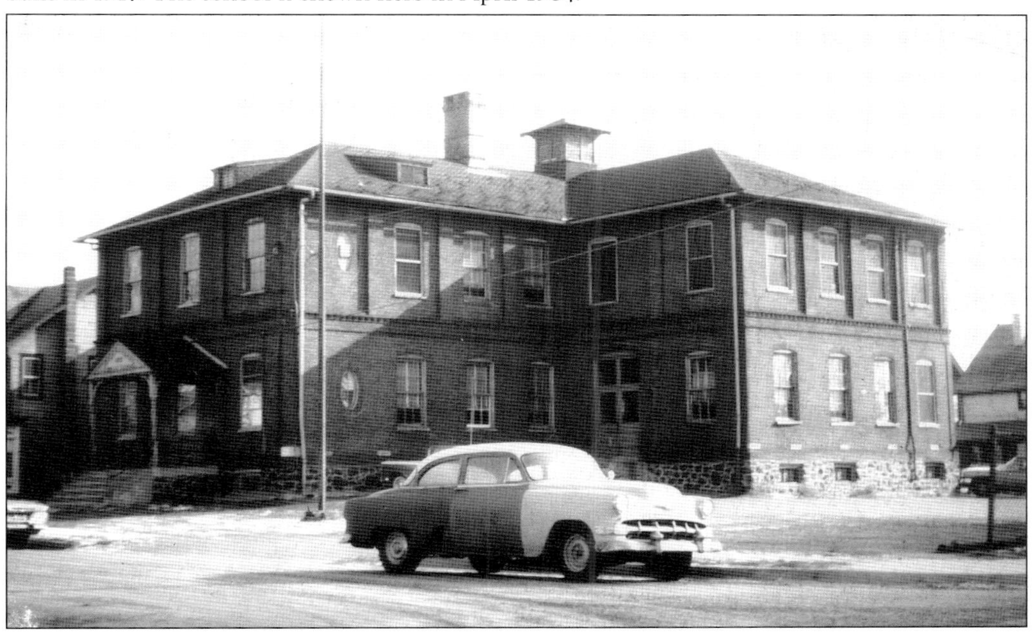

SEVENTH STREET SCHOOL. Very few people in Marcus Hook are aware that a school stood at Seventh and Green Streets. The grades for the school were first, second, and kindergarten. The school was built in 1895 and razed in 1964. The building was closed and sold to Sunoco at the beginning of World War II because of the fear of explosions and possible sabotage in the nearby plant, and townspeople thought it would be difficult to get the children out of the school. The space is now a parking lot. (Ralph Montella.)

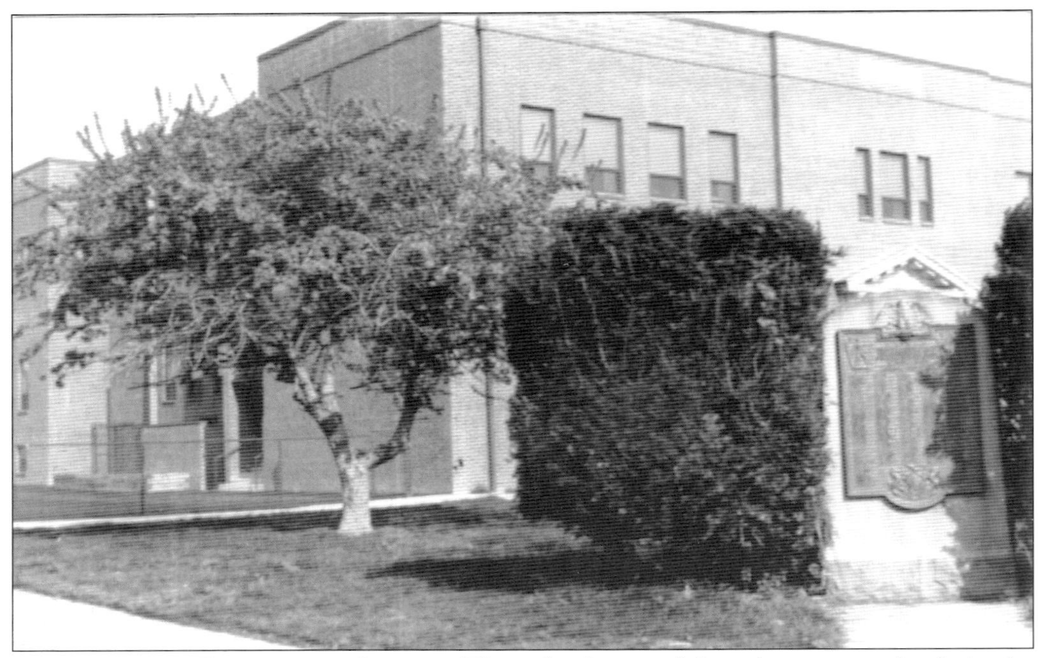

MARCUS HOOK ELEMENTARY SCHOOL. This school, one of four elementary schools in the Chichester School District, houses kindergarten through fifth grade. This photograph was taken by the author in April 1987.

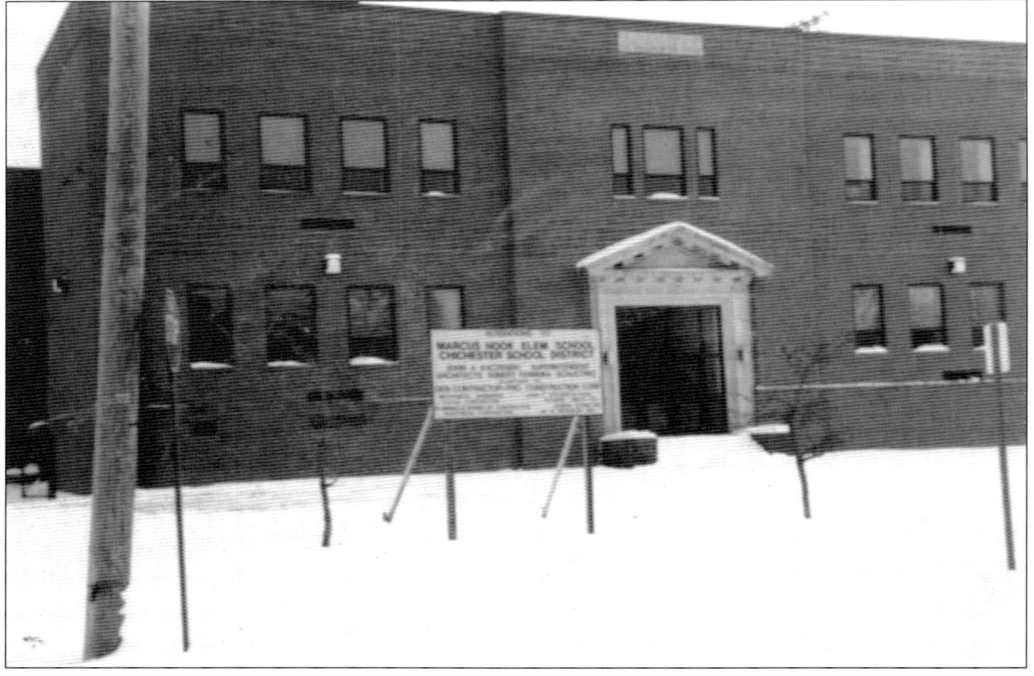

MARCUS HOOK ELEMENTARY SCHOOL, 1987. The renovated Marcus Hook Elementary School is pictured here in 1987.

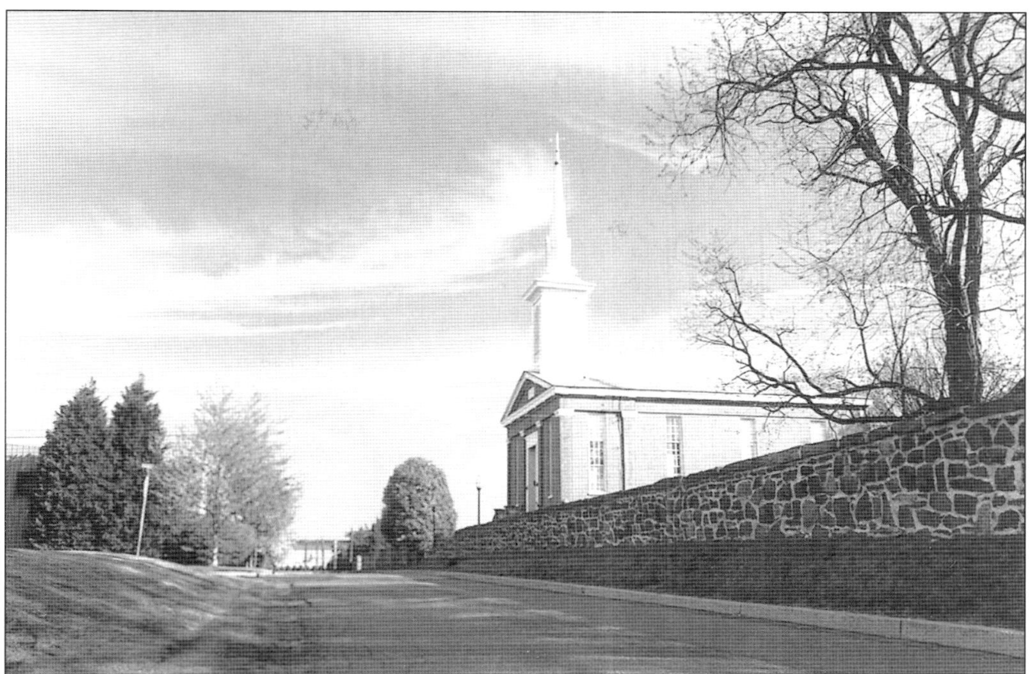

St. Martin's Episcopal Church. St. Martin's Episcopal Church, the second-oldest church site in the state and fourth-oldest in the nation, was founded in 1699 by local resident Walter Martin to provide an alternative place of worship and burial for non-Quakers. Services were held in a frame house purchased for five sterlings. It officially opened for service in October 1702. The current church building on the site (shown here) was built in 1845 and is the last of the 19th-century buildings that formerly constituted Marcus Hook's old Market Square district.

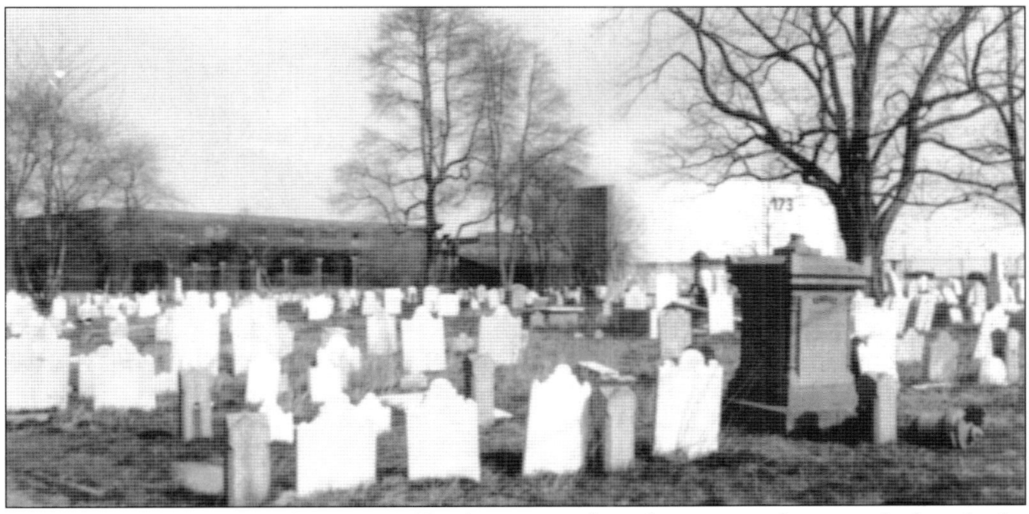

St. Martin's Church Cemetery. Tombstones within the graveyard are marked with the names of men who fought in the Revolutionary War, War of 1812, Mexican War, Civil War, Spanish-American War, World War I, and World War II. A noted grave in the cemetery is that of Elizabeth Smith, who lived in three centuries, having been born in 1699 and died in the early 1800s. This photograph was taken in April 1984.

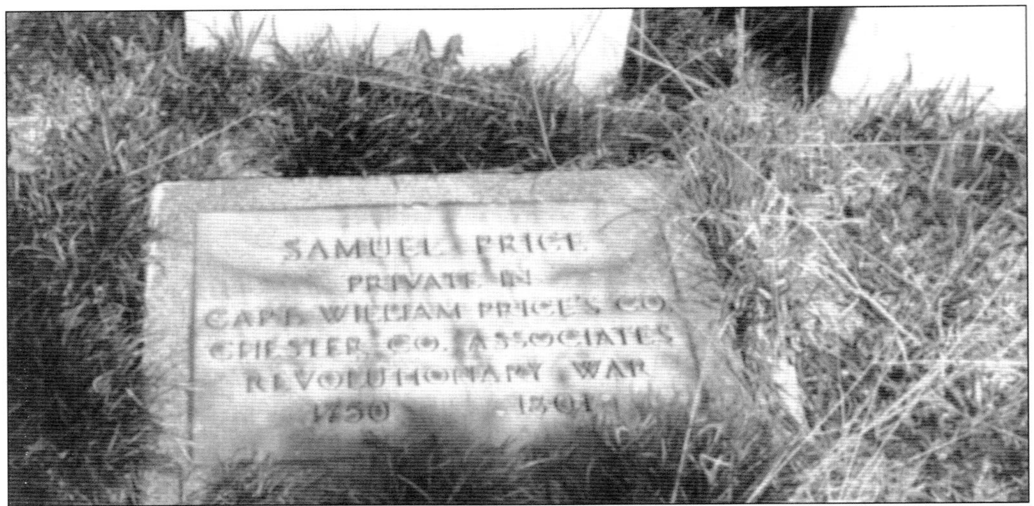

SOLDIER'S GRAVE. This grave marker is for Samuel Price, one of the many Revolutionary War soldiers buried at St. Martin's Church Cemetery. This photograph was taken in April 1984.

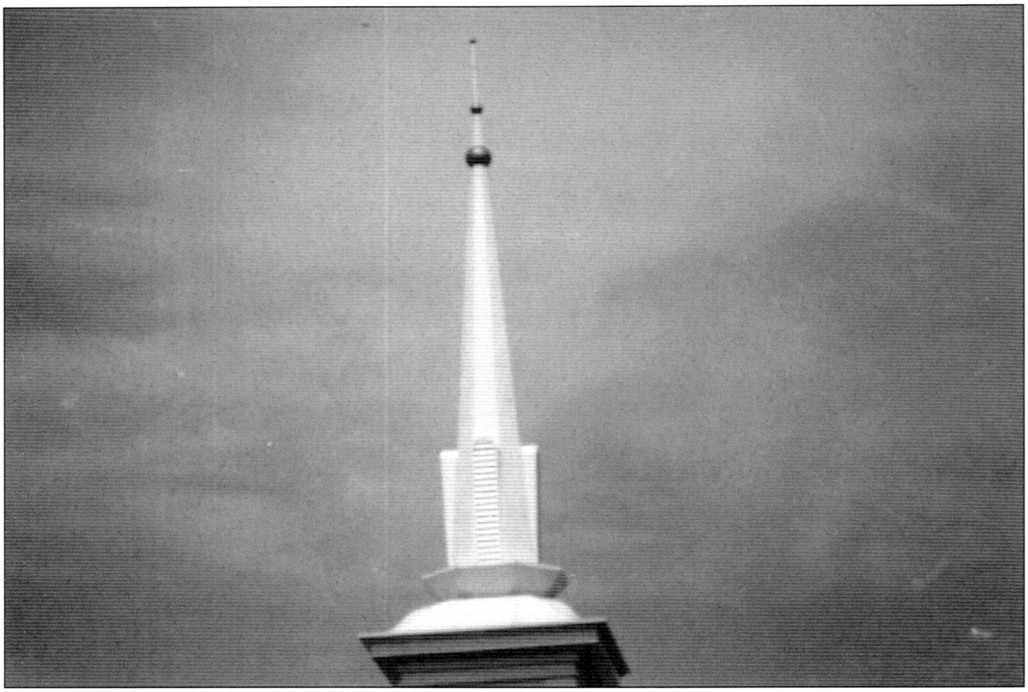

ST. MARTIN'S NEW STEEPLE. The new 46-foot steeple was installed atop St. Martin's Episcopal Church on March 3, 1988. The church property was gifted to the Marcus Hook Community Development Corporation on January 28, 1985. Soon thereafter a project to restore the church began. Over a two-year period, the exterior and interior were restored. The church is currently leased to the Bible Presbyterian Church congregation.

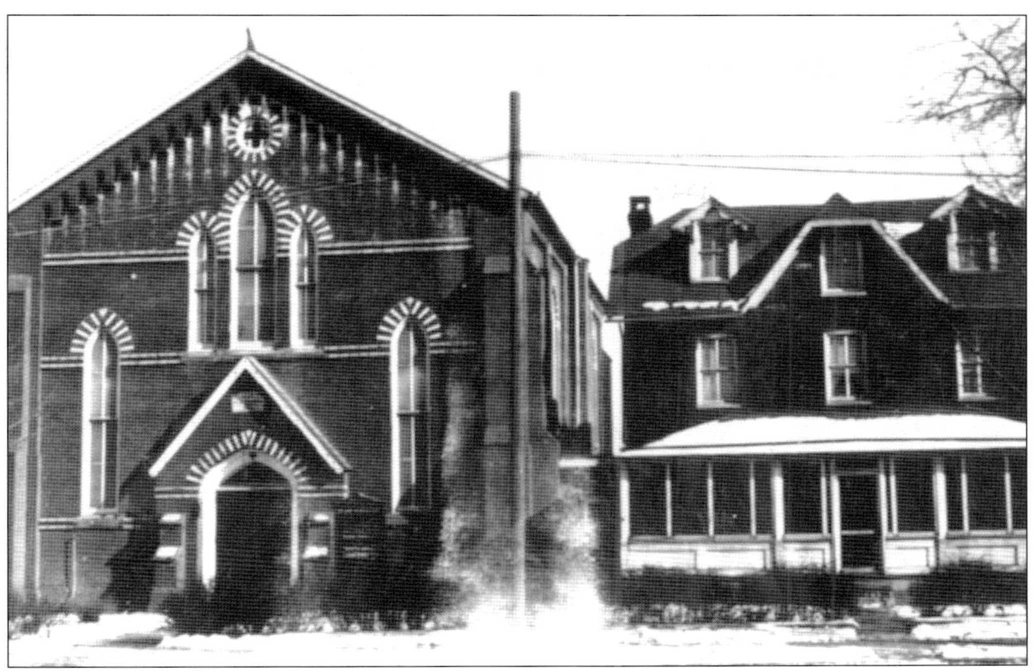

COKESBURY METHODIST CHURCH. This is the Cokesbury (Old St. George's) Methodist Church, on Market Street and Waggoner or Plum Street. It first started in a private home in 1833 and was originally called St. George's Church. The present brick structure was dedicated in 1871. This photograph was taken on January 23, 1946. (Delaware County Historical Society.)

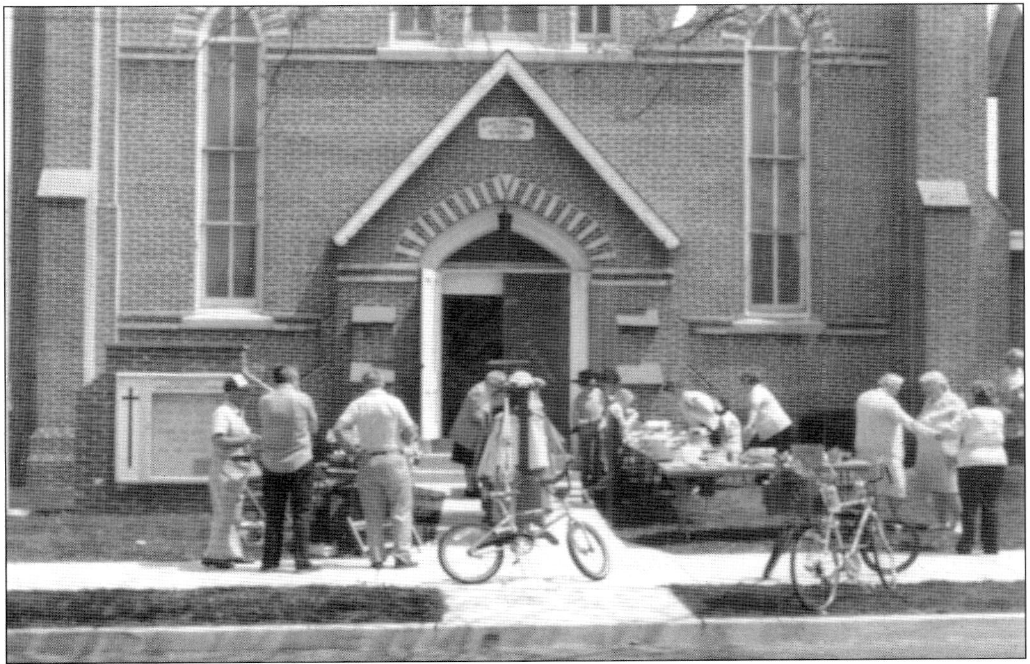

PRESENT-DAY COKESBURY METHODIST CHURCH. Cokesbury Methodist Church was named after the first two American bishops, Coke and Asbury. The church is pictured here in June 1983.

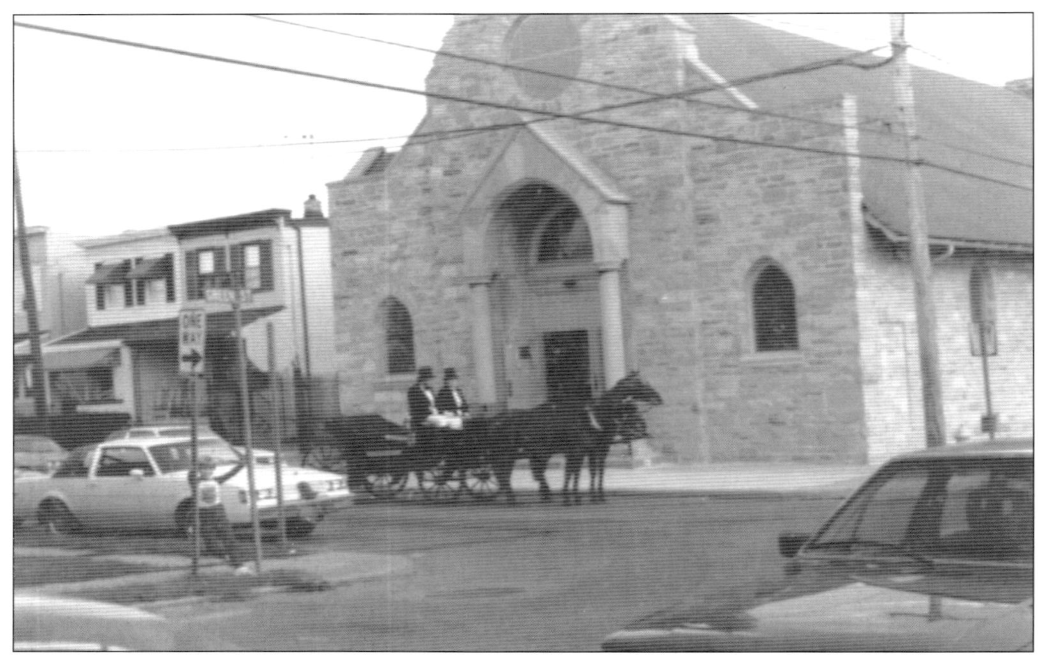

IMMACULATE CONCEPTION OF LOURDES ROMAN CATHOLIC CHURCH. The Catholic church began as a mission church for St. Anthony's parish in Chester. In 1917, the congregation built the present stone church in Marcus Hook. This photograph and the next were taken during the occasion of a wedding at the church in October 1985.

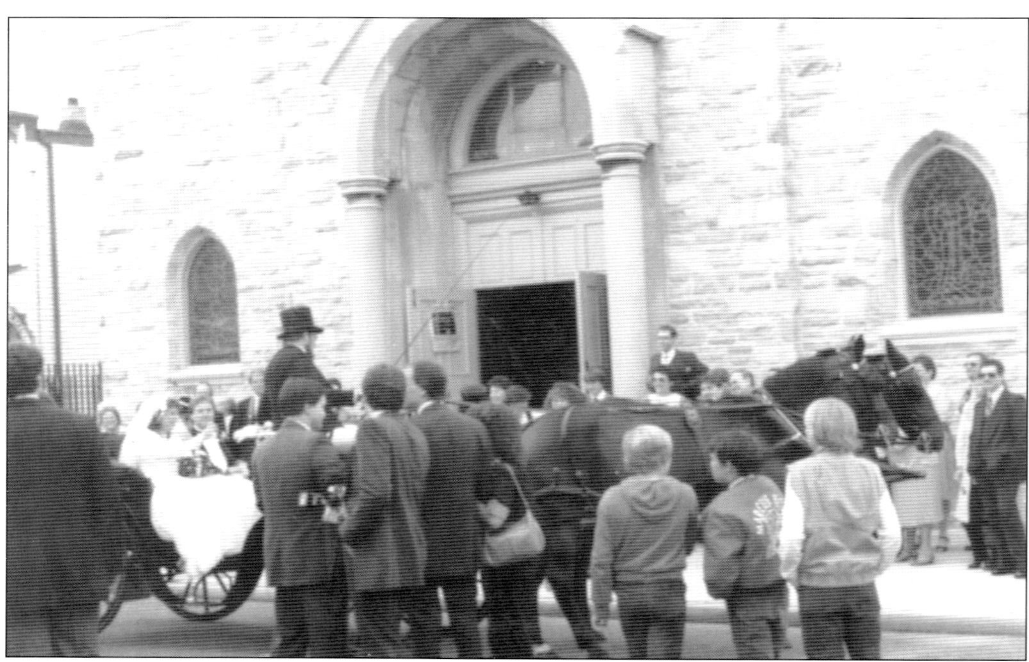

IMMACULATE CONCEPTION OF LOURDES ROMAN CATHOLIC CHURCH. Here is a close-up shot of the bride and groom in a horse-drawn carriage as many townspeople look on.

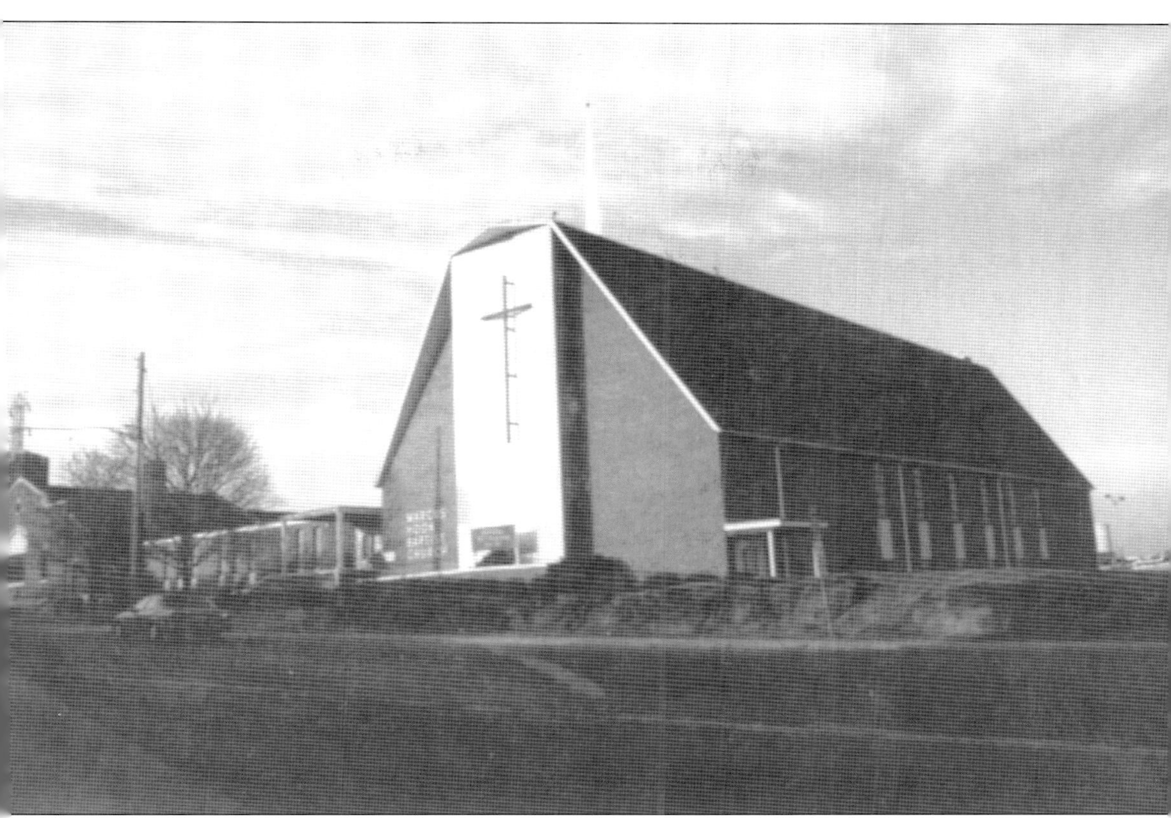

MARCUS HOOK BAPTIST CHURCH. This photograph is of the present site of the Marcus Hook Baptist Church just over the Market Street bridge, erected in 1927, in Lower Chichester Township. The church moved from Marcus Hook where it was located on the west side of Marcus Street, between Second and Third Streets.

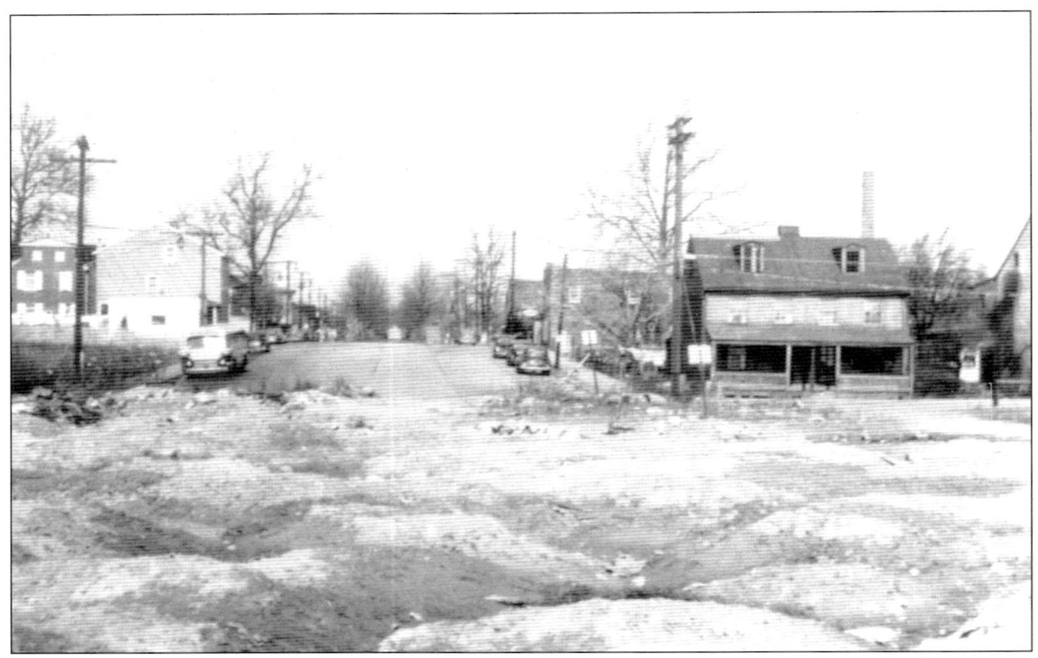

McClure Park. This is McClure Park, a park on the Delaware River, and its rocky beginning on March 17, 1949. This view is looking north toward Market Street. (Delaware County Historical Society.)

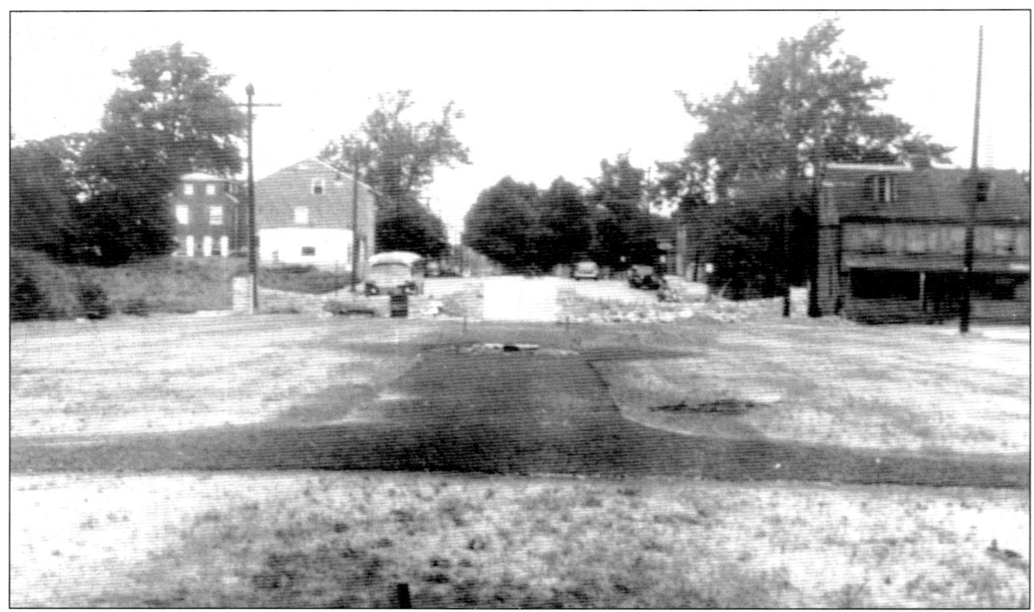

McClure Park, 1949. Later in the summer of 1949 there are the beginnings of a park. The park was named after burgess William J. McClure, for his many years of service to the community, and officially dedicated in 1951. McClure served as mayor for 28 years. Members of the McClure family were sportsmen with interests in gun shoots, foxhunts, and baseball. (Delaware County Historical Society.)

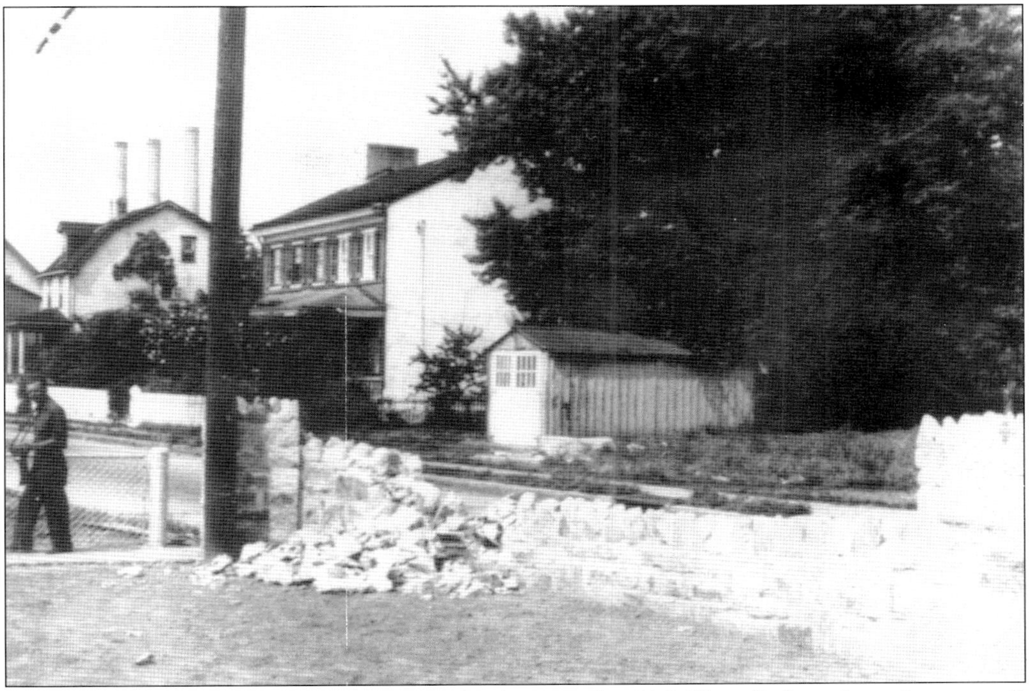

WALL AT MCCLURE PARK. This is an early photograph of McClure Fark with its famous wall crumbled. The date of this photograph is unknown. (Delaware County Historical Society.)

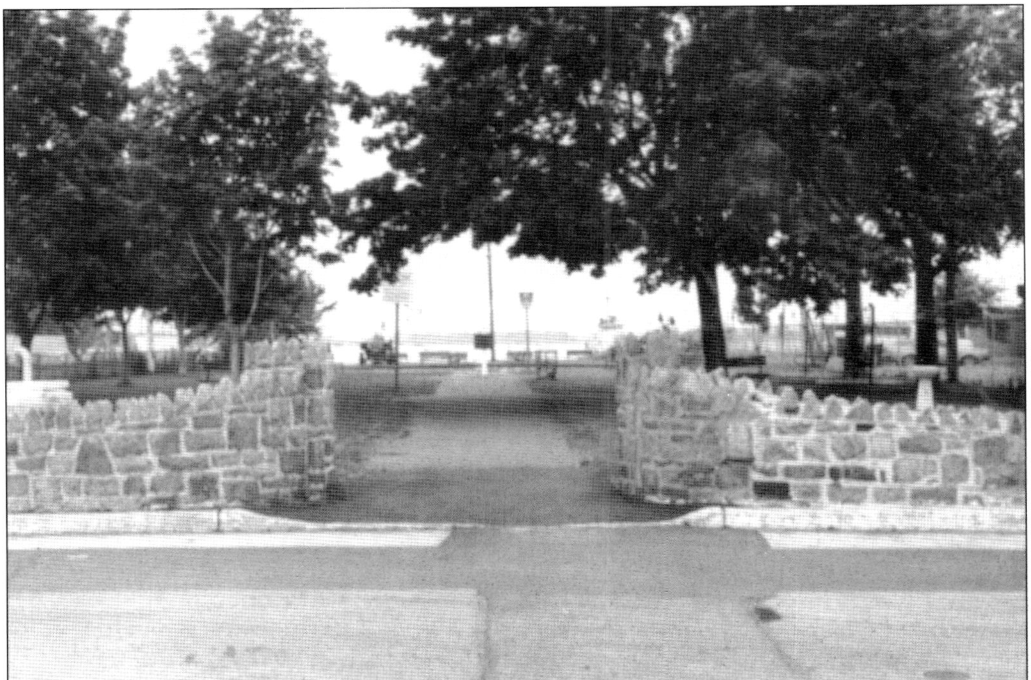

MCCLURE PARK ENTRANCE. The entrance to this park was made of stone that resembled the stone used for the house the author was born in. This photograph was taken in May 1981.

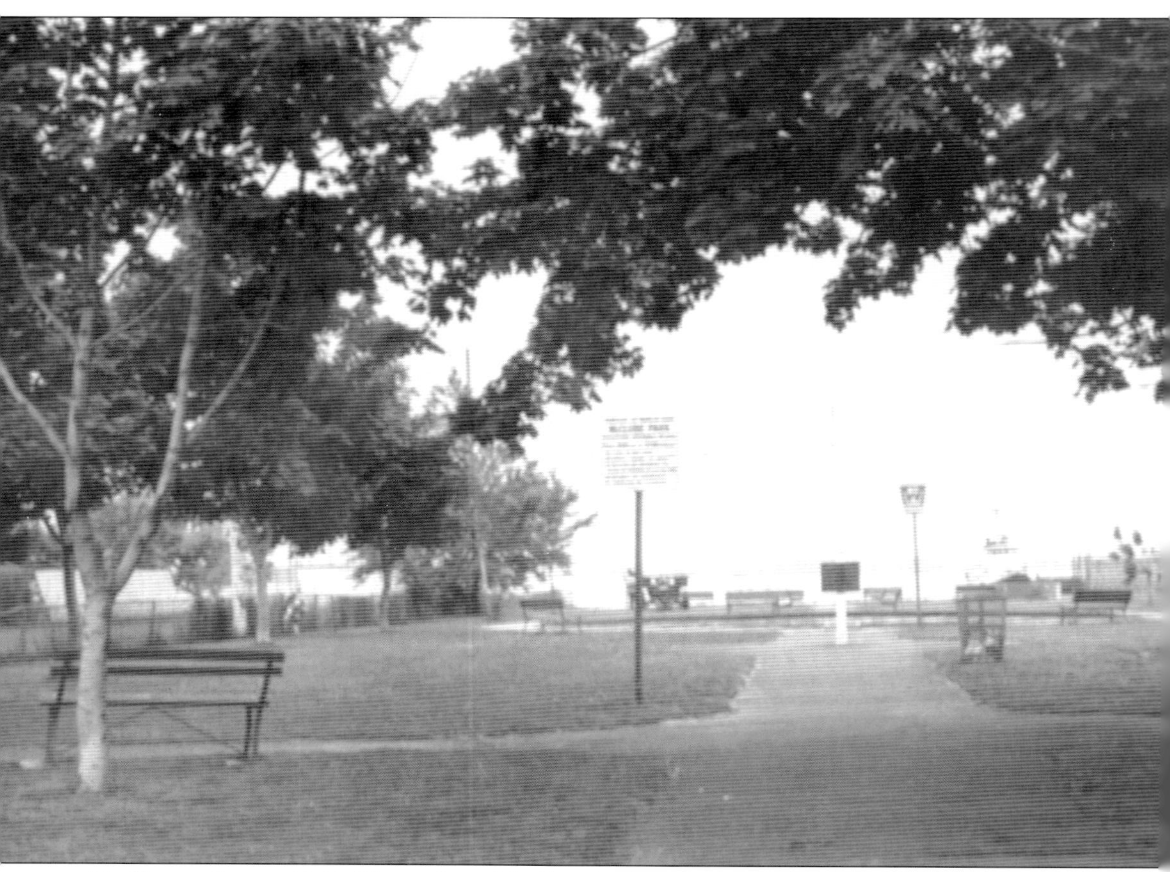

McClure Park, 1981. This is how McClure Park looked in May 1981. The park once had a fountain. A No Swimming sign can be seen. Little did the author know that the borough was working on plans to purchase adjoining property and expand the park.

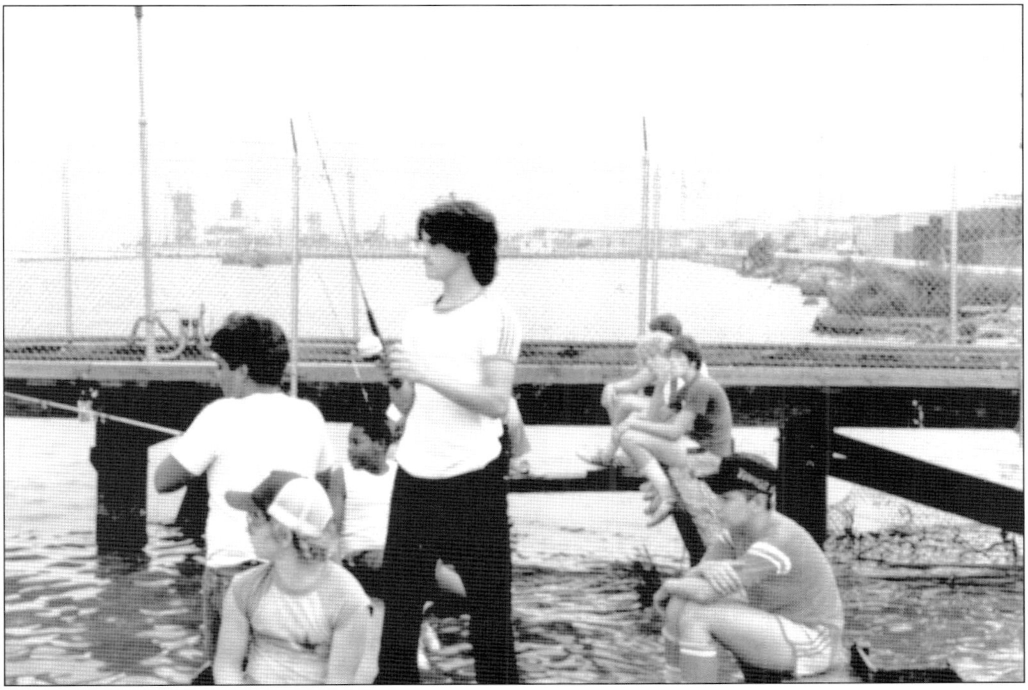

FISHING. These boys wait for the big catch in July 1984 before the new fishing pier was built.

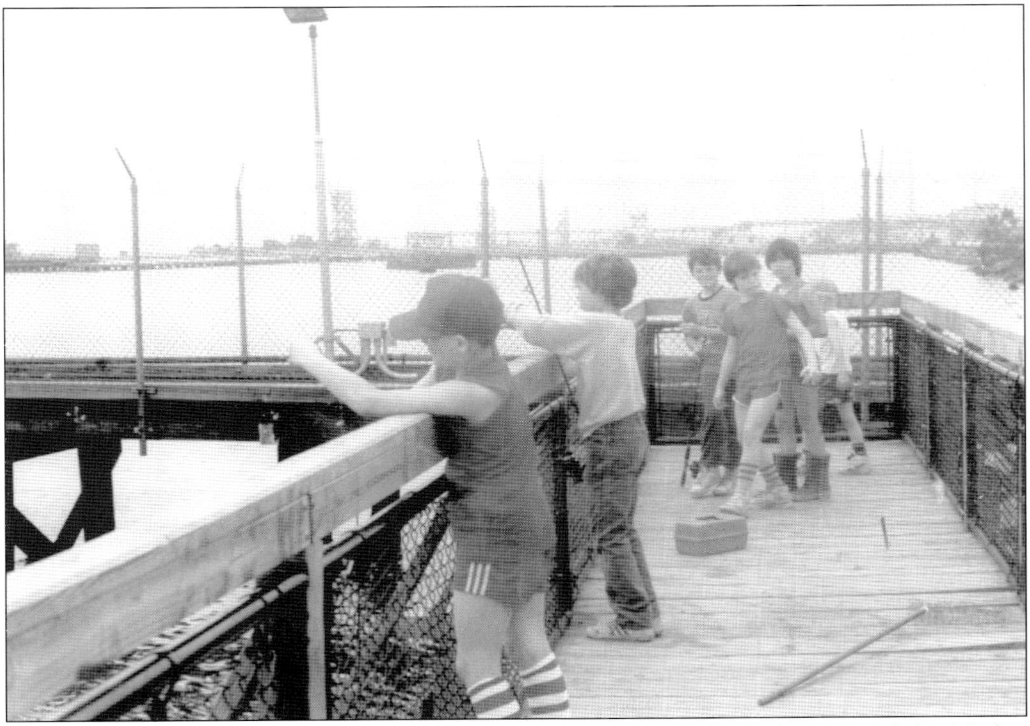

A NEW FISHING DOCK. In 1987, the new fishing dock was completed as part of the Market Square Memorial Park project.

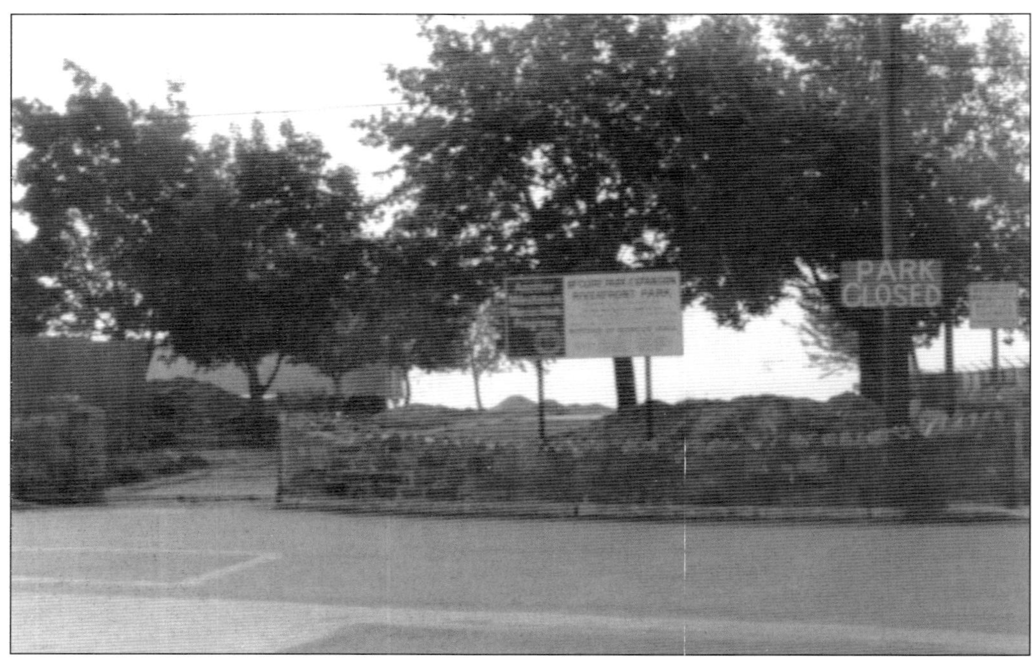

EXPANSION OF THE PARK. Construction of the new riverfront park began in the summer of 1986. The three-and-a-half-acre park, renamed Market Square Memorial Park, was dedicated on October 19, 1986.

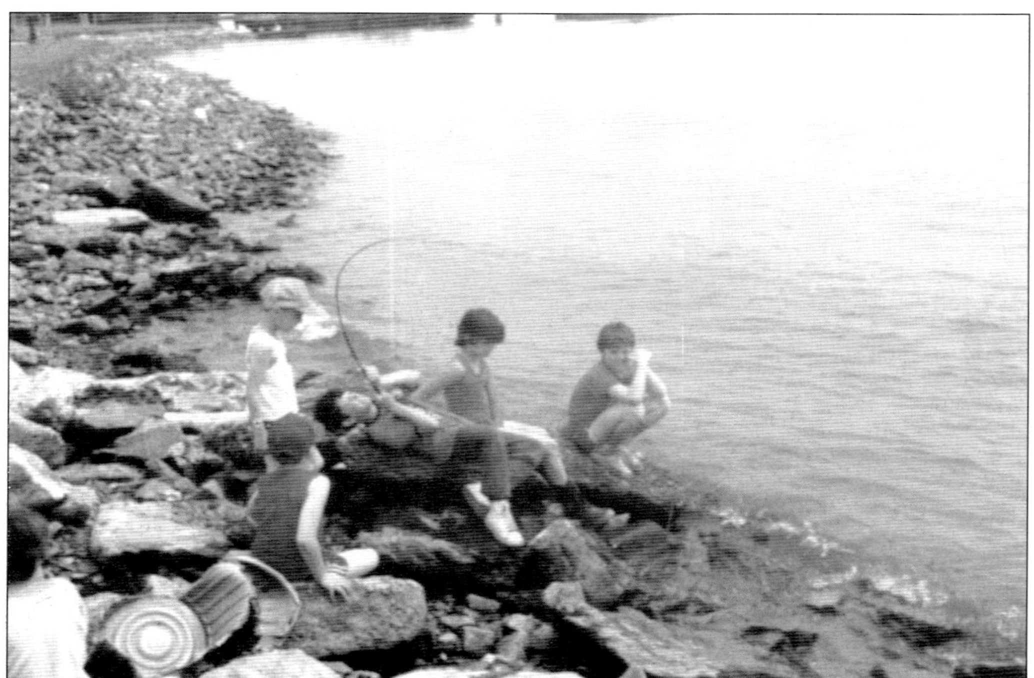

FAVORITE FISHING HOLE. The closure of the park in the summer of 1986 did not stop two young fishermen from hoping to catch the big one.

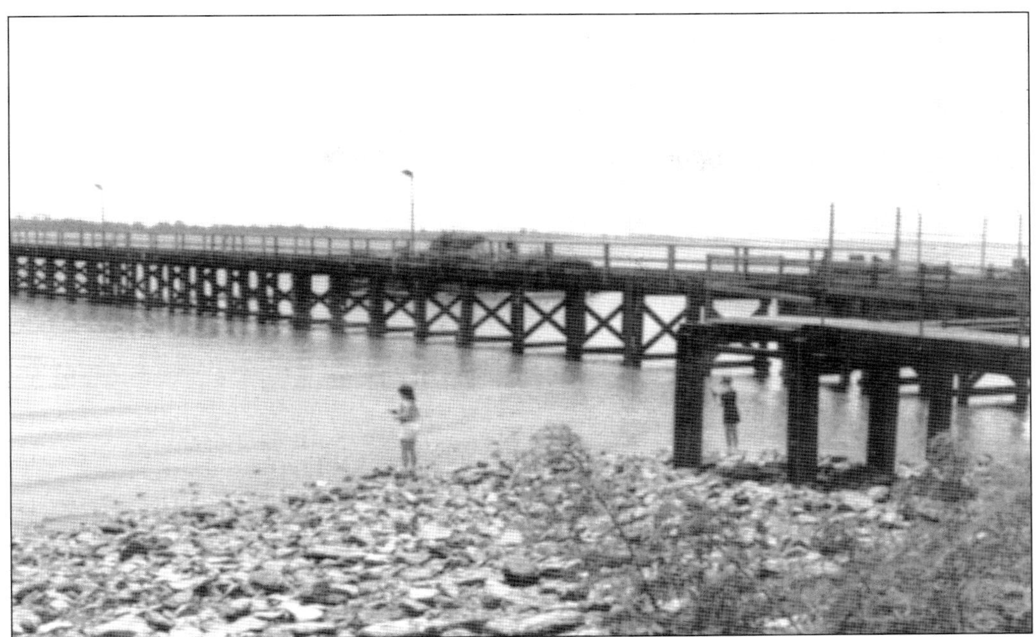

FISHING ON THE DELAWARE RIVER. Two fishermen are pictured here. At this same spot in the late 1800s and early 1900s, it was a common event for a boat and its two occupants to catch 300 or more shad and herring.

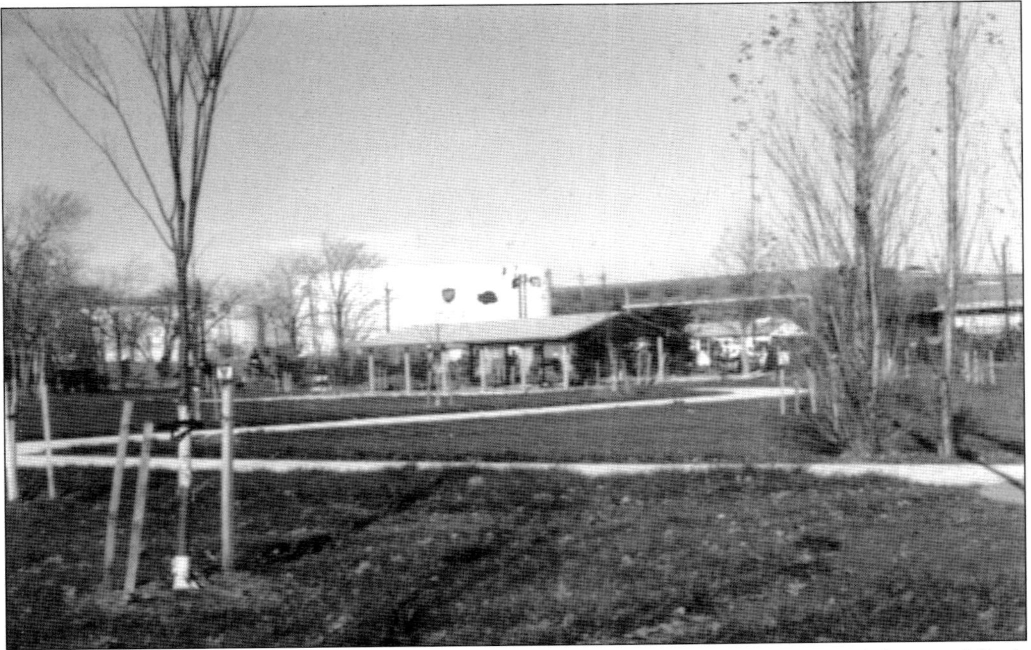

CONSTRUCTION COMPLETE. By the autumn of 1986, the new Market Square Memorial Park was complete. An outdoor pavilion with picnic tables lies at the end of clusters of newly planted trees. The park is located at the Market Street intersection and Delaware Avenue. At the time it was the only municipally owned riverfront park in Delaware County.

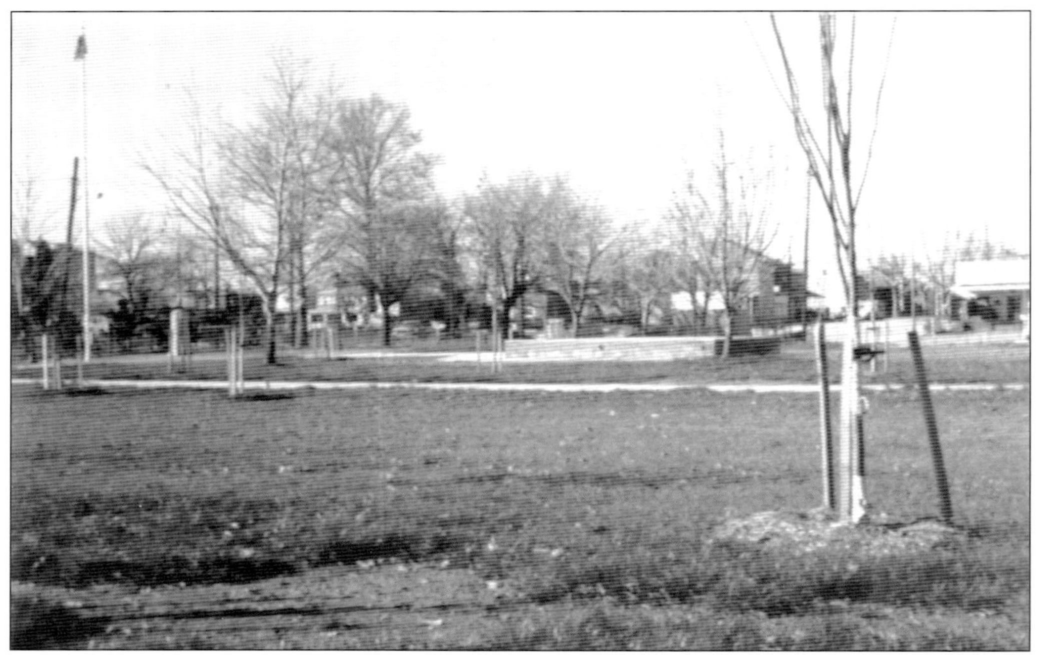

New Park Additions. The platform in the middle of this photograph will be the scene of summer concerts.

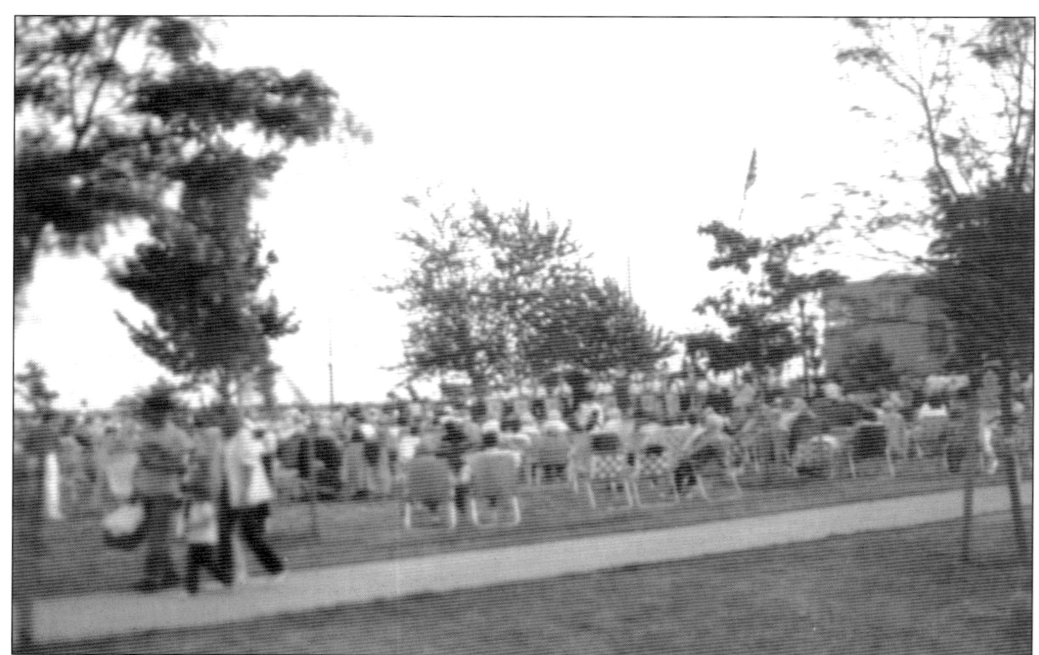

Al Raymond Band. In this shot of a summer concert in August 1987, the Al Raymond Band is entertaining area residents. Each week in the summer, a different musical group performs. Through the sponsorship of local business and industry, concerts have been offered free to the public since the program began in 1987.

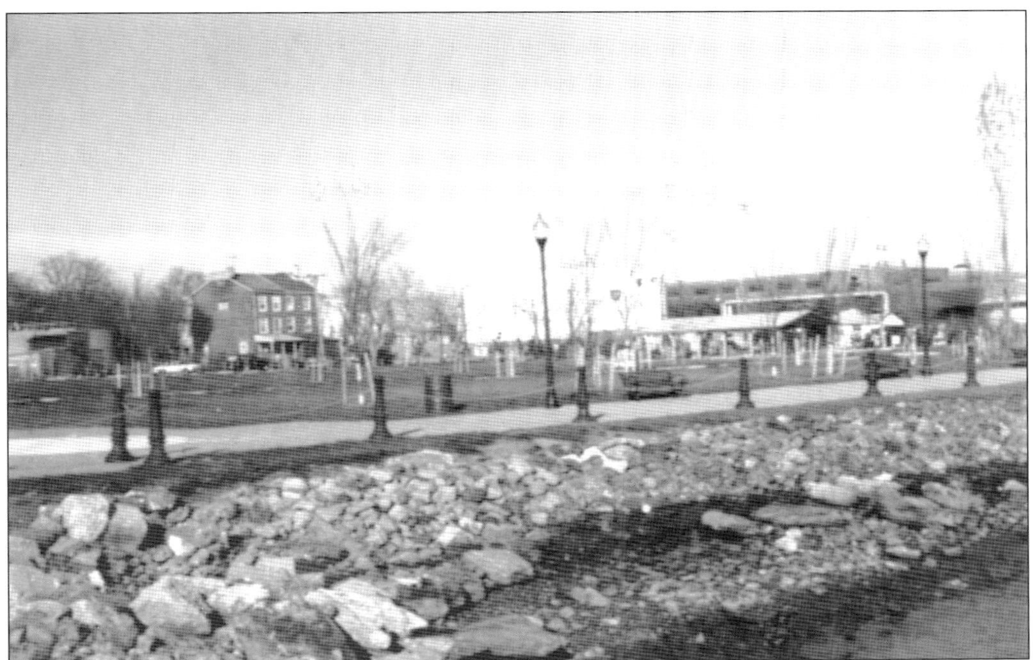

THE NEW MARKET SQUARE MEMORIAL PARK. This is a photograph of the new Market Square Memorial Park in late autumn of 1986. New park benches and tables, a pavilion, a platform stage, walkways, bollards and chain, historic walkway lights, and a refined shoreline make it an attractive park.

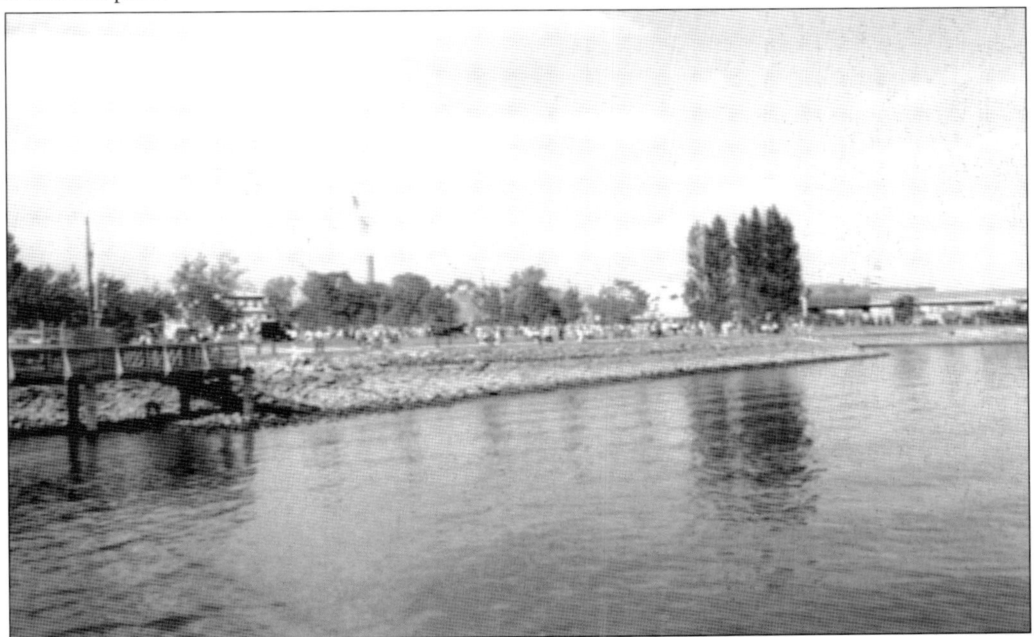

THE DELAWARE RIVER WATERFRONT, 1987. This is how the Delaware River waterfront looked in the autumn of 1987. The new riverfront park is now three and a half acres with 441 feet of river frontage.

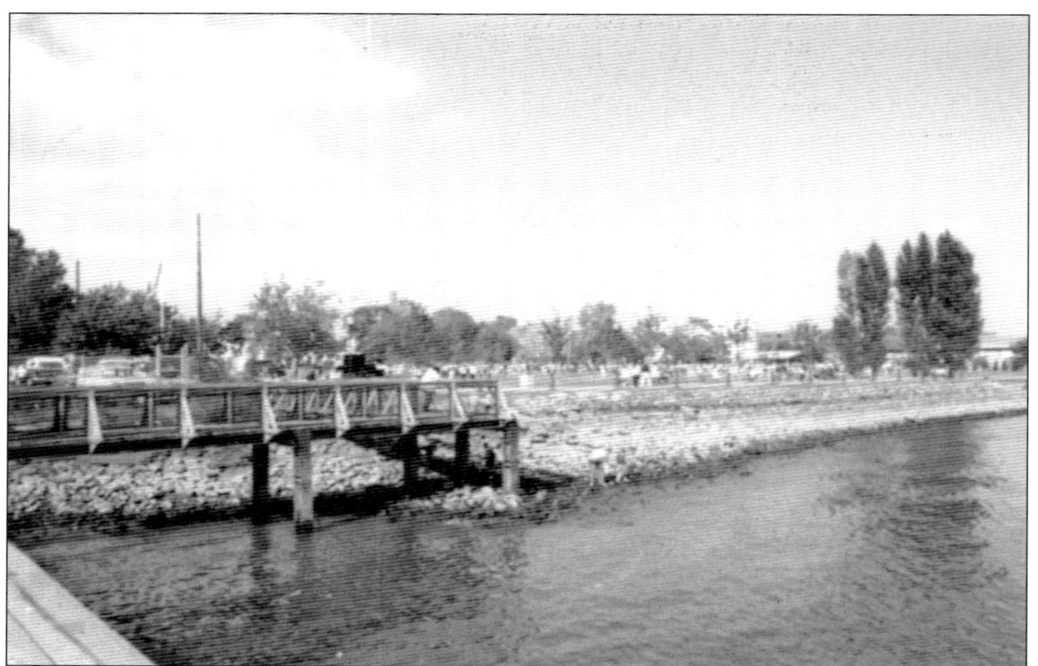

MARKET SQUARE MEMORIAL PARK. This is another shot of the new park. Planning of the park began with the completion of the McClure Park Expansion Study in 1980. This photograph was taken in the autumn of 1987.

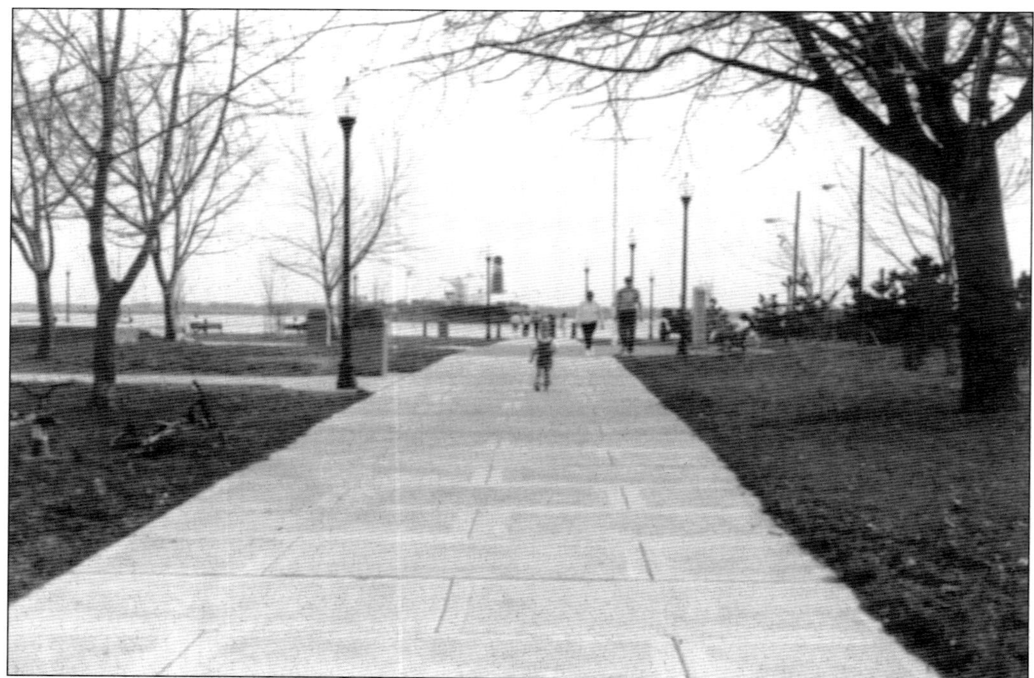

MARCUS HOOK'S NEW RIVERFRONT PARK. This child is taking small steps on the concrete walkway at Market Square Memorial Park.

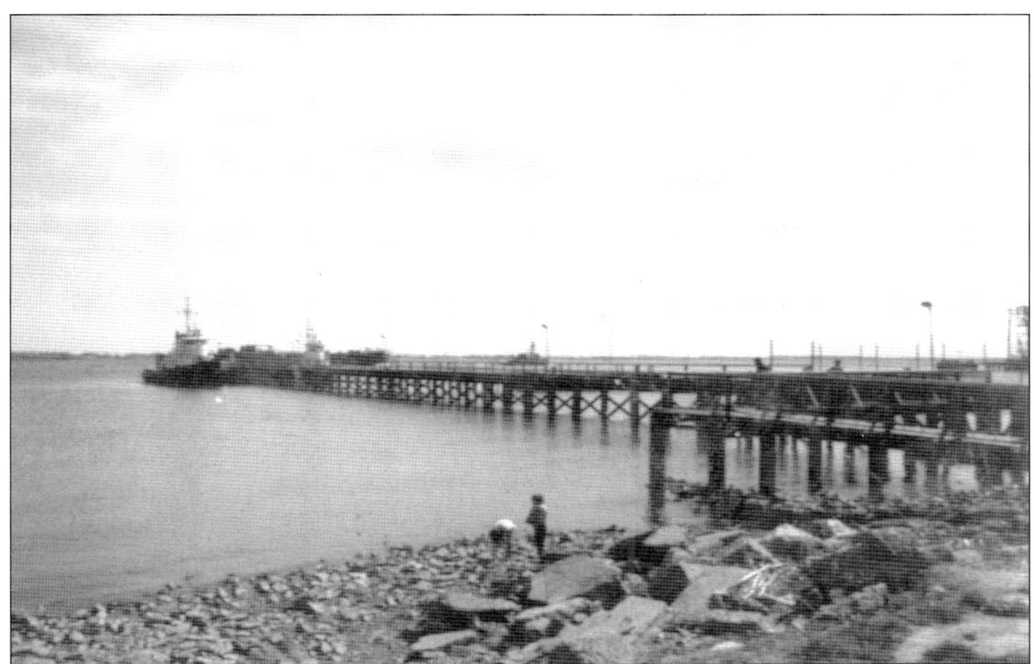

THROWING ROCKS IN THE DELAWARE RIVER. These young boys are enjoying their free time at the river's edge.

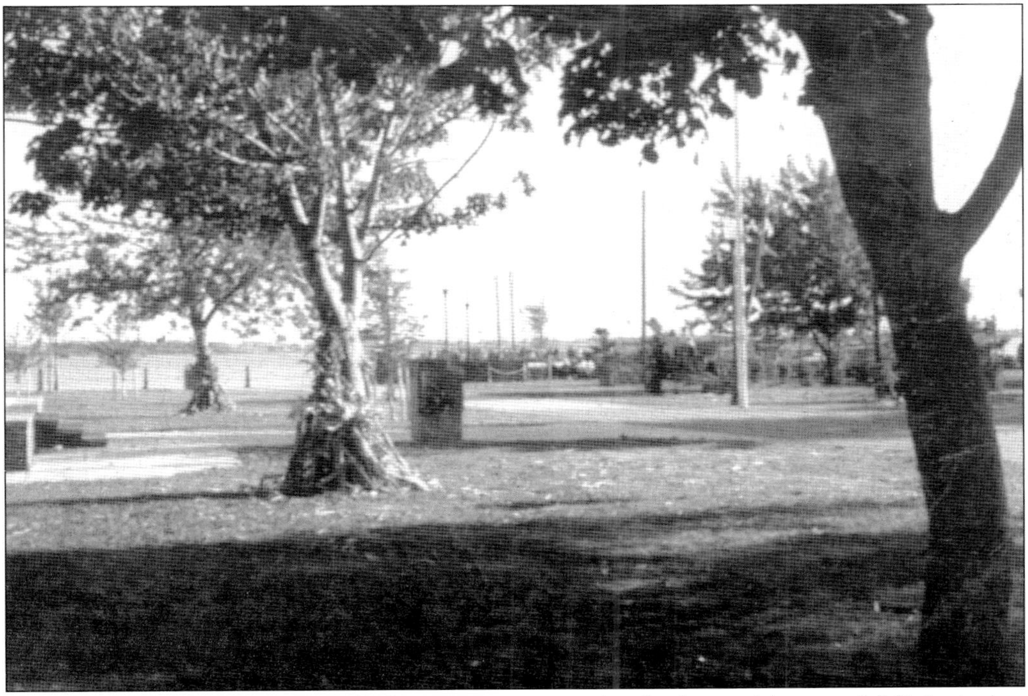

FALL FESTIVAL. This photograph depicts preparation for the borough's annual fall festival at Market Square Memorial Park.

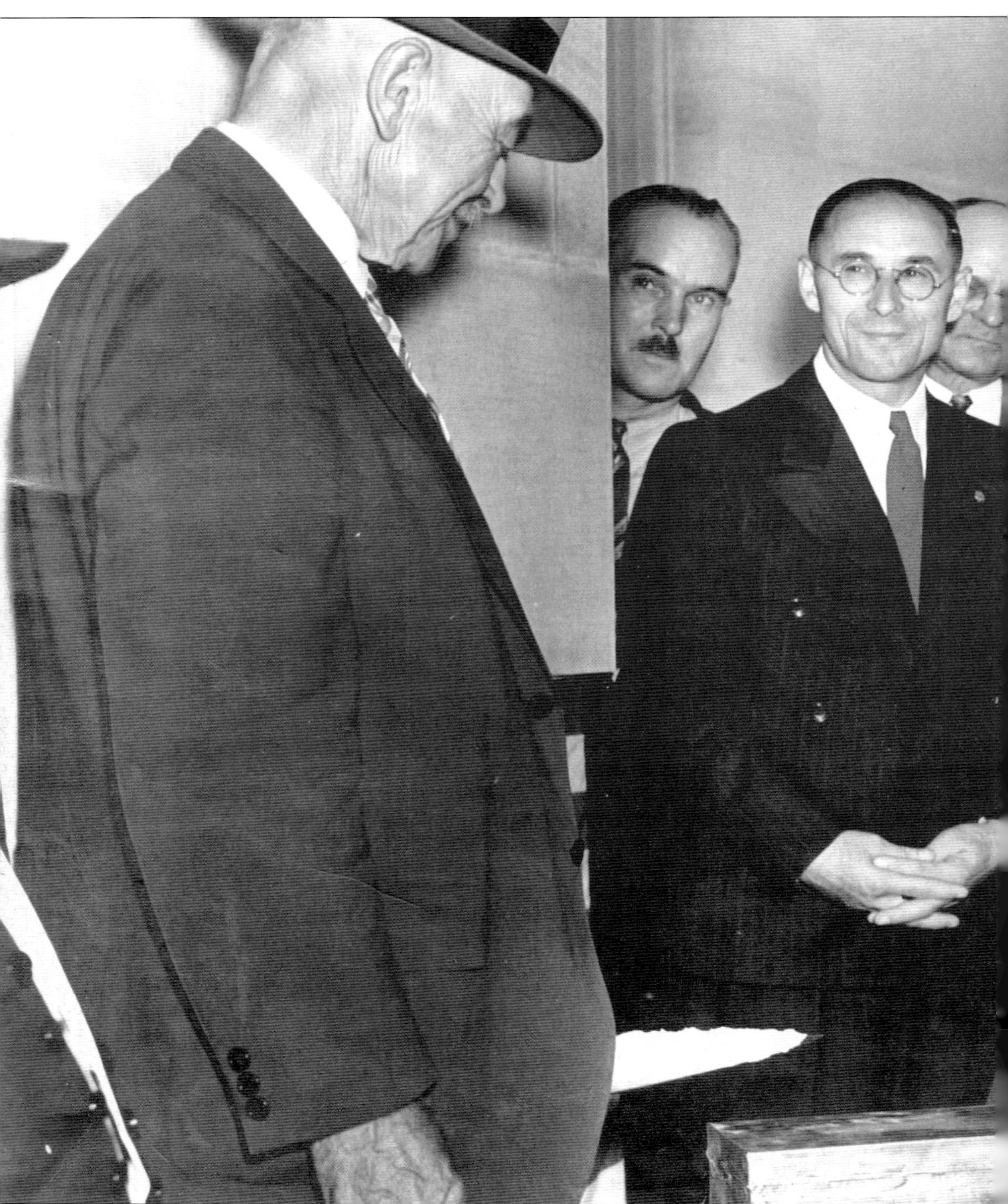

DEDICATION OF THE MARCUS HOOK MUNICIPAL BUILDING. Seen here is the official dedication of the cornerstone or metal of the Marcus Hook Municipal Building in 1939. Burgess Bill McClure can be seen wearing a hat with a trowel in hand. Members of the borough council are present. The only people who can be identified are Carmine Montella Sr. (left with dark suit and clasped

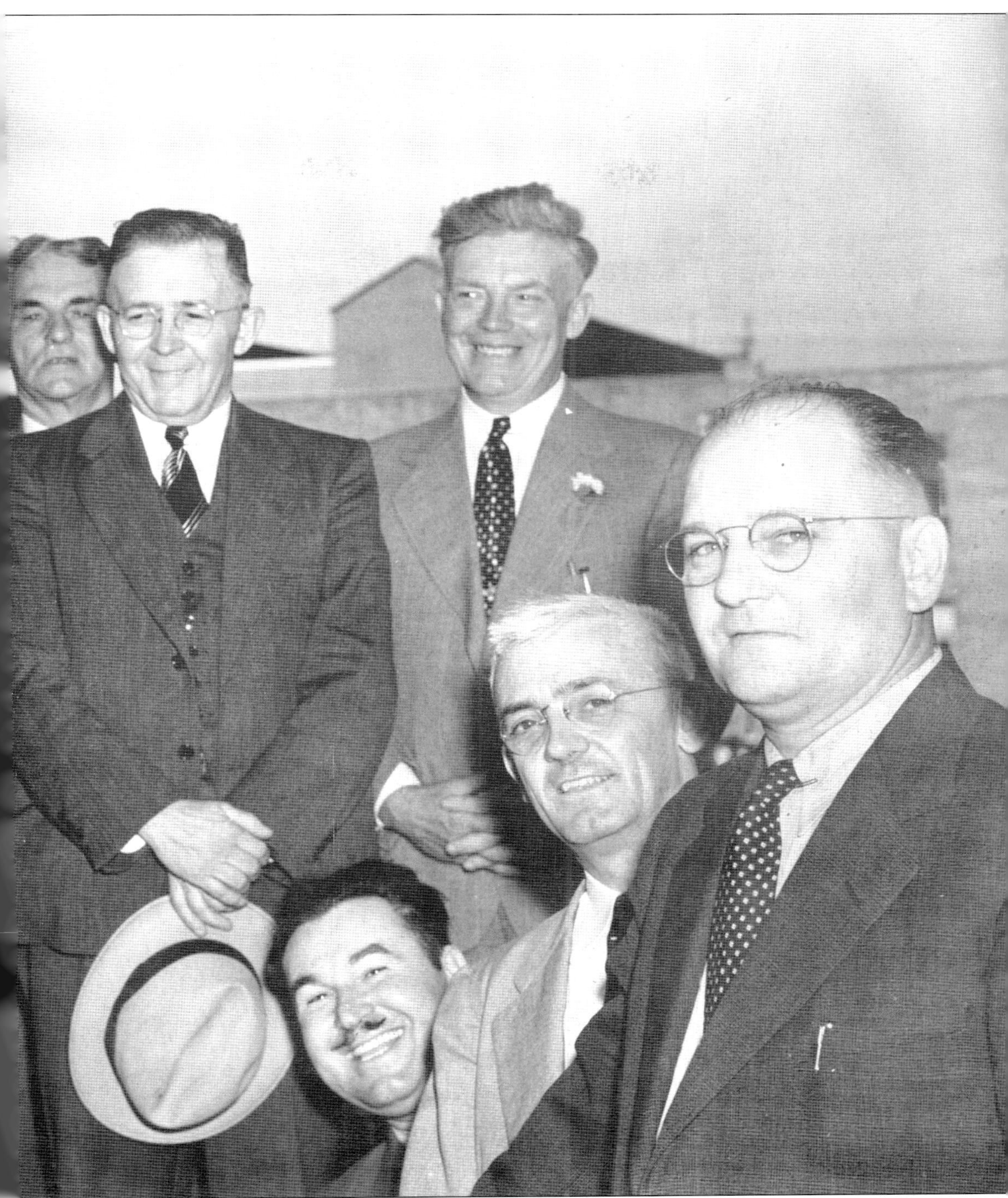

hands) and Elwood Hays Sr. (tan suit, light hair, flower in lapel). Carmine Montella came from Paolisi, Italy, and settled in Marcus Hook in 1911. He started as a water boy for Sunoco, making only 11¢ a day. He worked for Sunoco for 47 years, served on the borough council for 39 years, and was president of the council for 17 years. (Ralph Montella)

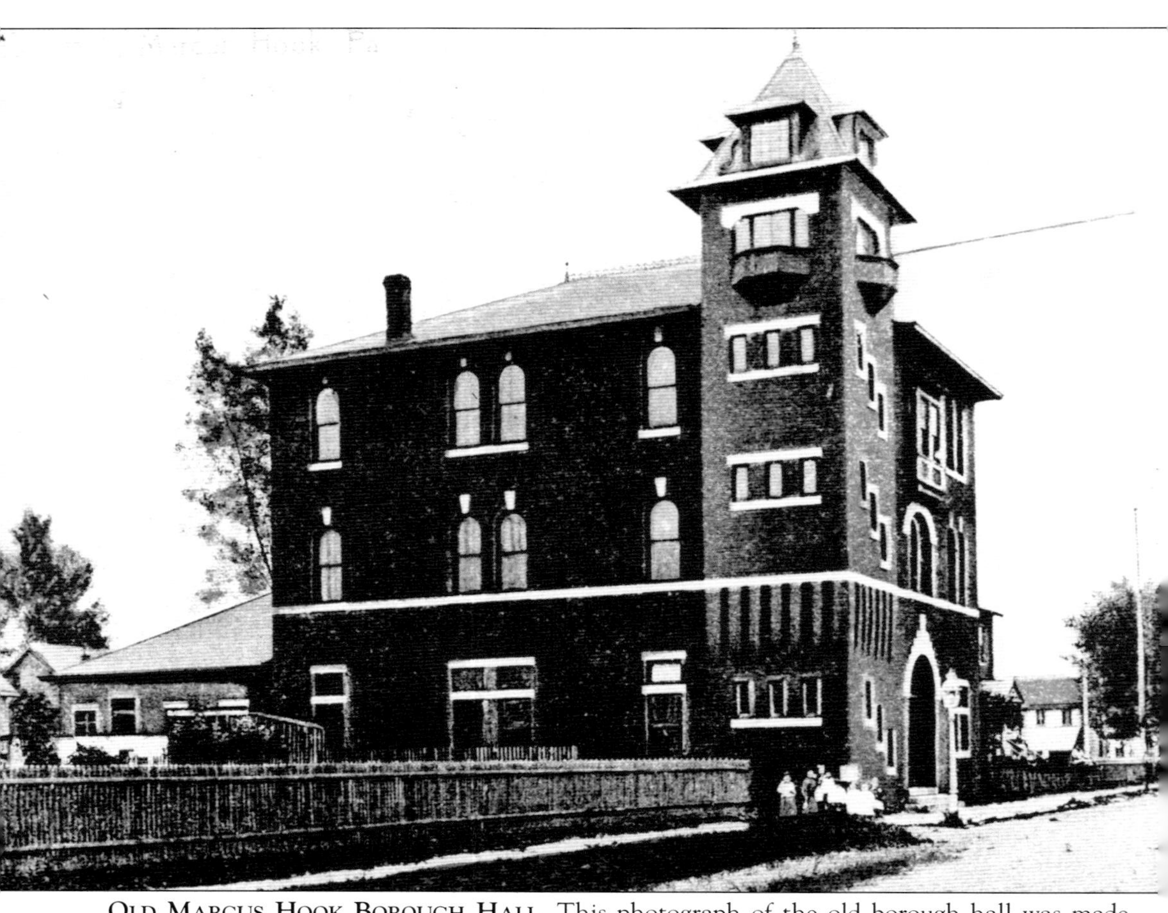

Old Marcus Hook Borough Hall. This photograph of the old borough hall was made from a 1903 postcard bought in Lancaster County in 1952. The old borough hall was located on Seventh Street at Maiden Lane. The original building was erected in 1893 and razed in 1938. (Ralph Montella.)

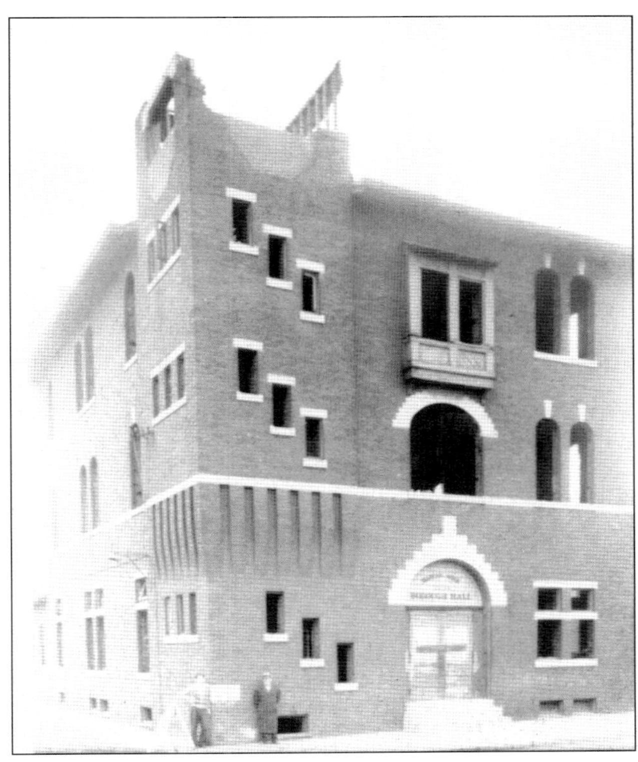

OLD BOROUGH HALL, 1938. In November 1938, demolition was under way on the old borough hall. (Delaware County Historical Society.)

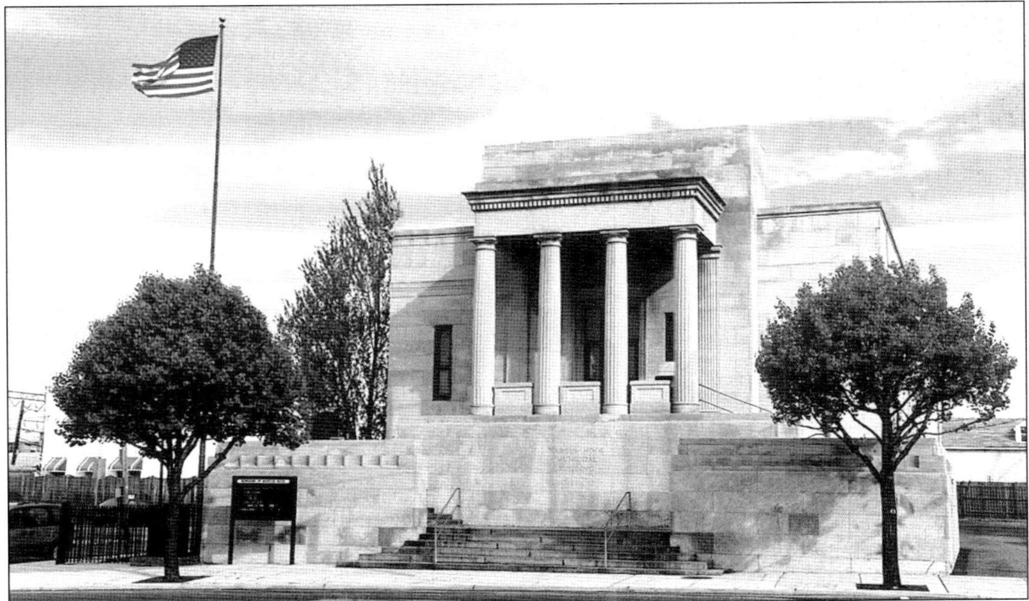

CURRENT MUNICIPAL BUILDING. This is how the current Marcus Hook Municipal Building looks in the classical Egyptian-Greek Revival style. It houses the library, police department, council chamber, and borough administrative offices. The municipal building is at Tenth and Green Streets and was erected in 1939. The cost of the new building was $98,300. The municipal building was a Federal Works Agency, Public Works Administration project.

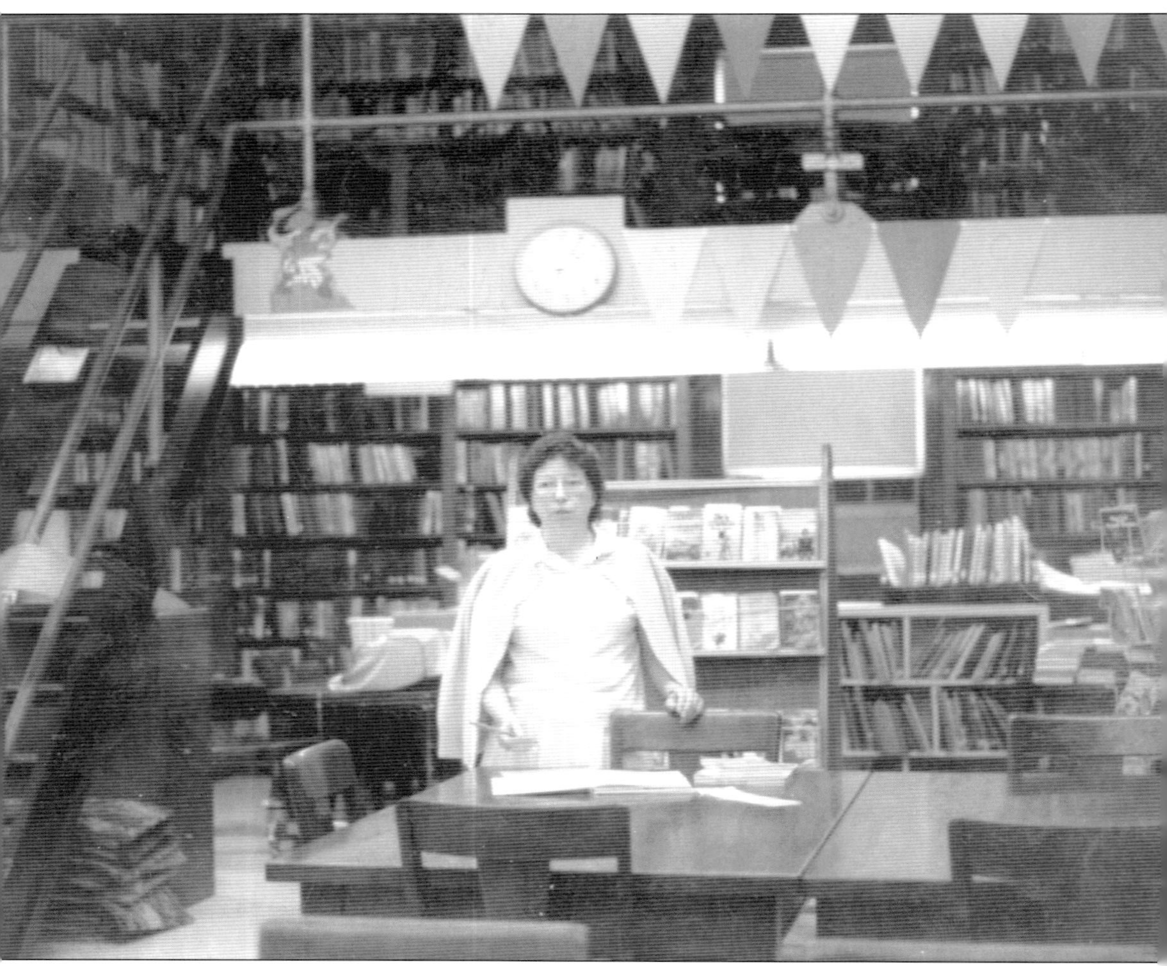

MARY M. CAMPBELL MARCUS HOOK PUBLIC LIBRARY. This is an interior view of the library. The librarian pictured here is Audrey Blossic, the librarian in 1983. It was Blossic who first gave the author the idea to do research on the history of the borough since she said it was not documented in a book.

Seven

PATRIOTISM

Patriotism has always been ingrained into the community character. There are signs of patriotism everywhere one looks in Marcus Hook. Throughout the borough, one can find nine war memorials in tribute to veterans from the Revolutionary War through the Vietnam War. The borough's Memorial Day parade is the largest in Delaware County. On parade day, Marcus Hook's main streets are alive and bustling with a variety of marching bands, military units, antique cars, and drill teams, all gathering to demonstrate affection for the nation, fellow citizens, and the proud inheritance they share. During World War II, Sunoco's bond drives raised thousands of dollars in support of the war effort. In these photographs are scenes of a community that never fails to honor American men and women who died in combat and those who served and survived the battle, came home, and continued to contribute to society.

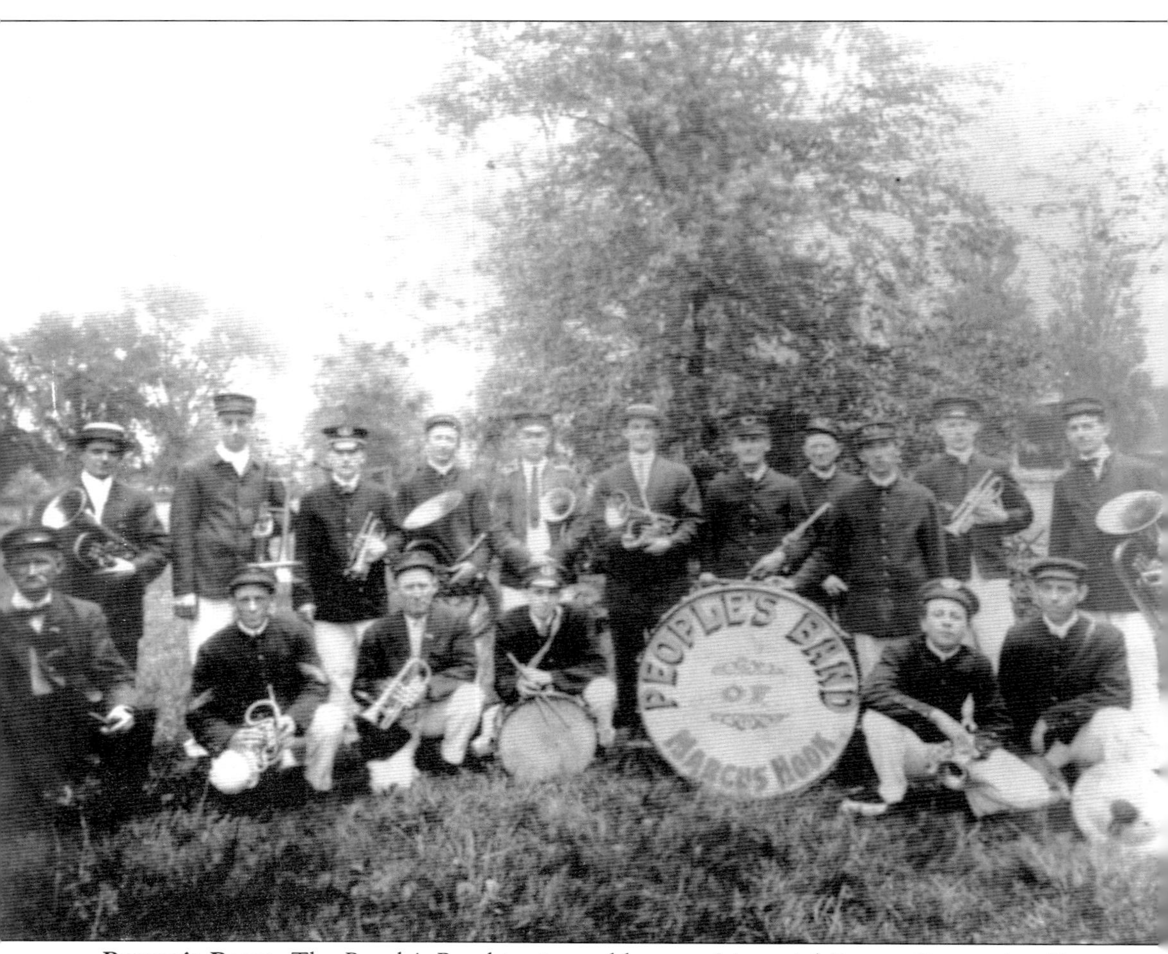

PEOPLE'S BAND. The People's Band is pictured here on Memorial Day, or Decoration Day, as it was once called. A group of bandsmen pose at the foot of Market Street on May 30, 1910. Among the band members pictured are William O'Donnell, William Barngarden, John E. Marshall, William Sims, Warner Ramsey, Ed Kane, George Palmer, Jon Larkin Sr., William T. Marshall, Frank Roberts, D. A. Capern, William Tobsen, and Jasper T. Martin. (Delaware County Historical Society.)

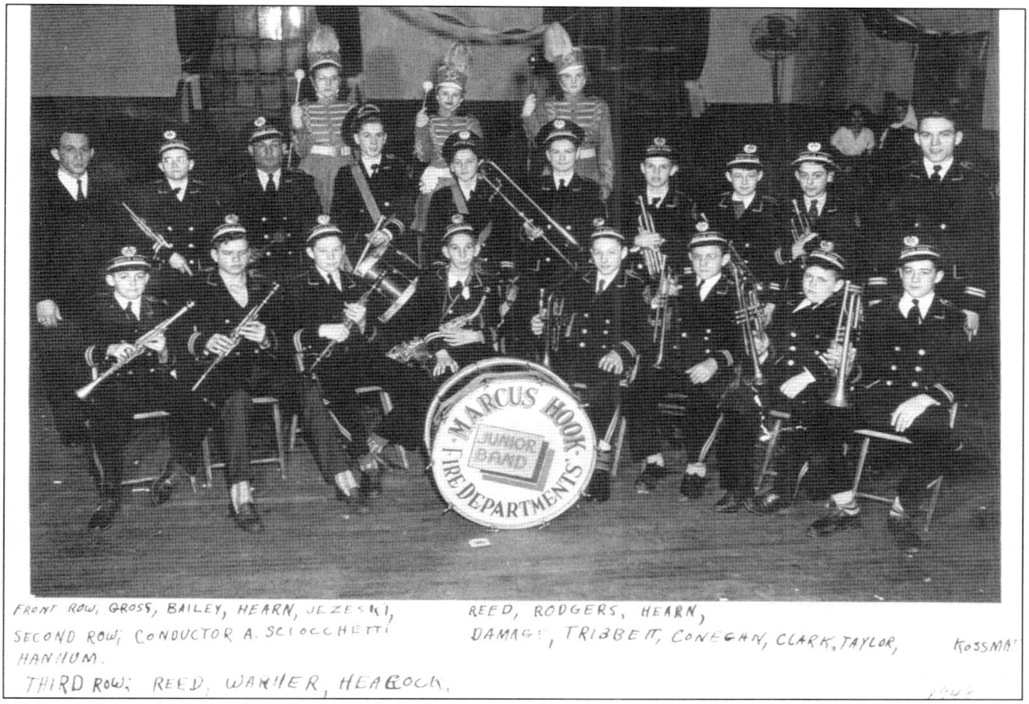

FRONT ROW, GROSS, BAILEY, HEARN, JEZESKI, REED, RODGERS, HEARN,
SECOND ROW; CONDUCTOR A. SCIOCCHETTI DAMAGE, TRIBBETT, CONEGAN, CLARK, TAYLOR, KOSSMAN
HANNUM.
THIRD ROW; REED, WARNER, HEACOCK,

MARCUS HOOK FIRE DEPARTMENT JUNIOR BAND. This photograph of the junior band in the old Marcus Hook Firehouse was taken around 1947. There is a great deal of significance in the location of the gentleman seated in the front left of the photograph. John Gross Jr., a band member, was killed in the Korean War. A memorial bench is dedicated in his honor at Eighth and Market Streets in Marcus Hook. (Chichester Historical Society.)

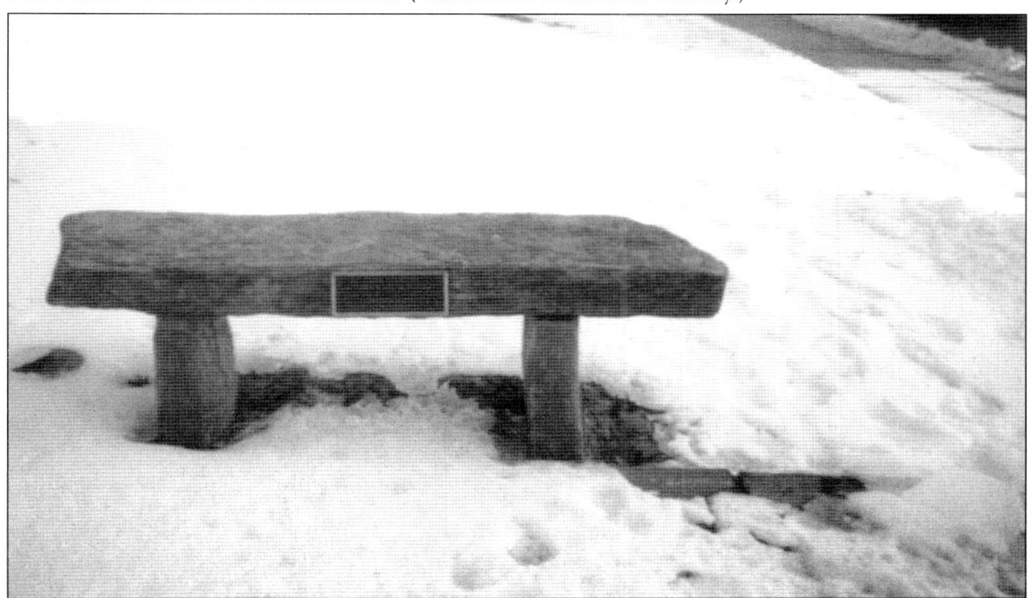

MEMORIAL BENCH. Pictured here is a close-up photograph of the memorial bench dedicated to Gross, who was killed in the Korean War.

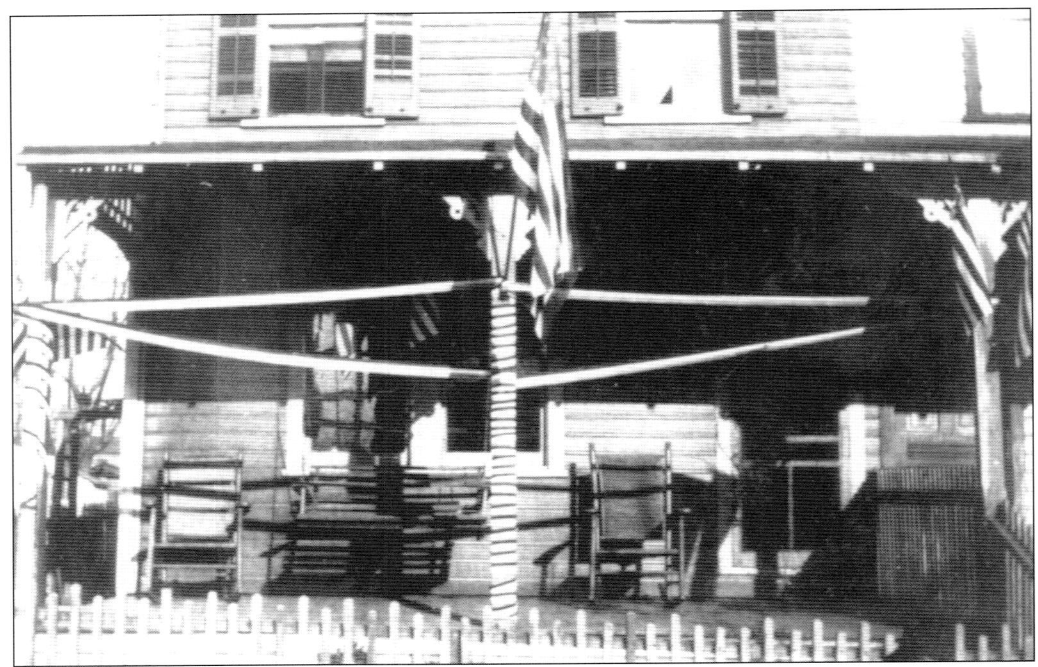

HOME ARMISTICE DAY. This is a photograph of the first Veteran's Day, or Armistice Day, as it was originally called in 1918, celebrated in Marcus Hook. This rare photograph from the Delaware County Historical Society is labeled "Home Armistice Day, 1918."

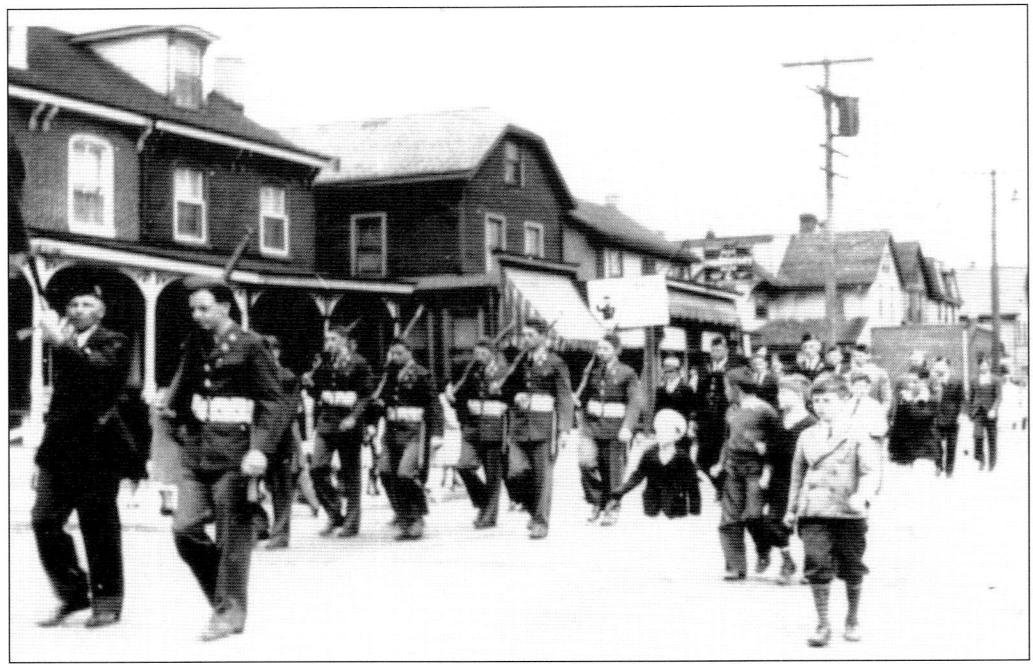

EARLY DECORATION DAY PARADE. This early view looks down Market Street in Marcus Hook. (Delaware County Historical Society.)

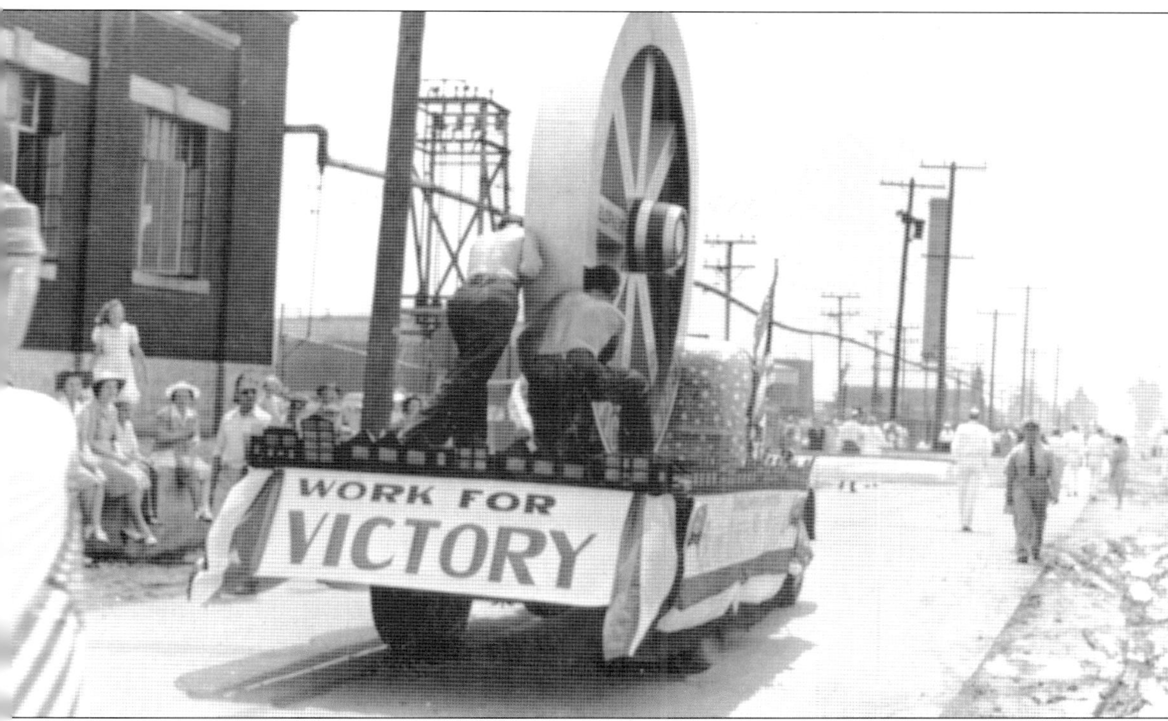

WORLD WAR II RALLY. Here is a photograph that captures two great qualities of Marcus Hook and the many small towns like it across the country—patriotism and hard work. This scene is on Blueball Avenue on July 4, 1942. In this particular parade 1,600 employees from Sunoco marched, and the impressive floats were built and paid for by employees themselves. The parade was meant to demonstrate the vital work being done in the area for the nation at war. A slogan for the parade was "we are working and we will work to win." (Hagley Museum and Library.)

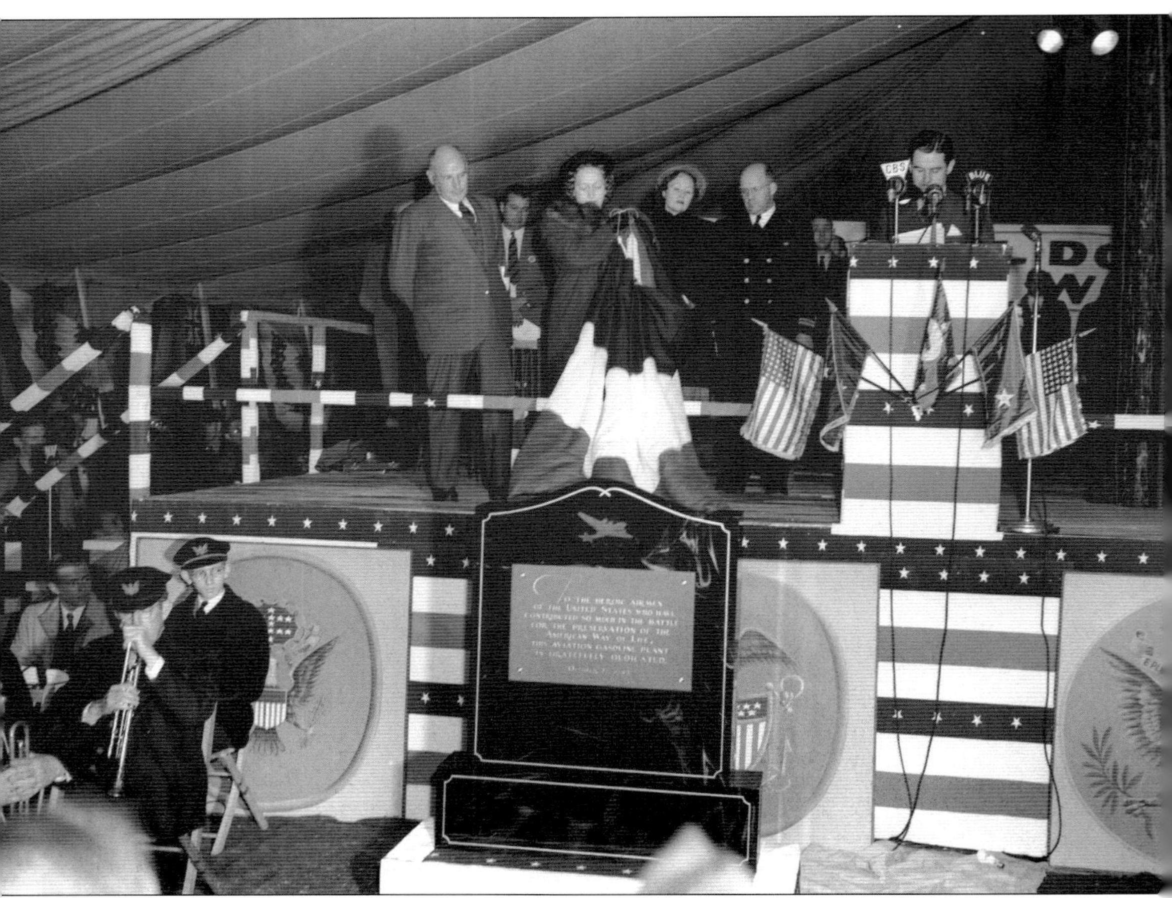

Unveiling of Plaque. With her husband by her side, Mrs. Andrew Sutton Sr. unveils a plaque at the Sunoco Marcus Hook refinery in 1943 for her son who was killed in World War II. The plaque was dedicated to heroic airmen of the United States who have contributed so much in battle for the preservation of the American way of life. It was also the official dedication of Plant 15 at Sunoco, the Houdry catalytic cracking aviation gasoline plant. The plant's cost was $13 million. The plant was later razed in 1968.

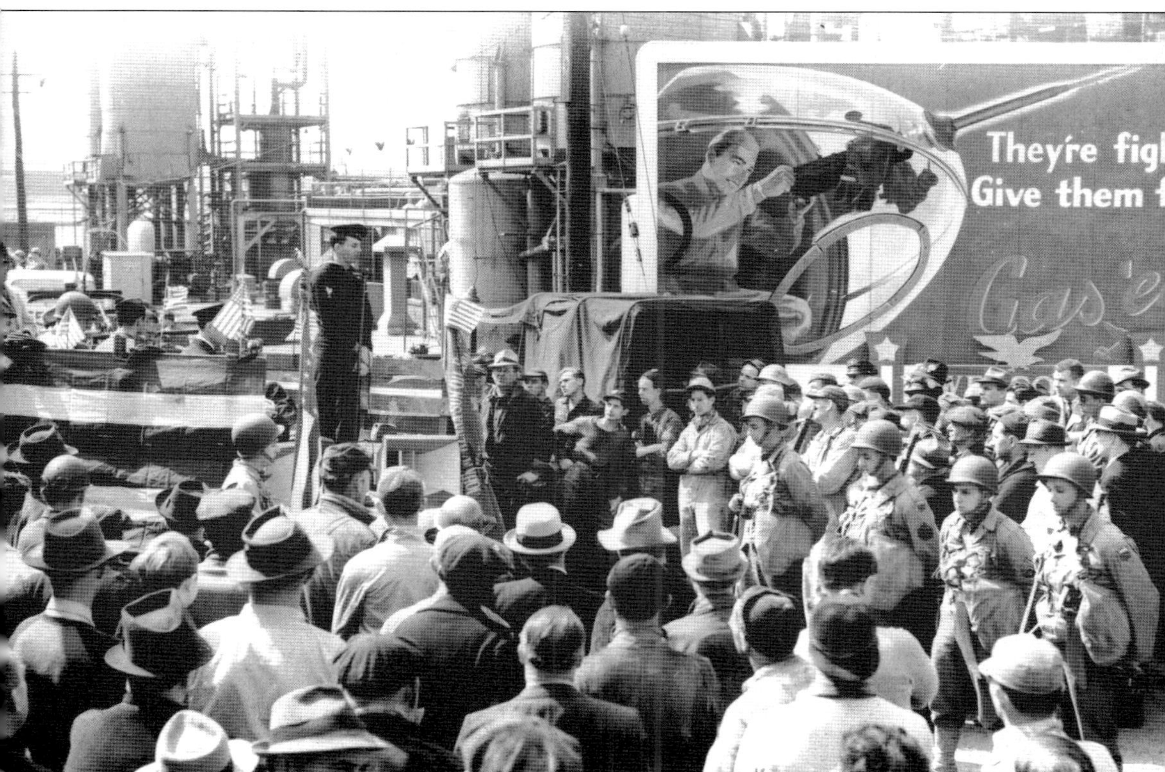

RALLY, 1943. In March 1943, a cavalcade from the 76th Calvary Reconnaissance Troop and naval personnel rode into the refinery and rallied crowds totaling over 2,500 men and women of Marcus Hook. They demonstrated the importance of the gas, oils, greases, and other petroleum products that Sunoco produced for the equipment they used, such as jeeps, tank guns, gas masks, bayonets, and so on, in their battle to win the war. About one month after this rally it was reported that students from the Marcus Hook schools had raised $19,231 to purchase army jeeps.

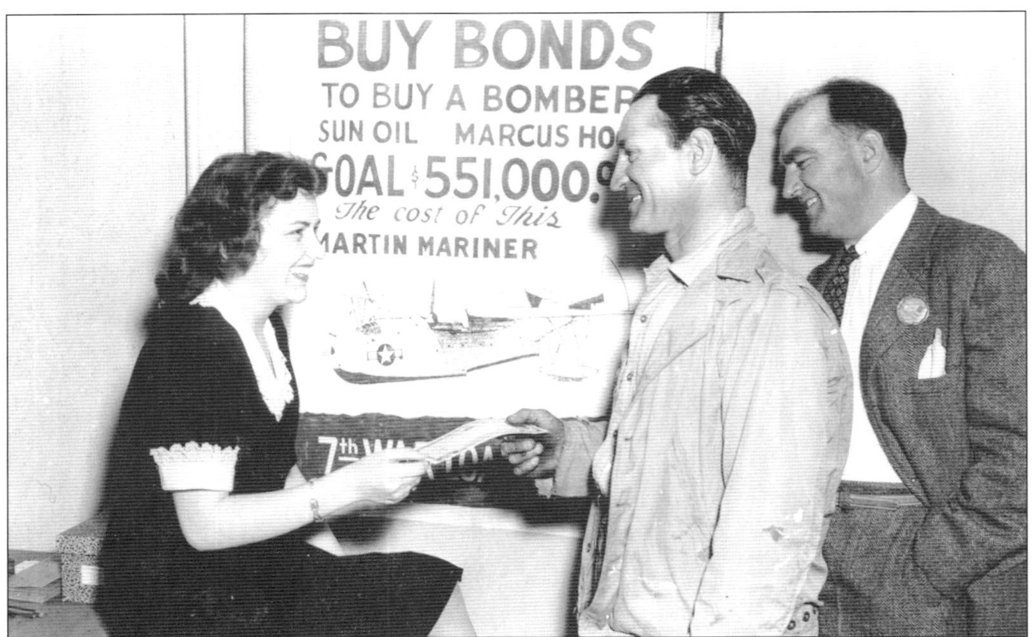

LOAN DRIVE. In May 1945, Louis Dicave was the purchaser for the first bond at the seventh World War II bond drive at the Marcus Hook Sunoco refinery. "The Mighty Seventh" was a war loan drive that received a lot of support at the Marcus Hook refinery. Through payroll deductions of Sunoco employees, war bonds were bought. In all, Sunoco employees bought $9,092,062 in war bonds during the World War II years.

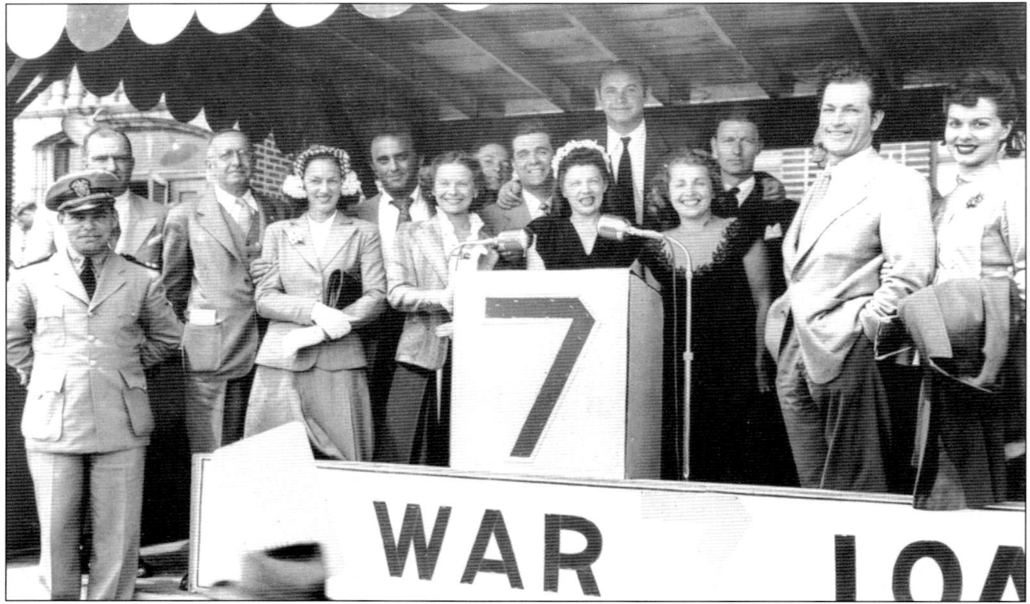

CAST OF *OKLAHOMA*. At the seventh World War II bond drive, the cast of *Oklahoma* performed. They stand here in May 1945 at the Marcus Hook Sunoco refinery. Through bond drives like these at Sunoco and others throughout the country, many people got together to raise money to defeat the enemy and win the war.

VISCOSE VILLAGE WAR MEMORIAL. Situated in the center of Robert E. Haebel Plaza at Tenth Street and Plaza Street is a memorial dedicated to all residents of the 4th Ward who served their country in World War II and the Korean War. It was erected by the Model Village Civic Community. Across the street within the bus shelter was located a World War II plaque dedicated to the employees of the American Viscose Company who served in the armed forces or at home. The plaque is now in the borough's possession.

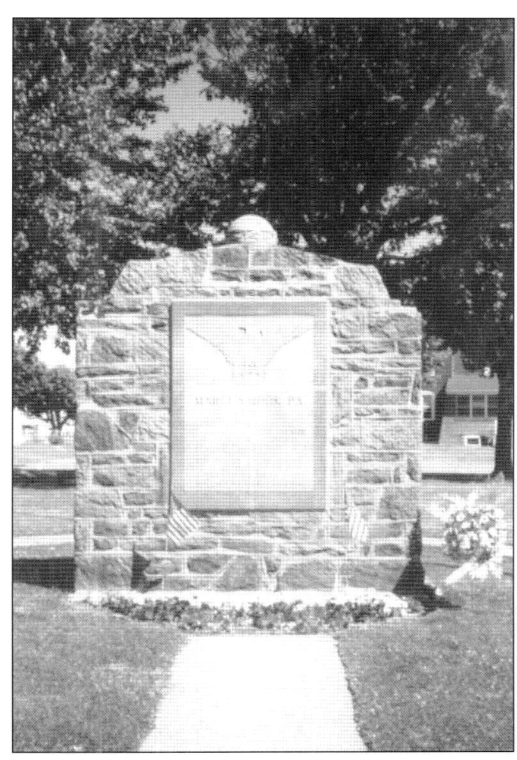

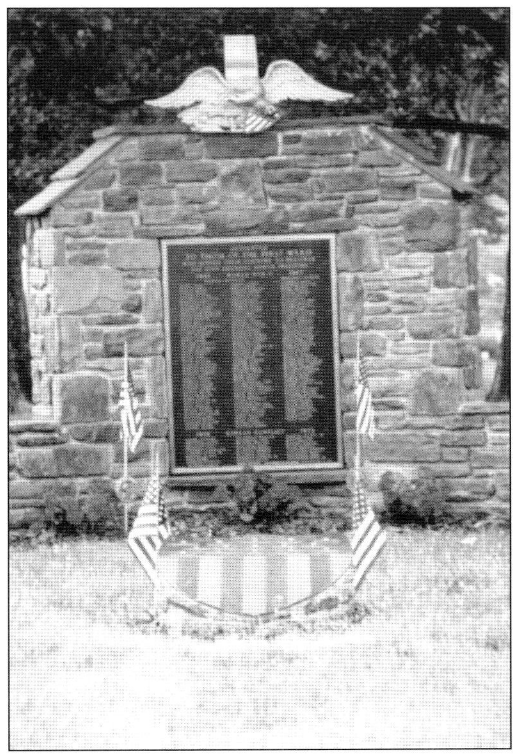

WAR MEMORIAL AT THIRD AND MARKET STREETS. At Market and Third Streets, located on the grass plot (Market Green), is a memorial dedicated to those in the 1st Ward who served their country to preserve the four essentials of human freedom during World War II, 1941–1945, and the Korean War, 1950–1953.

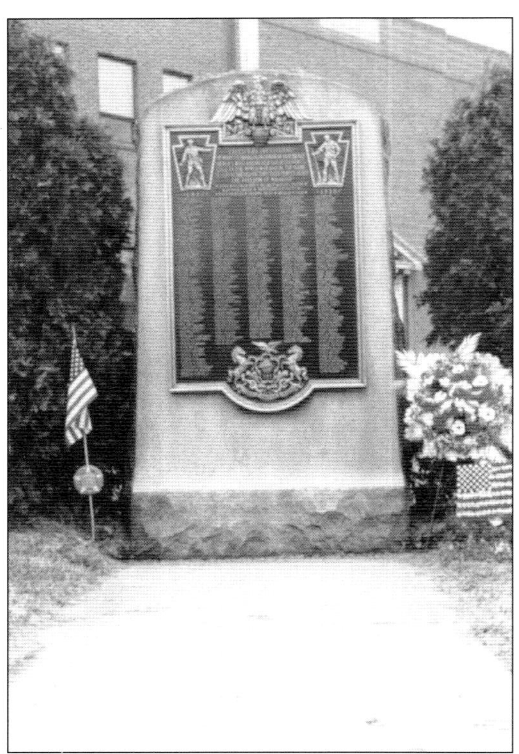

WORLD WAR I WAR MEMORIAL. Located on the corner of Eighth and Market Streets is a memorial erected by the citizens of Marcus Hook in honor of the brave heroes who answered their country's call in World War I, 1917–1918.

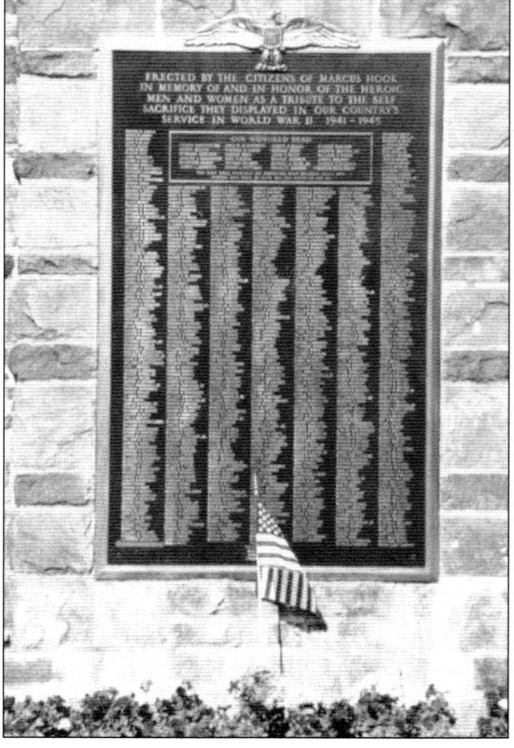

WORLD WAR II WAR MEMORIAL. On Market Street next to the Recreation Hut, is a World War II memorial in memory and in honor of the men and women of the borough as a tribute to the self-sacrifice they displayed in their country's service, 1941–1945. The money for this memorial had been raised by a committee called the Marcus Hook Honor Roll Committee.

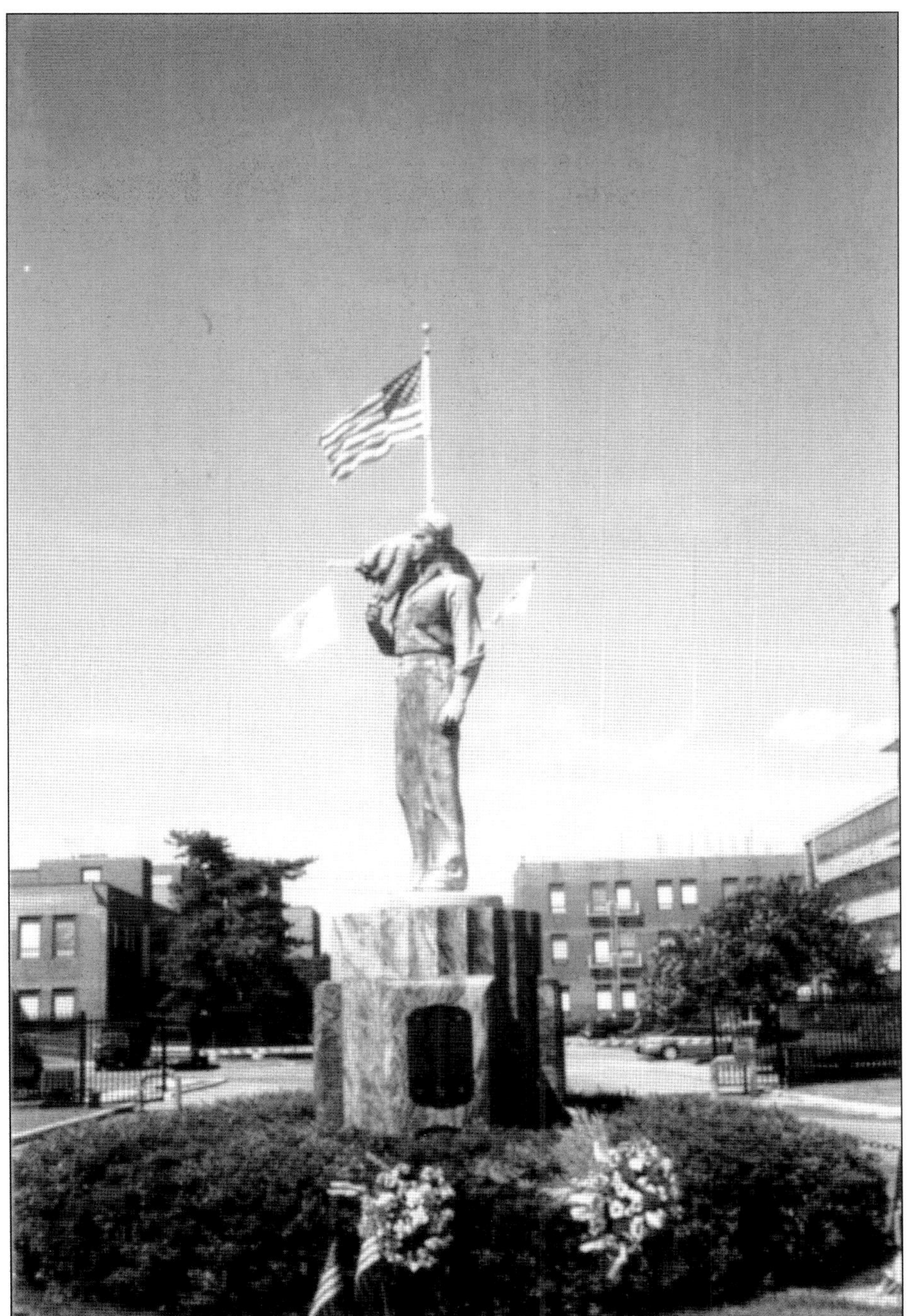

Sun Seaman's Memorial. Pictured here is the Sun Seaman's Memorial located at the main entrance to Sunoco's Marcus Hook refinery at Green Street and Delaware Avenue. Embossed in bronze, on October 8, 1949, it was dedicated by Sunoco employees to 141 brave officers and seamen who lost their lives in World War II while serving on Sunoco tankers. The building cost of the memorial was $50,000, raised by Sunoco employee contributions. (Urban Archives of Temple University.)

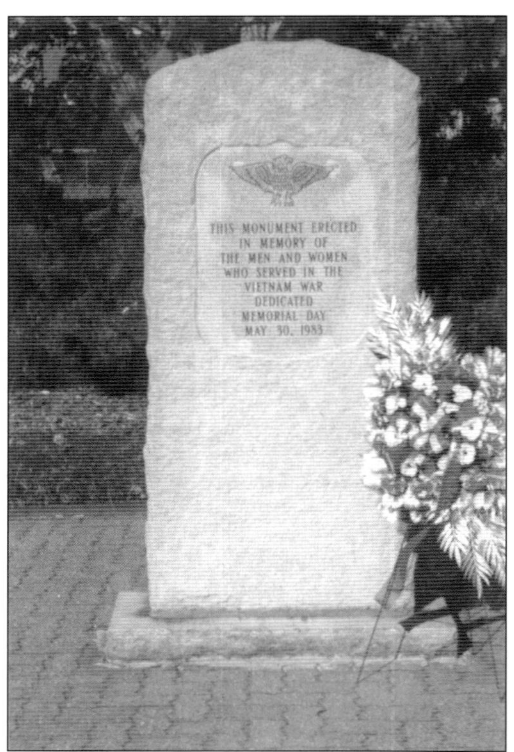

VIETNAM WAR MEMORIAL. On May 30, 1983, the Vietnam War monument was dedicated at the borough's riverfront park (then called McClure Park). This monument, the first of its kind in Delaware County, stands as a lasting tribute to residents of Marcus Hook Borough and the country who served in the Vietnam War.

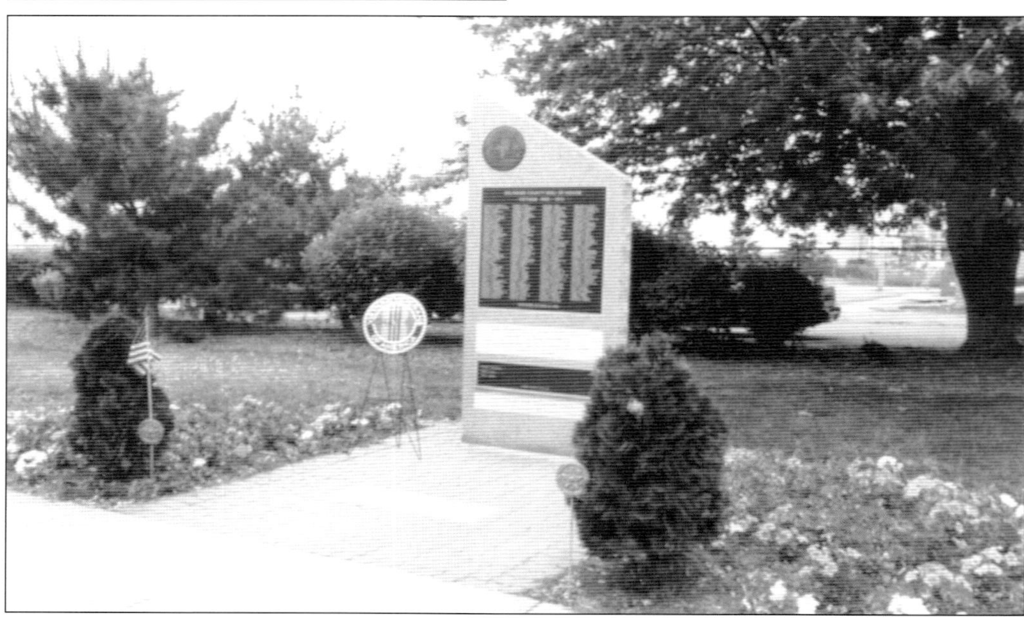

VIETNAM WAR MEMORIAL DEDICATION. The elegant polished granite memorial at Market Square Memorial Park was dedicated on October 12, 1992, to the Delaware Countians killed in service or missing in action in the Vietnam theater of operations. Individual names are listed on the memorial. The memorial is situated on the west side of the north–south walkway to the river.

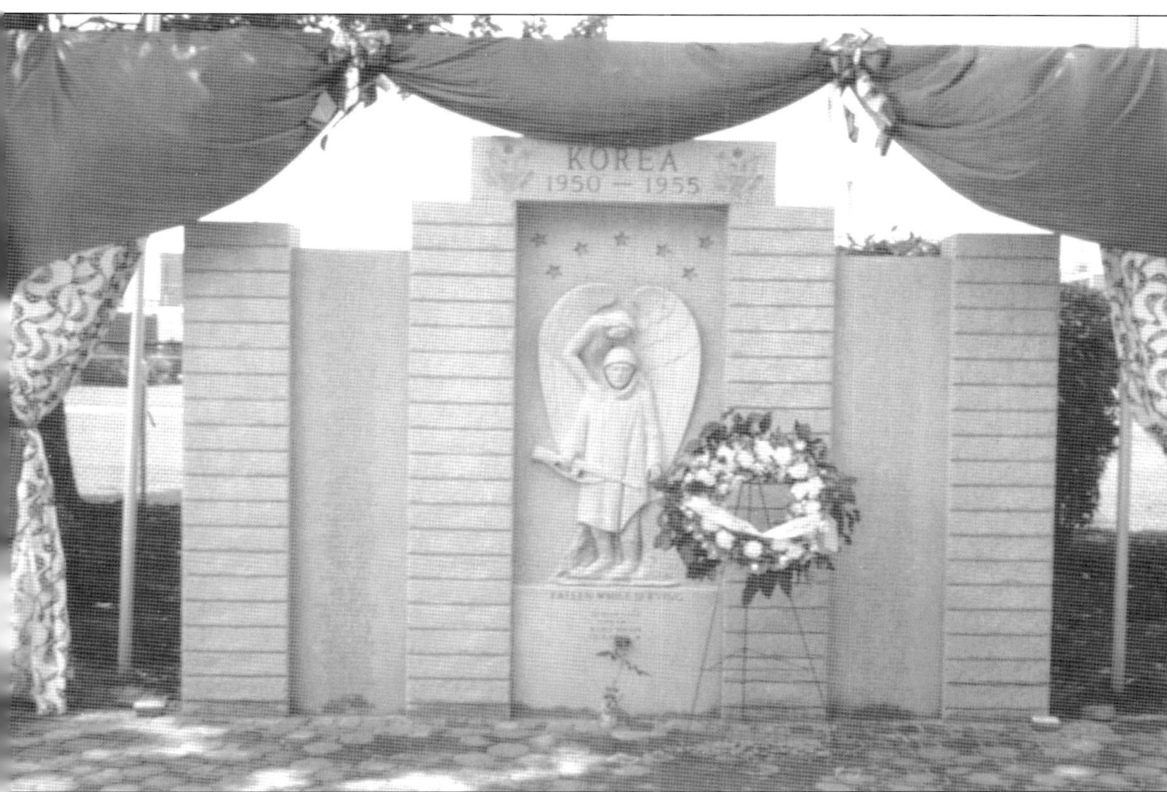

KOREAN WAR MEMORIAL. The Marcus Hook Korean War Memorial was dedicated at Market Square Memorial Park on May 26, 2001. This beautiful memorial pays tribute to Marcus Hook residents who served during the Korean War. Their names are inscribed on the memorial. On March 22, 2001, the borough sponsored a dinner in honor of its Korean War veterans. A PowerPoint presentation was shown picturing past veteran programs in the borough. Included were photographic remembrances from the many Memorial Day parades and dedications of war memorials.

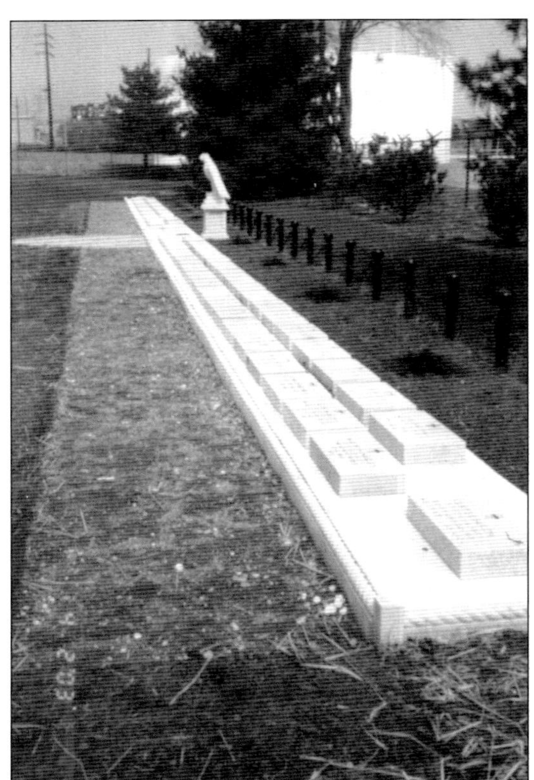

SOLDIER AND SAILOR WALK MEMORIAL. The Soldier and Sailor Walk Memorial was the result of a three-year project by the Marcus Hook Community Development Corporation to identify war veterans buried at St. Martin's Church Cemetery. Local historian/genealogist Helen M. Imburgia conducted the research to confirm the 73 veterans were from the Revolutionary War, the War of 1812, the Mexican War, the Civil War, and the Spanish-American War. The memorial was dedicated on May 24, 2003.

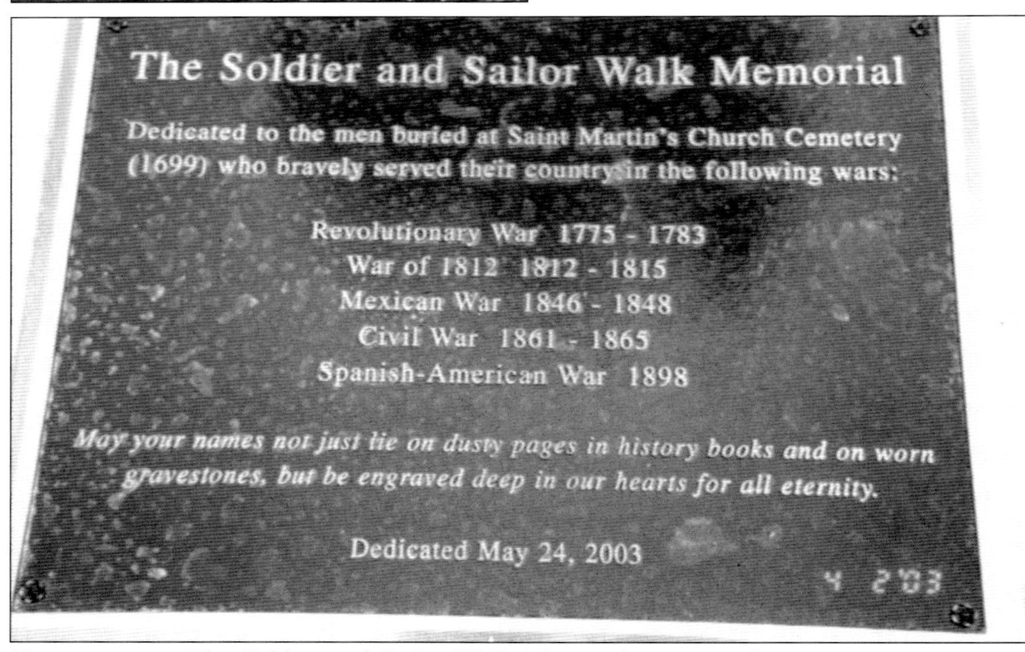

GRAVESTONES. The Soldier and Sailor Walk Memorial consists of government gravestones furnished by the U.S. Department of Veterans Affairs, Memorial Program Service. Each light gray granite marker is 23 inches long, 12 inches wide, and 4 inches thick, weighing 130 pounds.

Eight

Famous Marcus Hook Personalities

This chapter includes a selection of noted Marcus Hook personalities who left their mark on the borough's history. They are Mary M. Campbell, Joseph N. Pew, Mickey Vernon, Jasper R. Phillips, Robert E. Haebel, Curt Weldon, and Billy "White Shoes" Johnson. The last personality featured is Clara Young, who provided the author with many old stories about the history of the borough. This is merely a small collection of the many notables who are a part of the borough's history.

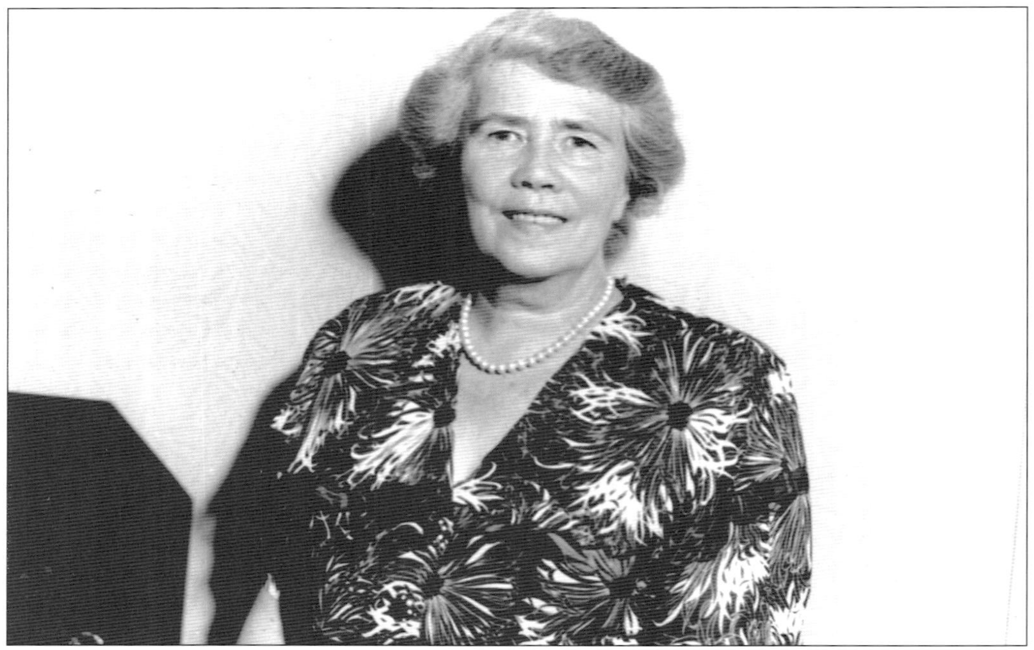

MARY M. CAMPBELL. Mary M. Campbell, the wife of a Marcus Hook dentist, was the first secretary of the library board and also was secretary of the local school board. The library in Marcus Hook was named after this famous resident. This photograph was taken on October 12, 1951. (Urban Archives of Temple University.)

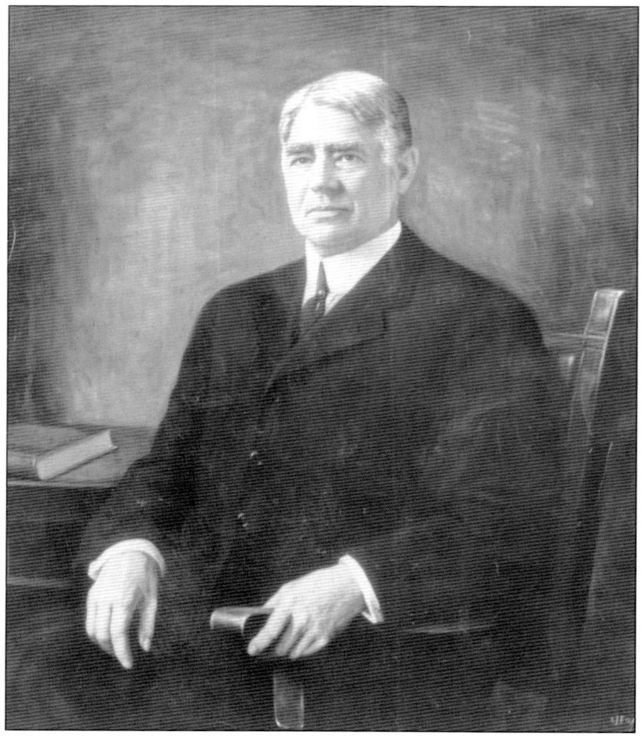

JOSEPH N. PEW. Joseph N. Pew, the founder of Sunoco, was a former schoolteacher and realtor. In 1901, Pew decided that a tract of ground at Marcus Hook offered the best possibilities for a refinery. It was at the end of the trolley line from Chester and consisted of 82 acres of level ground, 1,000 feet of river frontage, a small wharf, a mansion that could be converted into an office building, a stone house, and a frame cottage. (Hagley Museum and Library.)

MICKEY VERNON. Baseball great Mickey Vernon was born on April 22, 1918, in Marcus Hook and was a product of the borough sandlots. His family resided on Eighth Street. His grandfather Samuel had been the first mayor of Marcus Hook. Mickey played in the major leagues with the Washington Senators, Boston Red Sox, Cleveland Indians, Milwaukee Braves, and Pittsburgh Pirates. He was a two-time winner of the American League batting title (1943 and 1946). In this picture, he holds a baseball with "2000" imprinted on it, signifying 2,000 career hits. He ended his career with 2,465 lifetime hits, and his final game was on September 27, 1960. (Urban Archives of Temple University.)

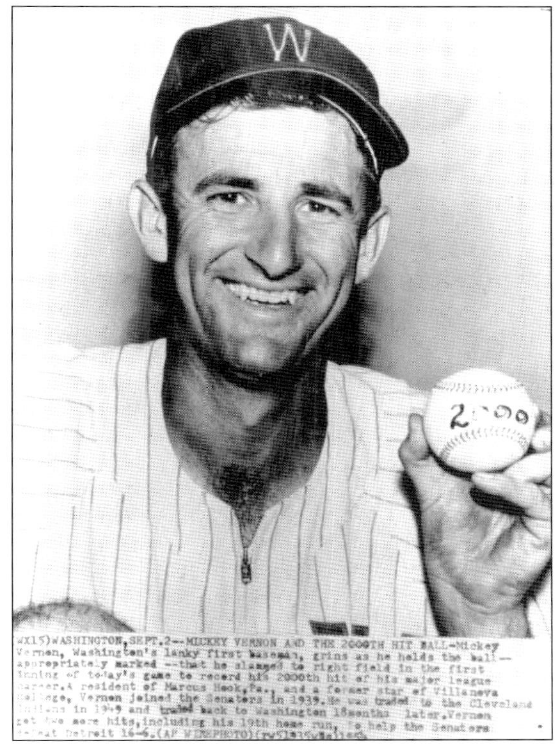

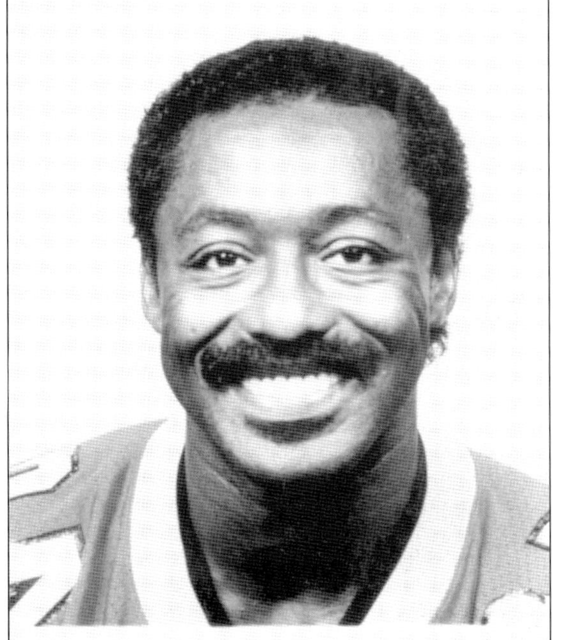

BILLY "WHITE SHOES" JOHNSON. Billy "White Shoes" Johnson was born in 1952 in Boothwyn (an adjoining town to Marcus Hook). He was a standout football player with the Houston Oilers from 1974 to 1980 and later played with the Atlanta Falcons. He was a wide receiver and punt returner. Johnson was voted into the College Football Hall of Fame. His trademark was the white football cleats worn since his days at Chichester High School and Widener College. His father, Leonard, was a Marcus Hook police officer.

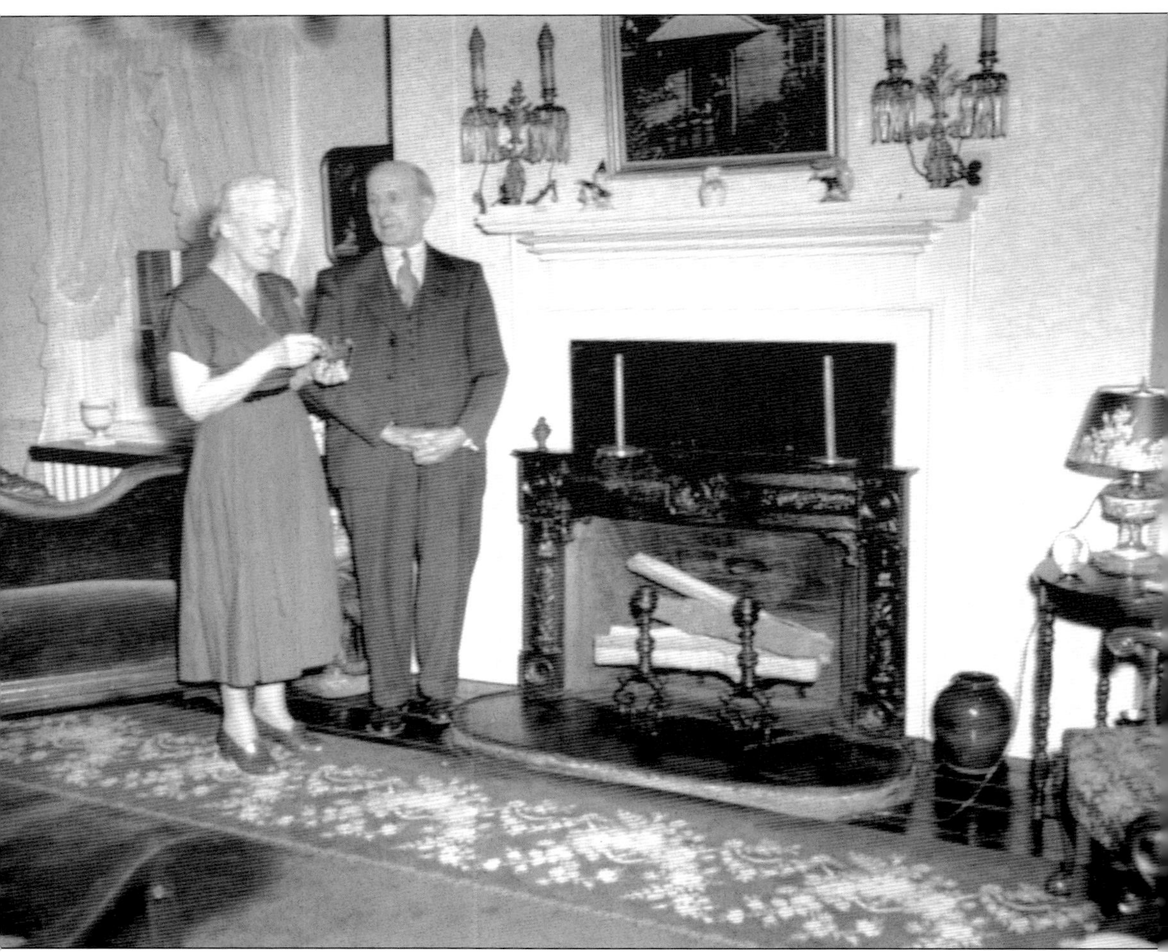

JASPER R. PHILLIPS. Jasper R. Phillips and his wife are shown by the side of a Franklin stove, one of the many antiques and heirlooms in this house, bought by Phillips in 1890. The house was built with bricks brought from England and had once been an inn when it was built in 1748. Phillips had the distinction of being a descendant of early settlers in Marcus Hook before William Penn landed in Chester. This photograph was taken on March 13, 1953. (Hagley Museum and Library.)

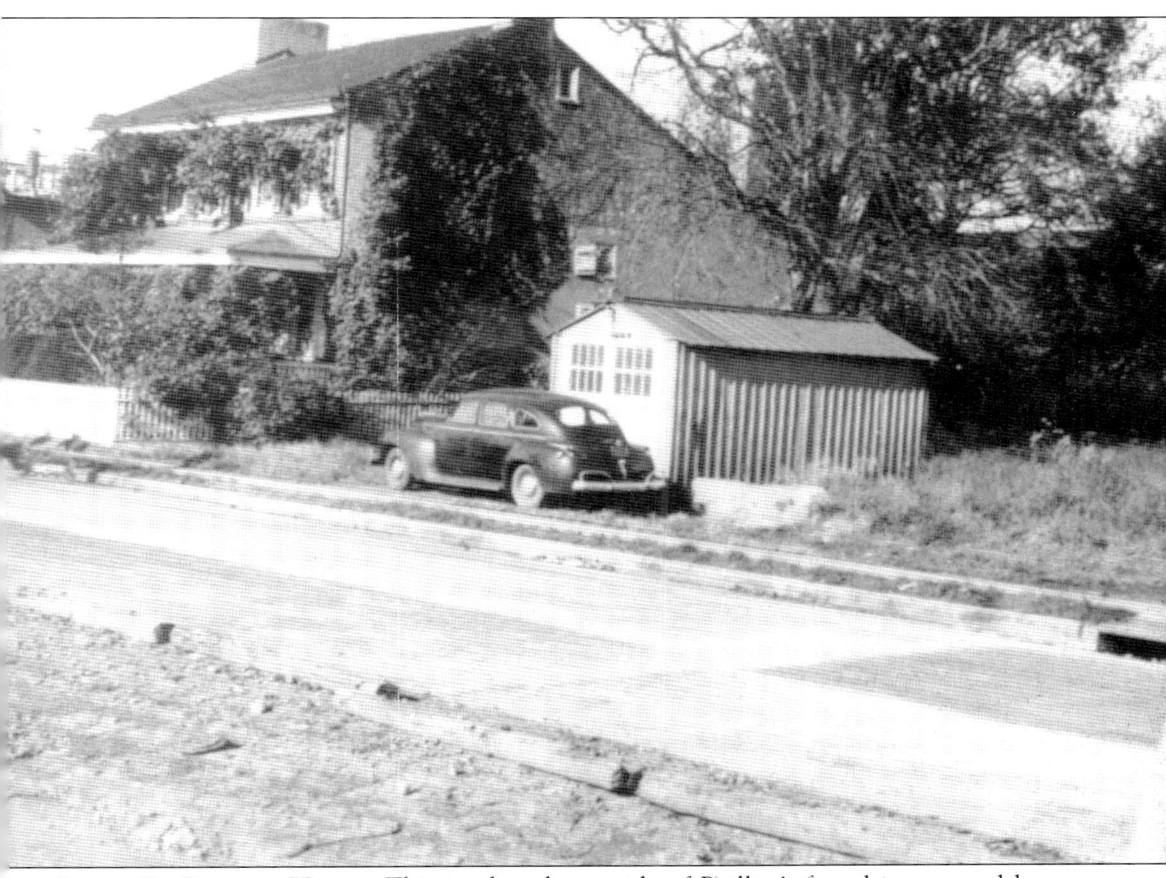

Jasper R. Phillips House. This is what the outside of Phillips's famed ivy-covered house looked like on Delaware Avenue. It was the third-oldest building in Marcus Hook and was once an inn before the Revolutionary War. Phillips was the head pressman for the *Chester Times* and wrote *1876 Life in Marcus Hook*.

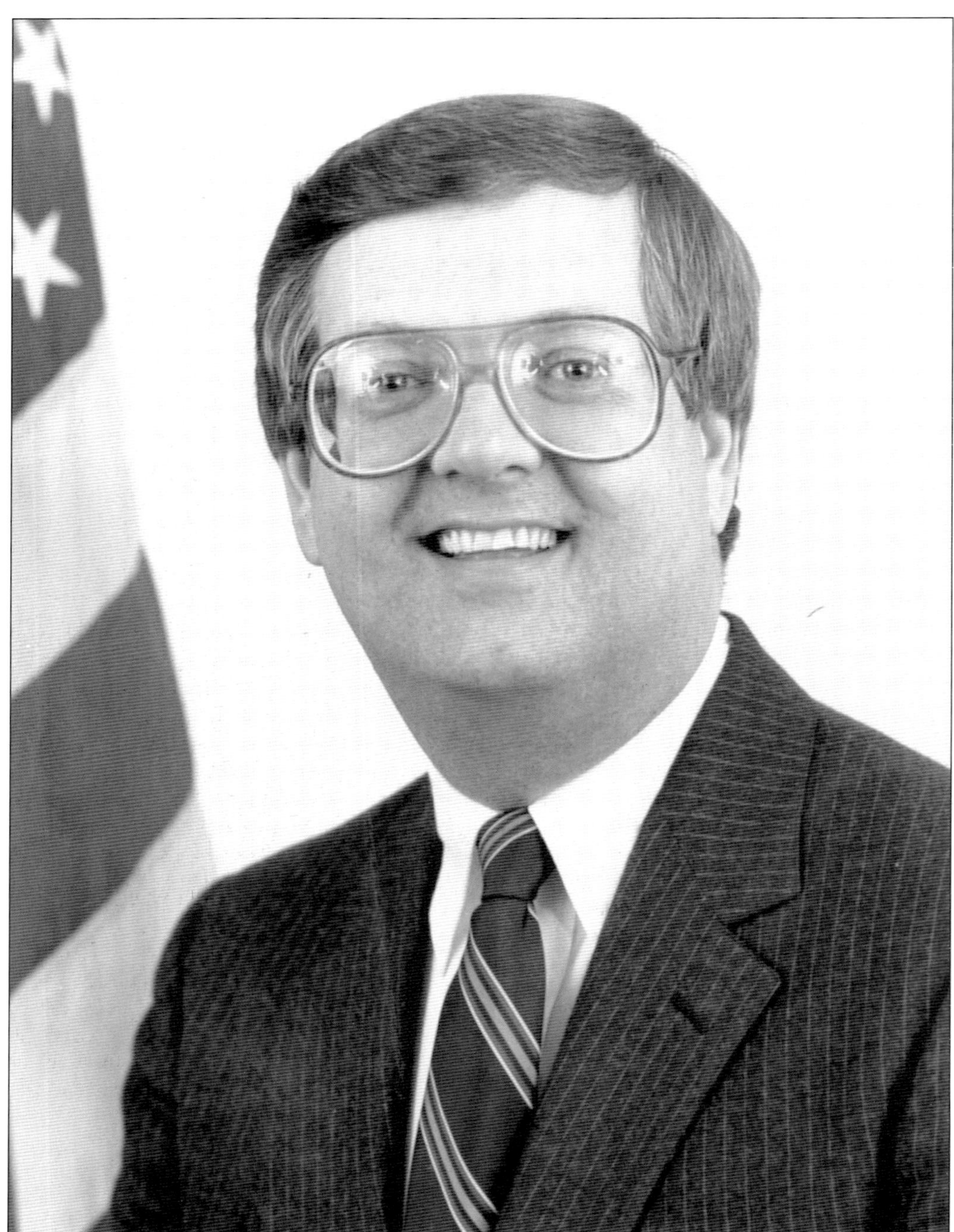

CURT WELDON. Former mayor of Marcus Hook and former congressman Curt Weldon was born on July 22, 1947. He served as mayor of Marcus Hook from 1977 to 1982 and was involved in much of the borough's revitalization. He went on to serve as a Republican member of the United States House of Representatives from 1987 to 2006, representing the 7th District of Pennsylvania.

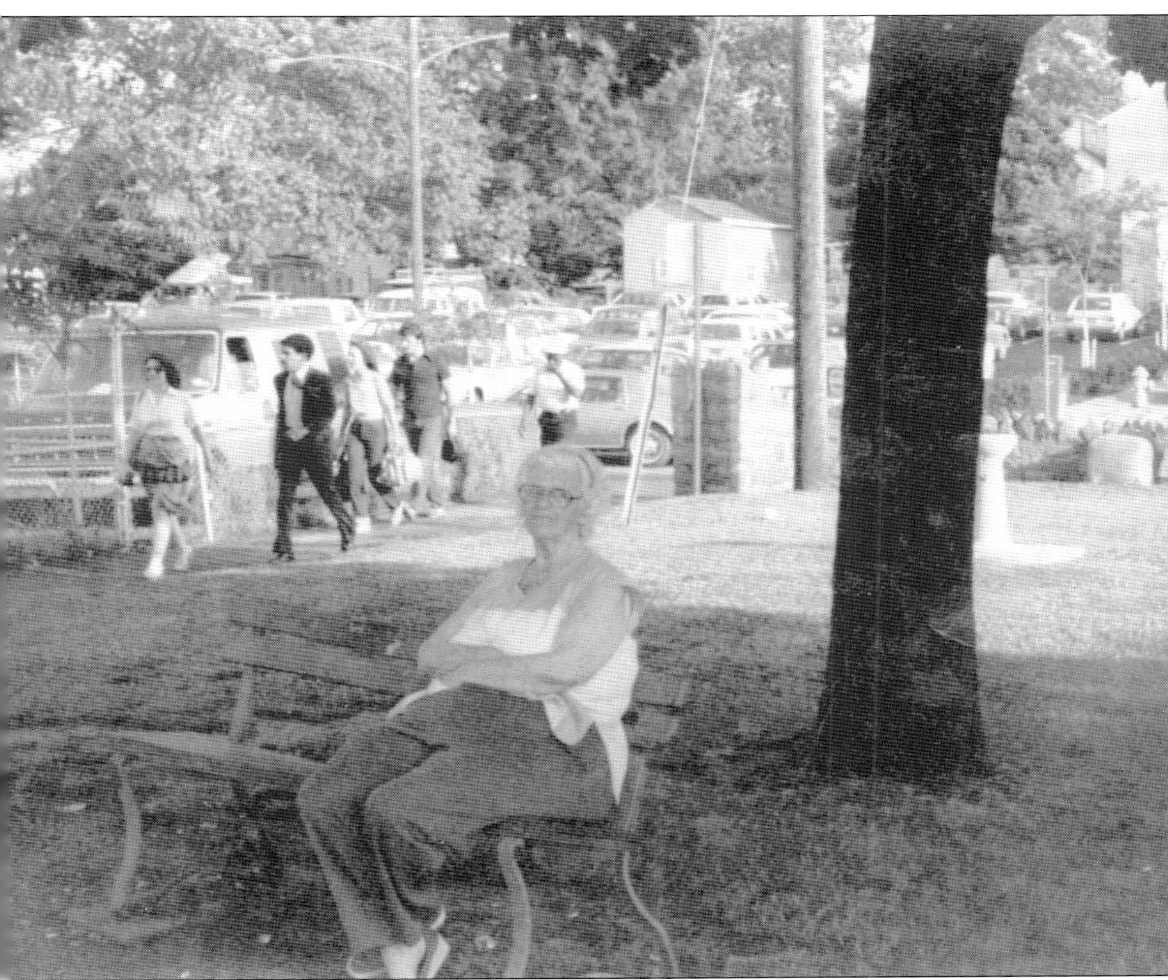

CLARA YOUNG. A fascinating personality is Clara Young, the aunt of baseball player Mickey Vernon and a member of the Marcus Hook senior group. This photograph was taken by the author one day in the old McClure Park when the tall ships came to town. Young told many stories about the old Marcus Hook, such as when she and her friend sank up to their necks and almost got swallowed up in quicksand on the Marcus Hook Beach (before Sunoco bought the property). Her account was likely to be true as a similar story was found while doing research at the Hagley Museum manuscript department, which related how a minister sank in the quicksand near Eighth and Market Streets and was never seen after that.

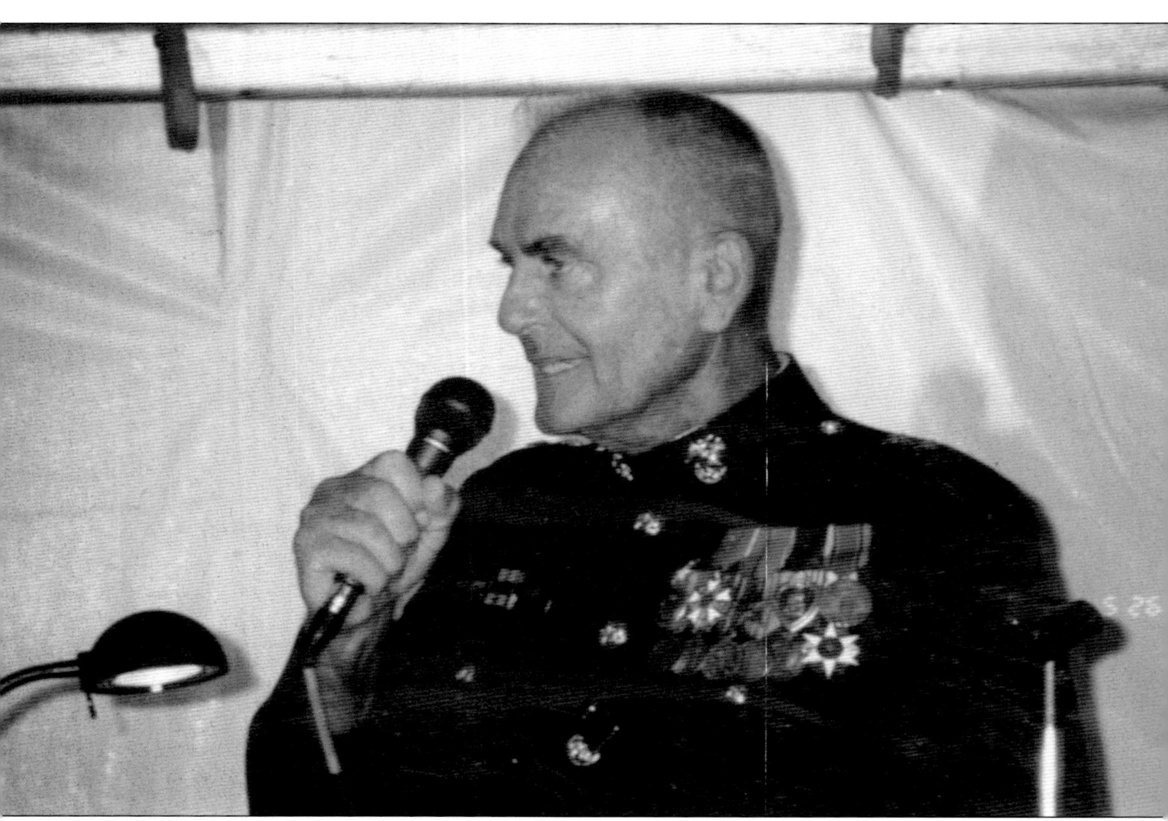

ROBERT E. HAEBEL. Retired major general Robert E. Haebel is a native of Marcus Hook. He was born in a Viscose Village house on July 18, 1927. He attended local schools and graduated from West Chester State Teachers College in 1951. During his distinguished military career with the United States Marine Corps, he advanced steadily in rank to positions of greater responsibility and respect and attained the rank of major general in July 1979. He last served as commanding general, Marine Corps Base Camp Pendleton, California, until his June 20, 1987 retirement. On May 23, 1987, the municipal park located at Tenth and Plaza Streets was named in his honor. The park, opposite 1 Plaza Street, where Haebel lived for many years, now bears a sign designating it as Robert E. Haebel Plaza. Haebel has often returned to the borough to march in the annual Memorial Day parade. In this photograph, he speaks at the dedication of the Korean War memorial on May 26, 2001.

Nine

Recent History

Marcus Hook Borough, located in the southeast corner of Pennsylvania, is commonly referred to as "the Cornerstone of Pennsylvania." If one visits Marcus Hook today, one will see tree-lined streets, well-maintained recreation areas, clean streets, and a beautiful riverfront park. Marcus Hook is a pedestrian-friendly community whose small-town charm is reflective of the borough's cultural and historical heritage.

Things have not always been as tranquil and peaceful as they are today. Marcus Hook suffered through a period of urban decline in the 1960s and 1970s. In an effort to reverse past trends toward economic, physical, and social decline, Marcus Hook embarked on a comprehensive effort of careful planning for the future. The results have been astounding, and Marcus Hook is recognized as a model of what can happen in towns throughout the United States through hard work, determination, and leadership. During the past three decades, Marcus Hook has reestablished itself as a community where all phases of life—living, working, playing—coexist in a harmonious manner.

Revitalization efforts that began in the late 1970s and early 1980s continue to this day. They are the cornerstone of ongoing community improvement and betterment projects that continue to inspire community pride. It is a belief in a better future, coupled with a practical sense of how to get things done, that is bringing about change in Marcus Hook and distinguishes its leaders.

Marcus Hook is a community with a restored vitality and a new sense of pride. The small-town feel and more personalized sense of community prevails in Marcus Hook. There is leadership, there is partnership, there is involvement, and there are countless achievements.

Marcus Hook is looking ahead to a bright tomorrow, having proved that a community can indeed shape its future.

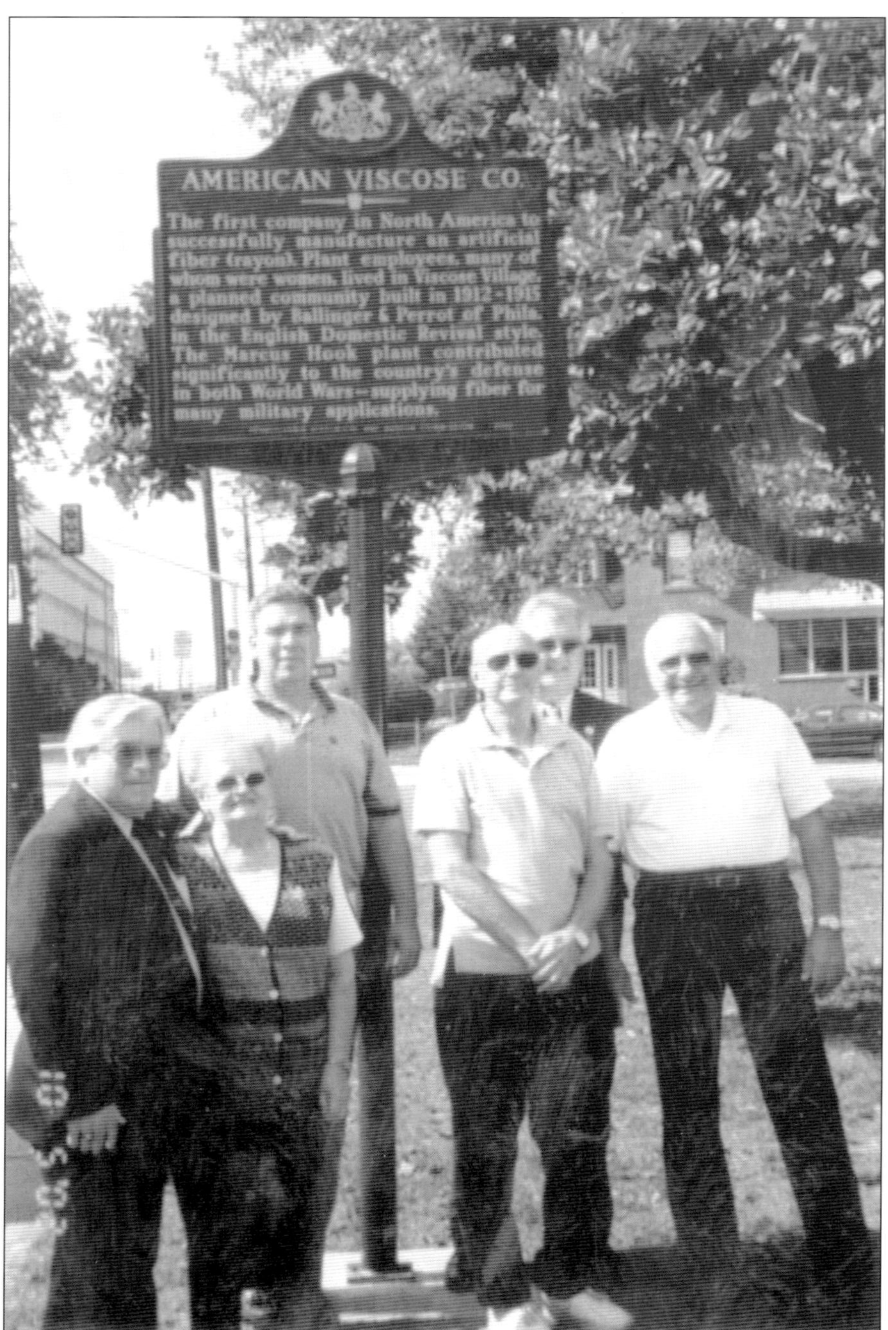

AMERICAN VISCOSE MARKER. The American Viscose Company memorial was dedicated on October 5, 2002. The borough's application for a roadside historical marker was approved by the Pennsylvania Historical and Museum Commission. Pictured here, from left to right, are Mayor George A. McClure; Joan Sylvester, member of borough council; Arthur E. Sutherland of the council; Mervin L. Boyer of the council; Congressman Curt Weldon; and Anthony A. Gallo of the council.

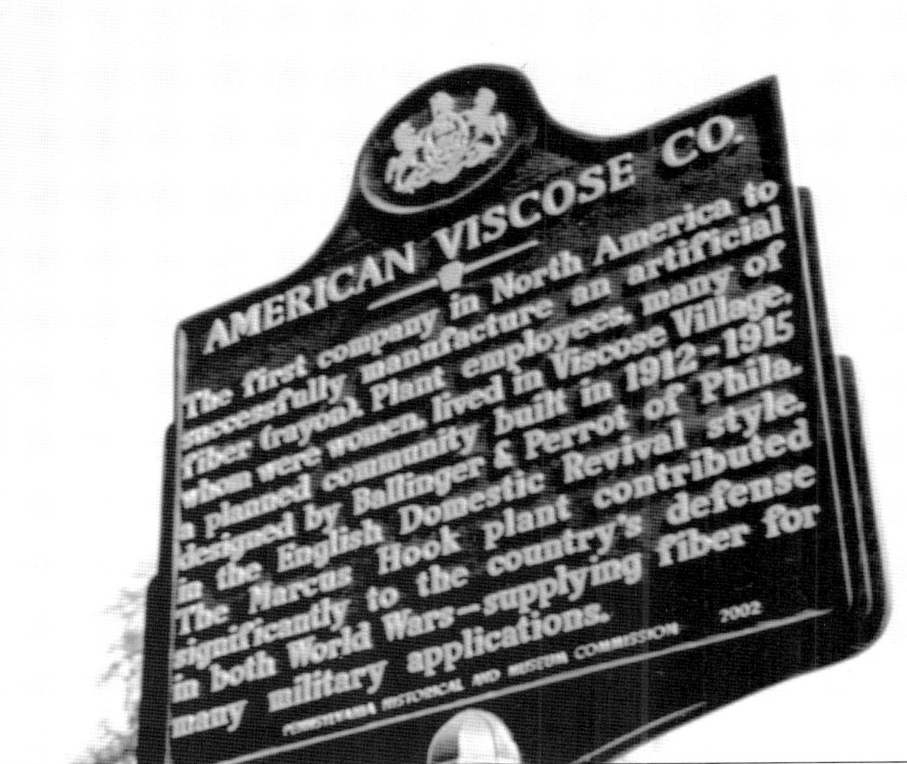

CLOSE-UP OF AMERICAN VISCOSE MARKER. Over 70 people were on hand for the dedication. In addition to Mayor George McClure and borough council members, attending were Christie Tate, who authored a dissertation on Viscose Village and the American Viscose Company, and six grandchildren of Emile G. Perrot, the architect of the village. A donation from the Perrot family covered the cost of the marker.

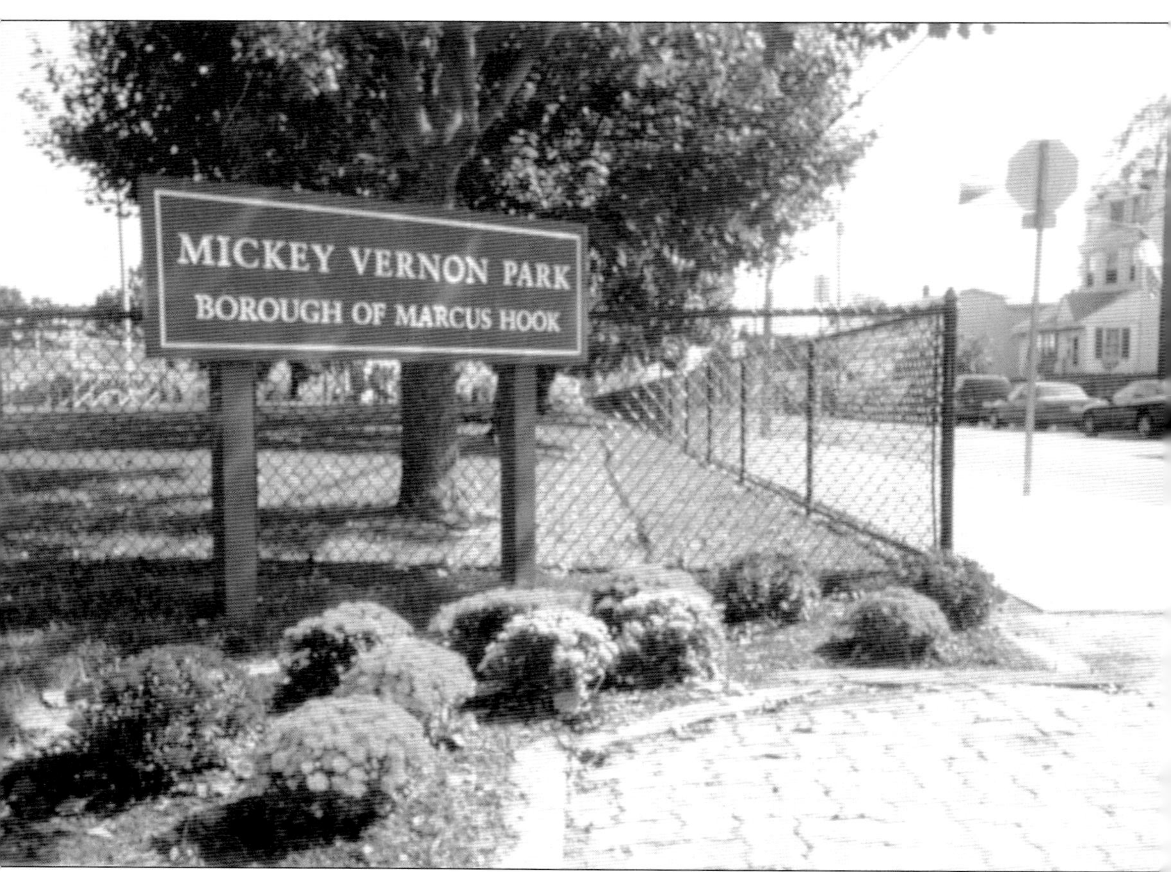

MICKEY VERNON PARK. September 20, 2003, was designated Mickey Vernon Day, and Memorial Field at Seventh and Market Streets was renamed in his honor. This honor was bestowed on him for being born and raised in Marcus Hook, attending local schools, and embarking on a 20-year, four-decade major-league baseball career.

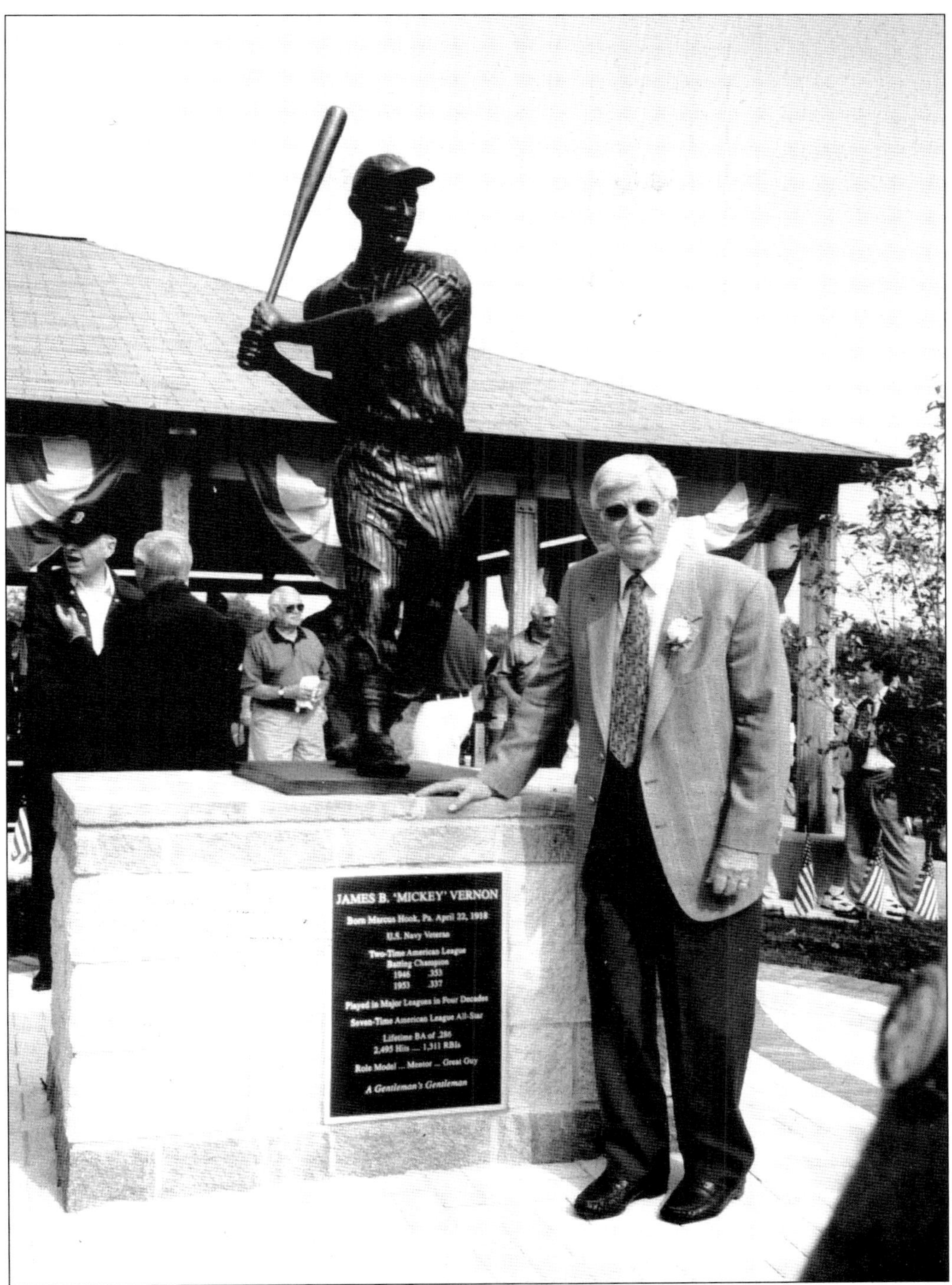

MICKEY VERNON STATUE. The Mickey Vernon statue was also dedicated on September 20, 2003. Mickey Vernon, at age 85, stands next to the statue. Vernon donated his time and talent over the years to many organizations and youth groups and always made himself available for appearances and autographs and never charged a fee.

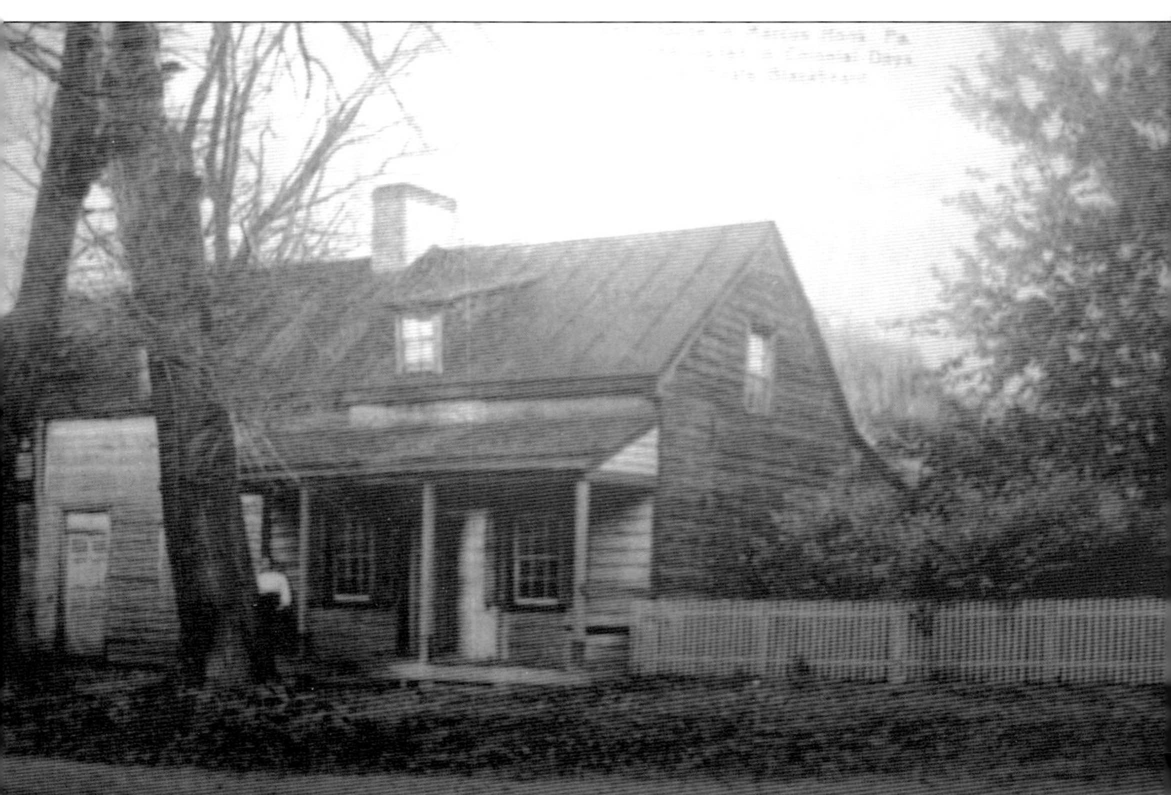

MARCUS HOOK PLANK HOUSE LOG CABIN. The MHPLCA was founded by its president, Michael Manerchia, to promote the research, documentation, and preservation of the architectural, archaeological, and historic resources of 221 Market Street. Since its establishment, the MHPLCA has arranged archaeological excavations, historical research, and public outreach programs and has a newsletter. The plank house has 20th-century stucco siding and a lean-to addition. Aided by a team of academics and volunteers, Manerchia has uncovered more than 10,000 artifacts, including a 4,000-year-old spear point, two cannonballs, and brass hardware from an 18th-century William and Mary cabinet. Underneath its modern stucco siding is a well-preserved plank house, an architectural style favored by early English settlers. Preservation Pennsylvania, a statewide nonprofit historic preservation organization, named the plank house one of the top 10 historic properties in the state. In the future, with more archaeological digs, possibly Blackbeard's treasure will be uncovered. (MHPLCA.)

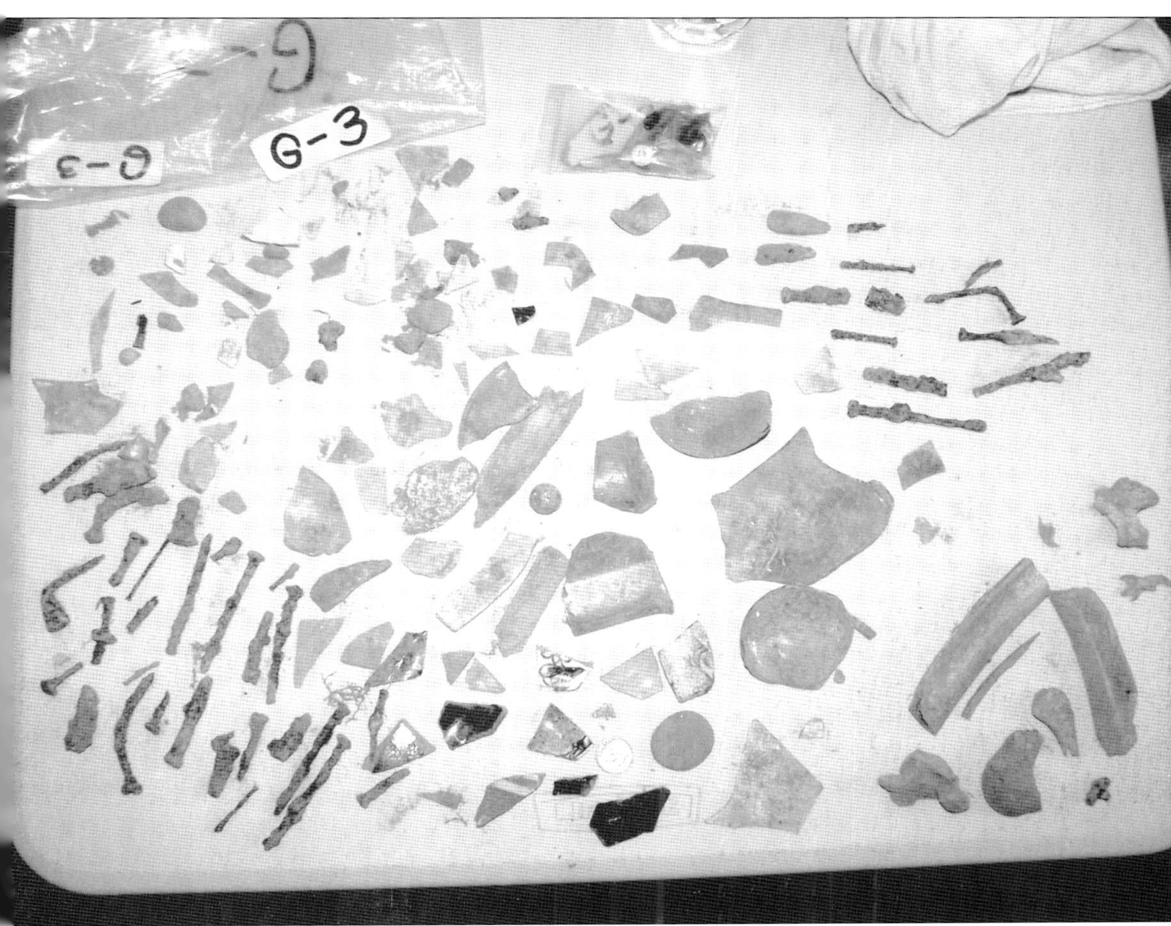

ARTIFACTS. Here is a picture of some of the 10,000 artifacts found at archaeological excavations. Many of the artifacts found were through the help of Temple University archaeologists Joe Blondino and Dr. David Orr. Volunteers are still needed for digging and cleaning. (MHPLCA.)

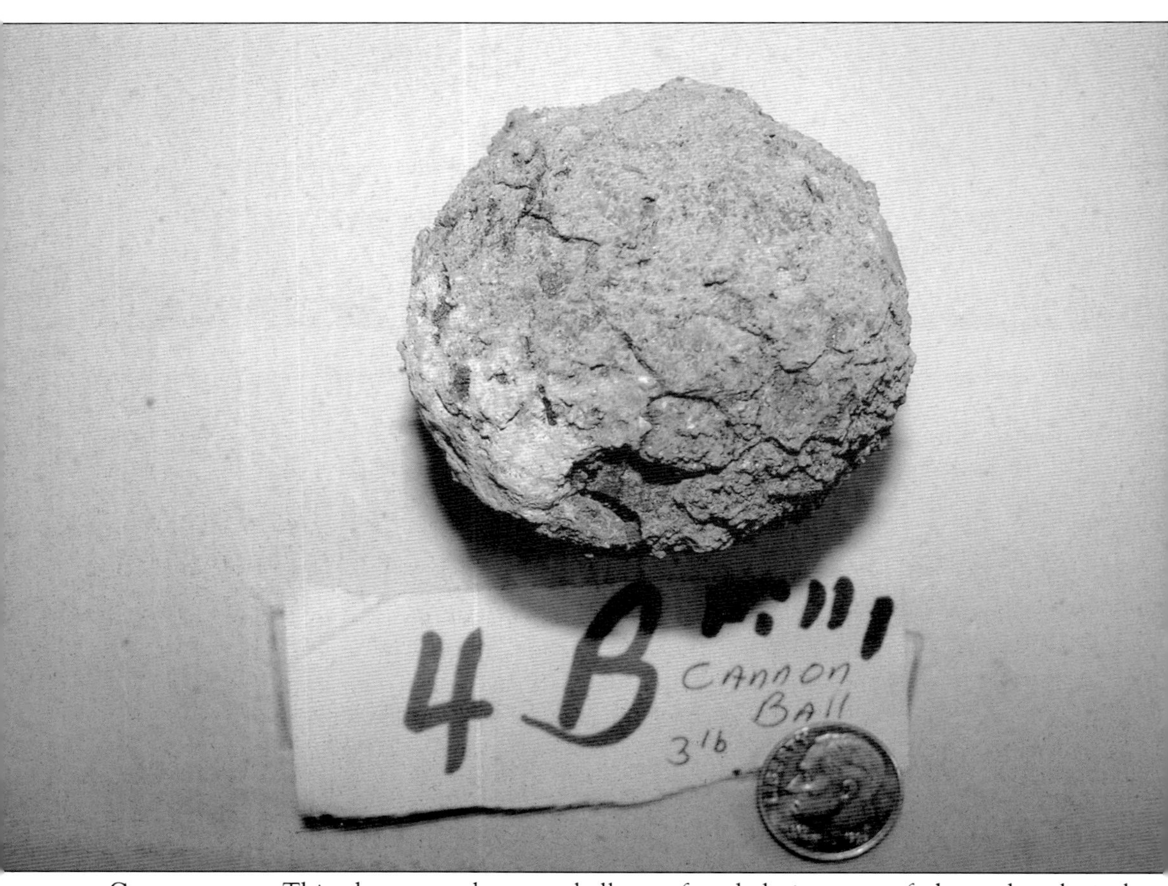

CANNONBALL. This three-pound cannonball was found during one of the archaeological excavations. This cannonball actually came from the British bombardment of Marcus Hook during the Revolutionary War.

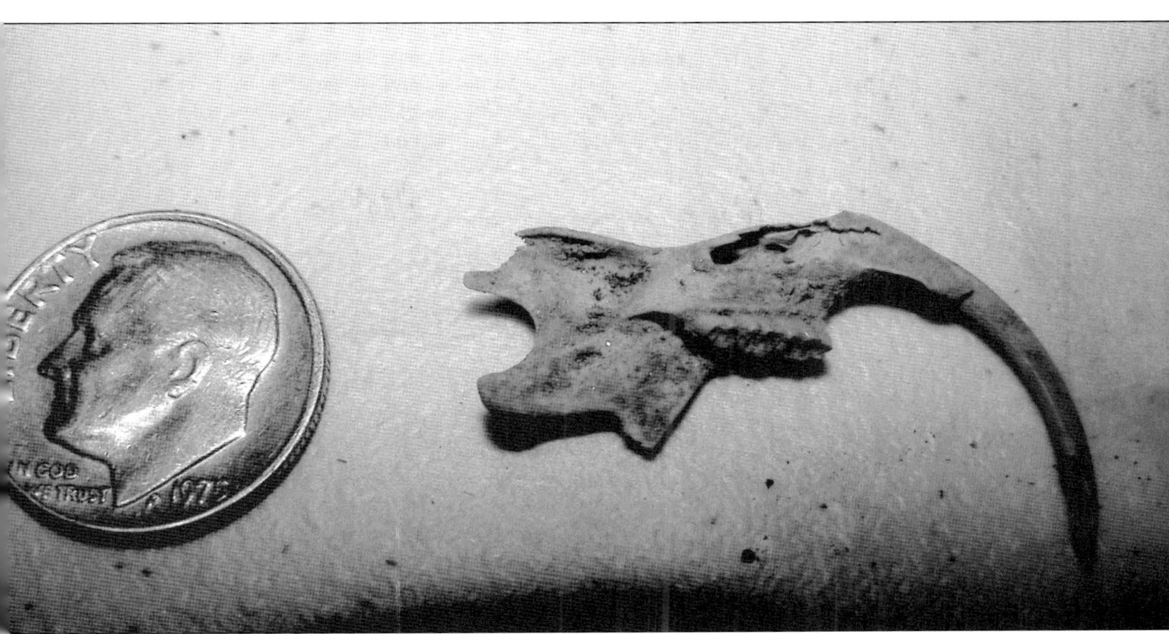

Tooth. This rodent's tooth, a fang, was also found during the excavations. The fang is sized by using a dime in this photograph.

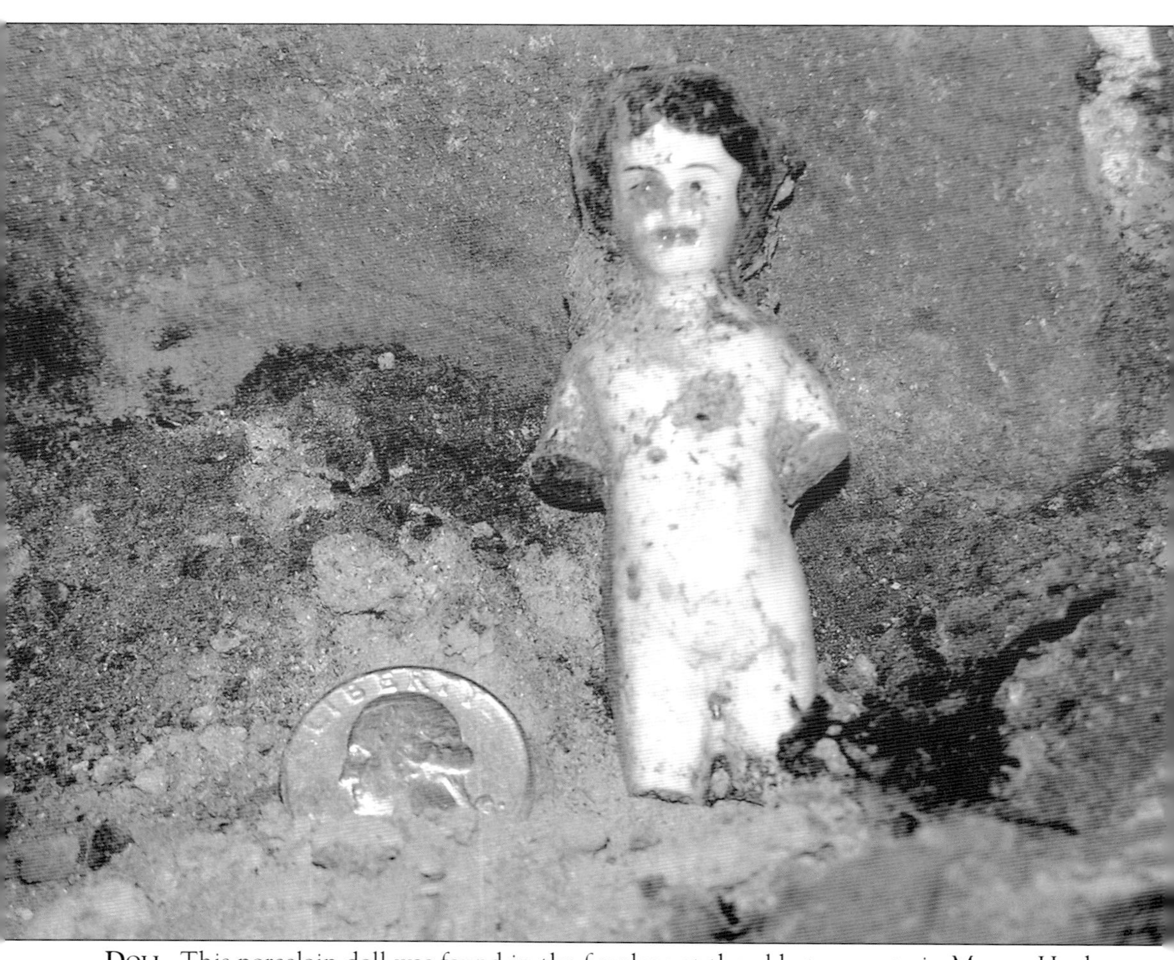

DOLL. This porcelain doll was found in the fireplace at the oldest property in Marcus Hook at 221 Market Street. Michael Manerchia plans to turn the house over to the Chichester Historical Society. Five porcelain dolls were found in all different sizes.

BIBLIOGRAPHY

Ashmead, Henry Graham. *History of Delaware County, Pennsylvania*. Philadelphia: L. H. Everts and Company, 1884.

Jordan, John W., LL.D. *A History of Delaware County, Pennsylvania, and Its People*. New York: Lewis Historical Publishing Company, 1914.

Marcus Hook Republican Club. *Our Hometown*. Marcus Hook, PA: October 17, 1964.

Palmer, Charles, Esq., ed. *A History of Delaware County, Pennsylvania*. Harrisburg, PA: National Historical Association Inc., 1932.

Tate, Christine. "Viscose Village: Model Industrial Workers' Housing in Marcus Hook, Delaware County, Pennsylvania" Ph.D. diss., University of Pennsylvania, 2002.

Wilbert C. Dubhorn Jr. Postcard Collection and History. Delaware County Historical Society.

Wiley, Samuel T. *Biographical and Historical Cyclopedia of Delaware County, Pennsylvania*. Richmond, IN: Gresham Publishing Company, 1894.